Deglobalization and International Security

Deglobalization and International Security

T. X. Hammes

Rapid Communications in Conflict and Security Series
General Editor: Geoffrey R.H. Burn

CAMBRIA
PRESS

Amherst, New York

Requests for permission should be directed to
permissions@cambriapress.com, or mailed to:
Cambria Press
100 Corporate Parkway, Suite 128
Amherst, New York 14226, USA

Library of Congress Cataloging-in-Publication Data

Names: Hammes, Thomas X., author.

Title: Deglobalization and international security / T.X. Hammes.

Description: Amherst, New York: Cambria Press, 2019. |
Series: Rapid communications in conflict and security series |
Includes bibliographical references and index. |
Summary: "Two trends-deglobalization and the evolution of cheap, smart weapons-
will fundamentally alter world economic and security orders. The return of production
and services to the United States will reduce the interest of the American people in
maintaining stability in the international system. Reinforcing this trend, resultant
employment disruptions, the oncoming U.S. debt and budget crises will force national
leaders to choose whether to allocate resources to domestic, particularly entitlement,
spending or to overseas efforts. Even more important, the new generation of weapons
will dramatically increase the cost in blood and treasure of U.S. military engagements.
In sum, the fourth industrial revolution will see major shifts in economic and military
conditions facing the United States. Fortunately, the United States is very well positioned to
exploit this opportunity to greatly improve both its economy and defense. Deglobalization
and International Security illuminates how the fourth industrial revolution will
fundamentally alter global economic and security arrangements and offers options
that allow U.S. leaders to exploit the fourth industrial revolution to provide economic
and military security for the nation. This is an important book for those in political
science, international relations, and conflict and security studies"-- Provided by publisher.

Identifiers: LCCN 2019031545 (print) | LCCN 2019031546 (ebook) |

ISBN 9781621964735 (paperback) |
ISBN 9781604979657 (hardcover) | ISBN 9781621964964 (epub)

Subjects: LCSH: National security--United States. | United States--
Economic policy. | United States--Foreign relations--21st century.
| Globalization--United States. | World politics--21st century.

Classification: LCC UA23 .H3634 2019 (print) | LCC UA23 (ebook) |
DDC 355/.033073--dc23

LC record available at https://lccn.loc.gov/2019031545

LC ebook record available at https://lccn.loc.gov/2019031546

TABLE OF CONTENTS

LIST OF FIGURES

ACKNOWLEDGMENTS

I required significant assistance to travel from the idea to the finished product you hold in your hand. I'd like to thank my colleagues at the Institute for National Strategic Studies, National Defense University for their assistance. They gave generously of their time in allowing me to explore the ideas and concepts that make up this book. In particular, Dr. Chris Lamb and Dr. Frank Hoffman took on the onerous task of reviewing and commenting on the entire book. The comments and conversations they shared with me significantly improved the quality of the work. Dr. Lin Wells also provided insights as I developed the ideas over the last couple of years. And the leadership of INSS and the Center for Strategic Research consistently supported and encouraged the effort.

Finally, I owe a great deal of thanks to the patience of my wife, Janet. Her humor and thoughtful observations were, as always, essential.

INTRODUCTION

Rapid, at times seemingly exponential, advances in a wide range of new technologies are pushing the world into what Klaus Schwab of the World Economic Forum has labeled the fourth industrial revolution. He stated the first industrial revolution (1760–1840), based on steam power, gave us mechanical production. The second revolution (late nineteenth and early twentieth century) was driven by electricity and led to assembly-line production techniques that created mass production. The third, the digital revolution, began in the 1960s with the widespread introduction of computers and continues with the rapid evolution of the internet. The fourth, a convergence of breakthroughs in bioscience, nanotechnology, robotics, artificial intelligence, autonomy, 3D printing, clean energy, and materials science, is evolving now.[1]

The previous industrial revolutions did not simply change the industrial base of society. They transformed services, finance, food production, defense, medicine, social, and political structures. In short, every aspect of society. This book argues that the fourth industrial revolution will have an impact even greater than the previous three. For decades, globalization— the global integration of trade, services, investments, and ideas enhanced by the free movement of people—has been reshaping our world. Since the

1950s, the combination of labor cost advantages, increasingly efficient freight systems, low-cost digital communications, and trade agreements have fueled a globalization surge by providing regional cost advantages for manufacturing and services.

That is changing. Driven by the fourth industrial revolution, the regional cost advantages, particularly for labor, are eroding dramatically in many areas. New methods of providing manufactured goods and services are fundamentally changing the competitive environment for businesses and nations. This will lead to major declines in the global movement of trade, services, and investments—in short, deglobalization. Obviously, this does not mean there will be complete cessation of global interactions. Key competitive advantages will remain in some areas such as gas and oil, aircraft, certain types of commercial ships, and other high-tech industries. And the global economy has, and will continue, to grow—but that growth will be focused in regional markets as opposed to interregional or global trade. Regional and local trade will continue to grow even as interregional trade declines as a percentage of global Gross Domestic Product (GDP).

Like all complex adaptive systems, world trade is not driven by a single factor but rather by the interaction of numerous large and small actors and factors. Historically, profit has been a primary driver of trade. If a company could not make a profit trading, it would fail. For a variety of reasons ranging from national security to social movements seeking to "civilize" the world, governments have periodically provided subsidies to companies to encourage international trade. However, for trade to grow, the subsidies had to be large enough to ensure that the companies made a profit. Conversely, periods of decline in global trade have usually been driven by political and security factors such as the Arab Oil Embargo or World War I, which increased the cost of doing business. With less profit, there was less reason to trade. But trade recovered when political or security conditions improved so that it was possible to make money again.

This period of deglobalization is shaping up differently. The convergence of new technologies is changing how and where people create wealth. *The Competitive Advantage of Nations* by Michael Porter argues that clusters of interconnected firms, suppliers, related industries, and institutions that arise in particular locations have superseded proximity to cheap labor and raw materials as a primary source of national advantage.[2] Rapid changes in how businesses provide both manufacturing and services are changing the locations of these clusters. At the same time, a growing demand for more responsiveness to customers needs and the desire for customized products is pushing business to locate in or near their markets. Quite simply, business will make more money by producing and selling both goods and services regionally and even locally than globally.

The overall manufacturing favorability of the United States is improving in a wide range of areas. As noted, the combination of rising labor costs globally and rapid improvements in automation has reduced the cost advantage of manufacturing overseas. The U.S. position is "further enhanced when one includes advantages in sophisticated supply-chain logistics, ease of doing business, and low corruption. Dramatically lower energy costs have handed firms located in the U.S. an enormous competitive advantage in energy-intensive production."[3] And of course, one of the biggest advantages to producing in the United States is proximity to the largest market in the world. In short, the unfolding fourth industrial revolution is very good news for the United States.

As always, political and social trends will have significant impacts on trade relations. But I contend the primary driver of the current deglobalization is technology. Political and social attitudes, particularly since 2014, have reinforced the trend, but they may well change as new political leaders take charge and social attitudes shift. However, the long-term technical trends are irreversible. They will continue to shift trade networks, supply chains, and, to some extent, service industries to regional rather than global structures.

From the early 1990s until 2008, globalization was increasing. Then the 2008 Financial Crisis brought a major decline in international trade. Several authors suggested this was the beginning of deglobalization, but surprisingly, trade recovered very quickly and by 2011 had reached pre-crisis levels. Talk of deglobalization ceased. However, for the next five years (2012–2016) trade as a percent of GDP steadily declined, even though global GDP increased during that period. The obvious question is "Why?" This book will grapple with that economic question.

The fourth industrial revolution is also driving changes in the character of war which, when combined with the changes in trade, is altering international security arrangements. The convergence of emerging technologies is creating a new generation of small, smart, and cheap weapons. These weapons will dramatically increase the ability of small states and even nonstate actors to challenge major powers. They may make the defense tactically dominant—and thus dramatically raise the cost of any outside intervention.

These two trends—deglobalization and the evolution of cheap, smart weapons—will fundamentally alter world economic and security orders. The return of production and services to the United States will reduce the interest of the American people in deploying military force to ensure stability in the international system. The employment disruptions inherent in an industrial revolution will also cause voter discontent that will force policymakers to focus more on national issues than international security. This will be reinforced by the oncoming U.S. debt and budget crises, which will force decisions on whether to allocate U.S. resources to domestic, particularly entitlement spending, or to overseas efforts. Even more important, the new generation of weapons will dramatically increase the cost in blood and treasure of military power projection. U.S. national security planning must take these changes into account.

The central thesis of this book is that the fourth industrial revolution is driving changes in trade patterns, the character of war, and international security arrangements. To understand how this is happening, chapter 1 will first explore the economic, political, and social factors that have been both drivers and indicators of periods of globalization and deglobalization historically. Next, it will discuss why the decline in the percent of GDP represented by international trade in both goods and services, cross-border financial flows, international shipping, and the changing pattern of foreign direct investment (FDI) all indicate a period of deglobalization. It will also examine how domestic political environments in the United States and Europe, as well as protectionism measures imposed around the world, form the next set of indicators of deglobalization.

This sets the stage for chapter 2 to explore the first three industrial revolutions briefly and then examine the fourth industrial revolution technologies that are most directly driving deglobalization. Robotics, artificial intelligence, 3D printing (as a key element of advanced manufacturing), energy and food production will be discussed to show how each is reducing international trade.

Chapter 3 will examine the accelerating economic impact of these changes. The discussion is then expanded to take a look at how changes in energy production and how state efforts to fragment the internet are putting additional pressure on global trade. It will examine the key question of why these changes are leading to reshoring of both manufacturing and services to the developed world.

Chapter 4 looks at the economic impacts on developed, developing, and underdeveloped countries. Obviously, these are very broad groupings that inevitably bring together very different states. However, these groupings can be used to identify broad issues that face each group. Clearly, the disruption in employment patterns for all three groups has the potential to create instability in their political systems. It will then look at the increasing regionalization of trade into three major trade blocs—North America, East Asia, and Europe. It will also examine very briefly the impact on South Asia, Africa, and Latin America.

Chapter 5 examines the specific technologies that will have the most immediate impact on military conflict. The convergence of advances in nanotechnology, drones (aerial, maritime, and ground), artificial intelligence, small warhead developments, and cheap space will create swarms of small but deadly autonomous weapons systems. These new systems will join the increasingly capable family of drones, cruise and ballistic missiles and the newly emerging, but expensive and complex, hypersonic weapons to render many of America's newest weapons— such as the F-35 and the *Ford*-class carriers—obsolete. The changes will go well beyond a Revolution in Military Affairs (RMA), it will result in a rare Military Revolution.[4]

Chapter 6 will turn to the tactical and operational implications of these technologies. First, the tactical impact of new technologies on each domain—ground, sea, air, space, cyber, and electromagnetic—will be examined. Next, we will turn to the five major operational changes that the convergence of these technologies will drive—range obsolescence, loss of immunity to attack, the emerging tactical dominance of the defense, the return of mass to the battlefield, and the resultant requirement for mobilization. The chapter will close with the cumulative impact of convergence and the way it will change the character of war.

Chapter 7 will bring together the different threads to suggest how the US military can manage the difficult transition to deal with the revolution of the small, smart, and many. The very long timelines involved in upgrading current U.S. weapons and the repeated failure to achieve the stated operational capabilities highlight the challenges of attempting to improve mature technology. After examining how to smooth the replacement of mature technology with new, this chapter recommends potential changes to the current force structures for conflict in each of the domains.

The final chapter looks at the cumulative impact of fourth generation on international security arrangements starting with why there is declining popular support for U.S. global engagement. Employment changes, reduced reliance on international trade, higher costs for future interventions, budgetary pressures, and debt servicing will all push

American voters to oppose committing major U.S. resources overseas when the United States has major unmet domestic needs. Yet, sustaining the international order should still be a priority to help America manage the five major threats identified by the 2018 U.S. National Defense Strategy —Russia, China, Iran, North Korea, and transnational violent extremism. Fortunately, the fourth industrial revolution can provide both means and opportunity for the United States to maintain its commitments to allies in an affordable way. The book will close with suggestions on how the United States can sustain its key alliances to deal with the identified threats and provide for its own security during this difficult transition.

The book reflects my research interests over the last three years. I previously published some of this material in papers through the National Defense University, CATO Institute, Hoover Institution, *The National Interest,* and *War on the Rocks* as well in as some shorter articles for other on online journals.[5] This book expands greatly on these articles and ties all the material together in a broader look at the interaction of technology, deglobalization, and the changing character of war. Like all predictions, this book represents one of many possible futures. Like all futures, it is based on deductions from an analysis of current political, social, and technical trends. And whereas the political and social trends have historically been subject to rapid shifts, technological progress has been a remarkably steady factor over the last two hundred years. The current technological advances are driving production, services, and financial transactions to regional or even local markets. Even if the political and social environment become more favorable to global trade, the profit motive will continue to drive deglobalization. The major shift in how wealth is generated driven by the fourth industrial revolution "will have a profound impact on the nature of state relationships and international security."[6]

Of particular concern is how the increasing cost of intervening, reinforced by the natural focus of the American public on domestic issues, will increase the reluctance of Americans to get involved in stability efforts overseas or even to sustain our current network of global security alliances. Thus, it behooves policymakers to be aware of the range of impacts this revolutionary shift could bring about. It is essential to investigate how the revolution will impact U.S. security while there is still time to make the necessary changes in our concepts, structures, and plans.

NOTES

1. Klaus Schwab, *The Fourth Industrial Revolution*, (New York: Crown Business, 2016), 6–8.
2. Michael E. Porter, *The Competitive Advantage of Nations*, (New York: Free Press, 1998).
3. Mark P. Mills, "The Coming Revolution in American Manufacturing," *MI*, December 2016, 15, https://media4.manhattan-institute.org/sites/default/files/R-MM-1216.pdf.
4. See MacGregor Knox and Williamson Murray's, *The Dynamics of Military Revolution: 1350–2050* (Cambridge: Cambridge University Press, 2001) for a thorough discussion of the difference between RMAs and Military Revolutions.
5. See, for example, "Technologies Converge and Power Diffuses: The Evolution of Small, Smart, and Cheap Weapons," CATO Institute, January 27, 2016, https://www.cato.org/publications/policy-analysis/technologies-converge-power-diffuses-evolution-small-smart-cheap; "Will Technological Convergence Reverse Globalization?" National Defense University, July 2016, https://ndupress.ndu.edu/Media/News/Article/834357/will-technological-convergence-reverse-globalization/; "America is well within range of a big surprise, so why can't it see it?, War on the Rocks, March 12, 2018, https://warontherocks.com/2018/03/america-is-well-within-range-of-a-big-surprise-so-why-cant-it-see/; "Navy Aircraft Carriers Are Expensive and Vulnerable to Attack. Here's How to Replace Them," *The National Interest,* October 17, 2018, https://nationalinterest.org/blog/buzz/navy-aircraft-carriers-are-expensive-and-vulnerable-attack-heres-how-replace-them-33681;" Technology Converges; Non-State Actors Benefit," Hoover Institution, February 25, 2019, https://www.hoover.org/research/technology-converges-non-state-actors-benefit.
6. Schwab, *The Fourth Industrial Revolution*, 80.

Deglobalization and International Security

CHAPTER 1

KEY TRENDS DRIVING DEGLOBALIZATION

The *Financial Times* defines globalization as "a process by which national and regional economies, societies, and cultures have become integrated through the global network of trade, communication, immigration and transportation."[1] The World Economic Forum defines it as "the integration of markets, trade and investments with few barriers to slow the flow of products and services between nations. There is also a cultural element, as ideas and traditions are traded and assimilated."[2] *The Economist* defines globalization as the "global integration of the movement of goods, capital and jobs."[3] The key elements of all these definitions are economic. Thus, the definition of globalization I will use for this book is the global integration of trade, services, investments, and ideas enhanced by the free movement of people.

For decades, the combination of labor cost advantages, increasingly efficient freight systems, low-cost digital communications, and trade agreements have fueled globalization by providing national competitive advantages for manufacturing and services. It has transformed agricultural societies into industrial powerhouses. Yet this is not the first wave of globalization.

Parag Khanna's *Connectography* stated globalization began in the third millennium BCE, when the Mesopotamian empires started trading with each other, Egypt, and Persia. Khanna expands the definition of globalization to include global supply chains, energy markets, industrial production, and flows of finance, technology, knowledge, and talent, stating that "the advance of global network civilization is the surest bet one could have made over the past five thousand years."[4]

In the long run, this has been true. However, Khanna fails to note that each expansion of globalization ended, often with a severe contraction. Some contractions, like the misnamed Dark Ages, lasted for centuries. Others, like the collapse of trade caused by World War I, lasted decades. Increasing connectivity between regions has not been a one-way phenomenon. It has repeatedly been subject to long periods of deglobalization where the key elements of globalization—the movement of goods, services, investments, people, and ideas—have declined.

The World Trade Organization (WTO) focuses on modern globalization and marks its beginning as the start of the Industrial Revolution.

> The immense technological advances in transportation and communications that it unleashed—from steamships, railroad and telegraphs to automobiles, aeroplanes and the internet—steadily reduced the cost of moving goods, capital, technology, and people around the globe.[5]

Further, the WTO divides it into two "ages of globalization." The first age stretched from the start of the Industrial Revolution in the early 1800s until World War I. During this period, the convergence of technologies created cost advantages for those nations that could also master the advances in production, transportation, finance, and communication. These advances were reinforced by a political and social environment among the developed nations that pushed hard to expand trade as a way to both generate wealth and "civilize" the non-Western world. As the leader in both the Industrial Revolution and global finance, Britain was in the best position to profit from global trade, and its government made key decisions that supported it. It placed the pound on the gold standard in the early 1820s. Other nations followed suit in the 1870s so that, by the 1880s, Britain had effectively created a global financial system. Pegging the value of their currencies to a single commodity virtually eliminated foreign exchange risks and reduced the friction inherent in international payments.

Britain also led the way in negotiating bilateral trade agreements to dramatically lower trade tariffs, thus increasing international trade among developed nations. To prevent being undercut by British policies, the other nations of Europe followed suit. To bolster their empires, the tariff rates between colonies and the home countries were the same, thus drawing large parts of the world outside Europe into the growing global network of trade. Finally, the Royal Navy provided security so that all trading nations could take advantage of the huge cost benefits associated with sea trade compared to overland shipments.

The combination worked. The gross world product (the summation of national gross domestic products [GDP]) grew at a rate of 2.1 percent from 1870 to 1913, but exports expanded at almost double that rate—3.8 percent.[6]

Western domination of manufacturing also led to the destruction of growing industrial capability in the rest of the world. India's cotton cloth industry was an early casualty.[7] The growth of Britain's textile industry and the collapse of India's was only one example of how the Industrial Revolution reallocated wealth around the world. Those nations that mastered and applied the new technologies grew much wealthier. Those that could not saw the destruction of large segments of their economies.

One exception was the United States. Although a major agricultural and rising merchandise exporter, it maintained high tariffs to protect its young domestic industries from advanced European competitors. Politics and profits provided the motivation for a pushback against international trade. When Italy (1861) and Germany (1871) were each finally unified, they each applied tariffs to protect their own industries and encourage the economic integration of their newly formed nations. The last three decades of the nineteenth century saw a rising tariff lobbying effort by domestic industries that were losing profits to overseas competitors. Across the globe, governments responded by imposing tariffs. Despite this pushback, global trade continued to grow faster than gross world product because colonial powers continued to exempt their colonies from tariffs to consolidate and expand their empires.[8] The home countries made high profits in selling overseas and gained from cheaper raw material imports.

Then, in August 1914, global trade crashed because of World War I. Trade as a percentage of gross world production had reached a high of 11.9 percent in 1913 but collapsed at the start of the war. It would not approach the 1914 level again until 1973.[9] After World War I, the recovery of trade was severely hindered by the political reaction to the Great Depression. Responding to social pressure from their voters, governments raised tariffs sharply. The U.S. Congress passed the infamous Smoot-Hawley Tariff Act in June 1930 over the objection of a majority of economists who believed the Act "would exacerbate the U.S. recession into a worldwide depression"[10] The Act was not driven by economic calculation but by American voters' fear and their desire for protection.

The WTO's second wave of globalization started after World War II. Unlike the first, this wave was assisted by specific international efforts to establish a global trading system. At the 1944 Bretton Woods conference, Western leaders strove to create an overarching legal, political, and financial system to encourage world trade. They created the International Monetary Fund (IMF) and the World Bank that remain central to the global economic system today.[11] The United States also resourced the European Recovery Program (Marshall Plan) to kick start the recovery. These governmental efforts set the conditions to rebuild international trade, but it was profit-motivated decisions by thousands of businesses, large and small, that provided the drive to see it through. They succeeded.

Assisted by major technological improvements in the field of transportation—air, sea, and land, world merchandise trade grew by eight percent per year from 1950 to 1973.[12] The advent of the jet age allowed leaders from all fields to travel much more regularly, and cheaply, to meet with international partners. At sea, ships increased in size by an order of magnitude. In the early 1950s, oil tankers averaged 16,000 deadweight tons (DWT) and dry cargo ships 10,000 DWT. Today, the largest tankers are over 500,000 DWT and bulk carriers range upward to 400,000 DWT. Size and efficiency greatly reduced the cost of shipping.

However, the truly important development in moving freight occurred in the mid-1950s with the development of the intermodal standard twenty-foot shipping container. They could be unloaded directly from ship to truck or train for onward movement in ports designed specifically to handle them. Bigger, faster ships tied to bigger ports with much higher throughput led to sharp drop in shipping costs that strongly encouraged long-distance trade.

Then, in 1973, the Organization of Petroleum Exporting States' embargo disrupted global growth. Pressured by second oil shock, the 1979 Iranian revolution, inflation, and inadequate trade and monetary policies, global trade slowed growth for two decades. Merchandise trade as a percentage of global GDP would not return to its 1974 level until 1993.[13] In the mid-1990s, China began to make itself felt in the global trade arena and the information technology revolution began to take effect with particular import for transportation costs.

Today, container ships can carry more than 19,000 containers. Managing that number of containers in an effective, tightly scheduled network required massive advances in information technology. The sheer volume of data involved in tracking these containers from factory to buyer would have been impossible to manage without advances not just in computers and software but in communications and peripheral hardware such as scanners. From 2000 to 2007, trade grew at a rate of six percent. This sustained the average from 1950 to 2007 at 6.2 percent, or about twice as fast as during the first wave of globalization from 1850 to 1913.[14] The remarkable burst of globalization increased the Global Trade (goods and services) percentage of the global GDP from 39.7 percent in 1991 to 60.8 percent in 2007.[15]

Then the 2008–2009 global financial crisis devastated global trade and led to concerns about deglobalization. Academics, think tanks, and respected news journals all speculated that the collapse would result in a rapid and long-term decrease in global trade. A Council on Foreign Relations–sponsored paper noted that the backlash would include both restrictive immigration measures and rising trade tariffs.[16]

In February 2009, in a short piece titled "Turning Their Backs on the World," *The Economist* outlined the key deglobalization indicators.

> World trade has plunged. As recently as the first half of 2008, boosted by rising commodity prices and a falling dollar, trade was growing at an annualised 20% in dollar terms. In the second half of 2008, as commodities sagged and the dollar rose, growth slowed fast; by September, says the IMF, it was in reverse. In December, says the International Air Transport Association, air-cargo traffic (responsible for over a third of the value of the world's traded goods) was down 23% on December 2007—almost double the fall in the year up to the end of September 2001, a result affected by the 9/11 terror attacks.[17]

Despite the sudden and very significant drops in global merchandise trade due to the financial crisis, the global economy showed remarkable resilience. It defied deglobalization predictions and bounced back. World Bank statistics show that global merchandise trade as a percentage of GDP recovered relatively quickly from the 2009 crisis, almost reaching pre-crisis levels by 2011 (see figure 1). Speculation about slowing globalization ceased. Optimism returned that global trade would continue to lead global economic growth.

Figure 1. Trade (% GDP).

Total Trade as a % of GDP

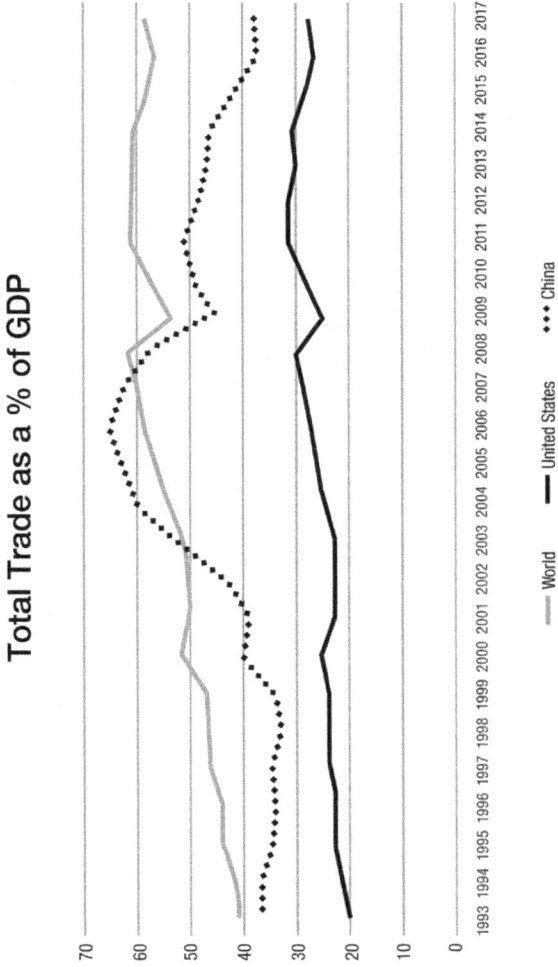

World   ▬▬ United States   ••• China

1993 1994 1995 1996 1997 1998 1999 2000 2001 2002 2003 2004 2005 2006 2007 2008 2009 2010 2011 2012 2013 2014 2015 2016 2017

Source: World Bank, "Trade (% of GDP)," http://data.worldbank.org/indicator/NE.TRD.GNFS.ZS/countries/1W-CN-US? display=graph.

Even as worries about deglobalization faded, trade (the combined value of merchandise and services), as a percentage of global GDP, flattened and then declined. Whereas the world economy continued to grow from 2011 to 2014,[18] the growth of international trade lagged behind instead of exceeding the growth rates. Both the global economy and global trade decreased sharply from 2014 to 2015, but although the global economy recovered, the decline in trade remained steep in 2016.[19] However,

> Global trade rebounded in 2017. ... The rebound springs predominantly from stronger import demand in East Asia, as domestic demand picked up in the region, supported by accommodative policy measures.[20]

For 2018, the World Trade Organization reported that world merchandise trade declined slightly for the first three quarters but then increased in the last quarter.[21] Reuters noted that some of the growth was attributed to the fact that in the last quarter of 2018, U.S. businesses built record inventories as they stocked warehouses in anticipation of new Trump administration tariffs.[22]

World Bank statistics (figure 2) show merchandise trade followed the same pattern. It increased sharply from 1995 to 2007, dropped sharply in 2008, then climbed steeply from 2009 until 2011, flattened in from 2012 to 2014 and fell sharply from $19.11 trillion in 2014 to $16.07 trillion in 2016.[23] By the end of 2018, world trade had rebounded to just above the 2014 figure but, by February 2019, the World Trade Organization predicted a sharp slowdown for global trade.[24] Scholars find these trends significant, with one noting,

> For a number of reasons, this stagnation in global trade may not be just a temporary disruption. One is a major shift in China, which imported vast quantities of commodities, industrial parts, and equipment as it became the assembly plant for the world. Lately, China has been importing less, as its economy slows sharply and as it make more of the parts it needs at home...[25]

Figure 2. Merchandise Trade (% of GDP).

Merchandise Trade as a % of GDP

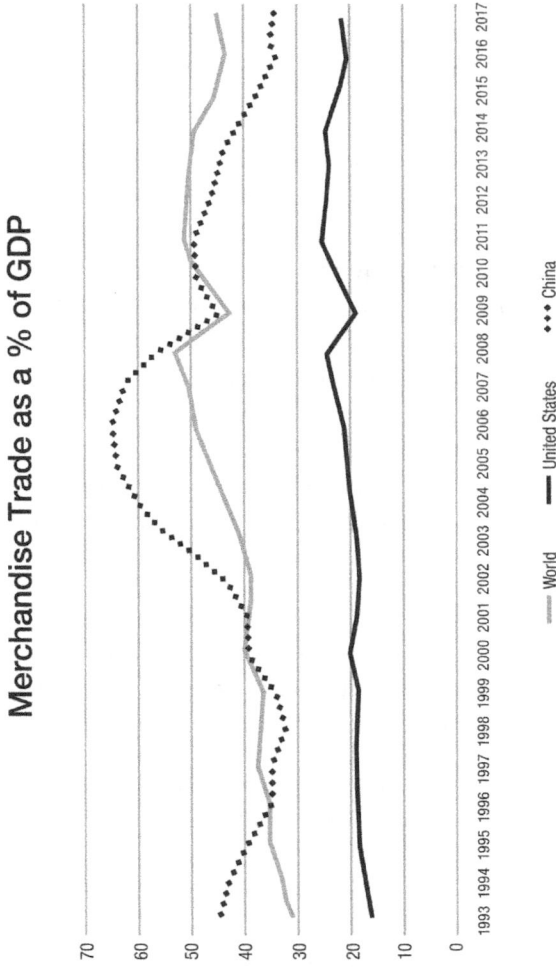

70 60 50 40 30 20 10 0

1993 1994 1995 1996 1997 1998 1999 2000 2001 2002 2003 2004 2005 2006 2007 2008 2009 2010 2011 2012 2013 2014 2015 2016 2017

—— World ——— United States ••• China

Source: World Bank, "Merchandise trade (% of GDP)," http://data.worldbank.org/indicator/TG.VAL.TOTL.GD.ZS/countries?display=graph

Thus, two of *The Economist*'s key measures of globalization—the movement of goods and services—declined from 2011 to 2016 and are predicted to fall farther in 2019. However, some dismiss the possibility of deglobalization because they feel the traditional trade statistics fail to account properly for services. Because each nation's GDP is used as a base figure for calculating foreign trade percentages, it is important to understand the problems with using this measure.

A good place to start is to ask where the term came from and what it measures. In 1940, John Maynard Keynes, a famed economist and investor, defined the gross domestic product as "the sum of private consumption and investment and government spending (with account taken for foreign trade)."[26] With some modifications, this remains the rough measure of a nation's production. There are a number of significant problems with using this measure. GDP does not do a good job of measuring unpaid activities such as home care, home schooling, or even housekeeping; new economic ventures such as Uber; or free online entertainment or social media like Facebook, YouTube, and Google. Furthermore, the bias toward manufacturing means that GDP does a poor job of measuring financial activities.[27]

Yet, for all its problems, GDP remains a central statistic in tracking and projecting the performance of the economy and has the considerable virtue of being familiar to the non-economist reader. Thus, I will use GDP as the best measure currently available to track trends in the economy.

As one would expect, another measure of international trade activity —global financial flows—declined sharply during the crisis. However, unlike global trade flows, financial flows did not recover between 2009 and 2011. The decade before 2008 saw rapid ramping up of international capital flows until they represented ten to fifteen percent of global GDP. Growth in the accumulation of external assets and liabilities were even greater than the growth in trade. Then the collapse of 2008 led to massive retrenchment with the reversal of flows equal to ten percent of the global GDP. Trade recovered but financial flows did not.

Figure 3. Total Net Financial Flows to Developing Economies.

Total Net Financial Flows to Developing Economies
(Billions of US Dollars)

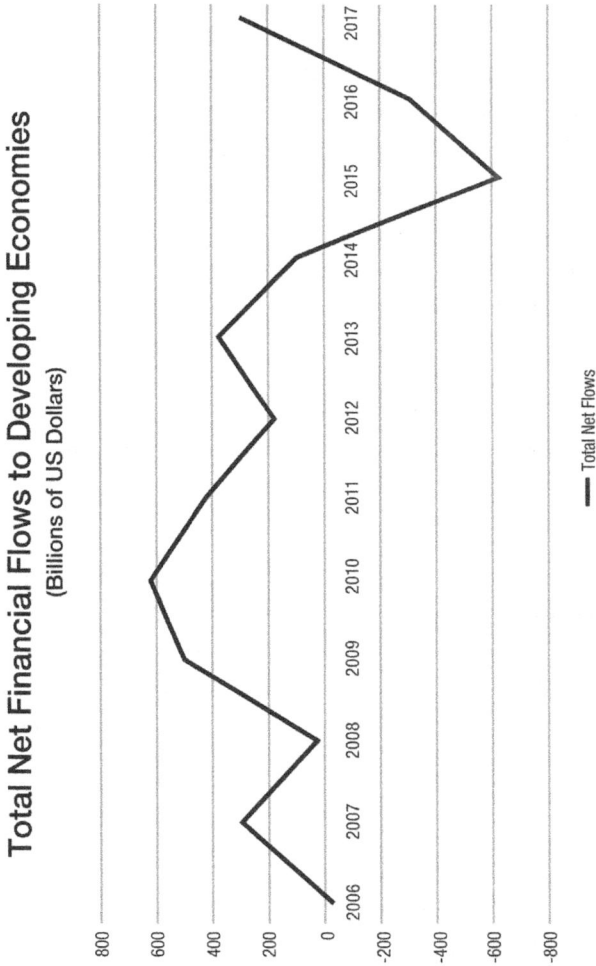

Total Net Flows

Source: "World Economic Situation and Prospects 2018," United Nations, 39, https://www.un.org/development/desa/dpad/wp-content/uploads/sites/45/publication/WESP2018_Full_Web-1.pdf

"The 'Great Retrenchment' that took place during the crisis has proved very persistent, and world financial flows are now down to half their pre-crisis levels..."[28] These decreases in financial flows hit developing countries particularly hard. Figure 3 shows capital inflows to these countries initially rebounded after the 2008 crisis but slowed again after 2010, then turned negative in 2014. The decline was driven by large net outflows from transition economies, particularly the Russian Federation. In 2015, over $700 billion in capital left developing economies, greatly exceeding even the $145 billion net outflows during the Great Recession.[29]

In August 2016, the European Central Bank released a working paper that stated: "The global financial crisis in 2008 led to a precipitous decline in international capital flows, representing an abrupt interruption of the financial globalisation process."[30] They have declined from 16% of the global economy in 2007 to only 2% in 2015—a level last seen in 1980.[31] Flows to developing countries remained heavily negative in 2016 as $300 billion in additional capital left. Whereas capital flows to developing economies turned positive in 2017, they did not begin to replace the outflow from the previous years.[32]

Despite these indicators, the March 2016 issue of *Harvard Business Review* argued that globalization was not slowing but still increasing rapidly. A team of authors noted that "globalization is becoming more about data and less about stuff...It has gone digital. Cross-border data flows have grown by a factor of 45 over the past decade, and they're projected to post another ninefold increase by 2020."[33]

Recent research from the McKinsey Global Institute also explored this new era of digital globalization. It found "over a decade, all types of flows acting together have raised world GDP by 10.1 percent...This value amounted to some $7.8 trillion in 2014 alone, and data flows account for $2.8 trillion of this impact."[34]

An increase from near zero to $2.8 trillion is very impressive growth, however, it should be kept in perspective. According to the World Bank, global GDP was $81 trillion in 2017.[35] Further, the authors of the study admit it is very tricky to translate the number of terabytes of data flowing across borders to a dollar value. One analysis of the flow indicated seventy percent of North American Internet traffic during peak hours in 2015 came from video and music streaming.[36] In addition, CISCO Systems attributed much of the increase in traffic to a "growing number of M2M [machine to machine] applications, such as smart meters, video surveillance, healthcare monitoring, transportation, and package or asset tracking, are contributing in a major way to the growth of devices and connections."[37] It is difficult to see how data that is heavily about entertainment and day-to-day operation of mechanical devices contributes heavily to globalization. This subject certainly requires further research.

In the two previous rounds of modern globalization noted by the WTO, profits have been the essential driver. Businesses did not expand out of their home countries for geopolitical or charity reasons. They went out to make money. In January 2017, *The Economist* noted a key indicator of deglobalization

> Central to the rise of the global firm was its claim to be a superior moneymaking machine. That claim lies in tatters...Returns on capital have slipped to their lowest level in two decades...the pain is too widespread and prolonged to be dismissed as a blip. About 40% of all multinationals make a return on equity of less than 10%, a yardstick for underperformance. In a majority of industries they are growing more slowly and are less profitable than local firms that stayed in their backyard...For many industrial, manufacturing, financial, natural resources, media and telecoms companies, global reach has become a burden not an advantage.[38]

The trend of multinationals withdrawing from the global market is a particularly powerful element in deglobalization. Although multinationals account for only two percent of the world's jobs, they own or run over fifty percent of world trade. The cross-border supply chains' share of trade has stagnated since 2007. Whereas the trade figures only stagnated, profits of the top seven hundred multinational firms headquartered in rich countries dropped by twenty-five percent over the last five years.[39]

Many firms expanded too quickly and into too many new markets. To correct these errors

> companies themselves are backing away from globalization. For several years, there's been a growing trend in business toward so-called vertical integration, in which companies put high-end jobs —in research and development or product design—closer to lower-end factory and logistics jobs...[they] now create multiple product hubs in regions, rather than building complex global supply chains based on where each element of a product can be sourced most cheaply. This "localization" is now being touted by companies from General Electric to Caterpillar and IBM.[40]

In its Global Connectedness Index 2018, Deutsche Post DHL reports that the combined measures of trade, capital, information, and people flows increased in 2017. Europe led on trade and people flows, however, seventy-five percent of that was intraregional.[41] Similarly, the United States led on capital and information flows, but most were intraregional. Thus, even the flows that are increasing are primarily regional rather than global. The report cautioned that "the policy environment for globalization darkened in 2018 as trade conflicts escalated and countries raised barriers to foreign takeovers, immigration, and other flows."[42]

The international shipping industry's dramatic decline in the last few years is a clear indicator of reduced volume of trade. In late 2015, massive container freight overcapacity drove spot freight rates from China to Europe down by thirty-two percent.[43] Shipping companies responded by scrapping one thousand ships with an average age of only fifteen years instead of the normal thirty. They also drastically reduced orders for new ships. Maersk Shipping, one of the three largest shipping firms in the world, announced it would not be exercising its options for six second-generation 19,630 TEU Triple E Class ships and two 3,600 TEU feeder vessels. It postponed the decision on eight optional 14,000 TEU vessels.[44]

Even these measures were insufficient. On September 4, 2016, Hanjin Shipping Company declared bankruptcy so suddenly that its ships and cargo were stranded at sea because they could not pay port fees.[45] Later that month, to protect itself, Maersk split its oil exploration and production, drilling rig, and oil tanker businesses into a new energy company separate from shipping. Soren Skou, the new chief executive A.P. Moller–Maersk Group, also known as Maersk, told the *Financial Times* that "We have nearshoring of manufacturing and the fact that containerisation has run its course—there's not much more you can put in a container that is not already in a container."[46]

In 2018, rates on the United States to Asia route fell well below 2017 rates until July. At that point, rates increased somewhat as the global economy continued to grow and shipping companies' capacity cuts began to take effect. However, the biggest boost in rates occurred when Trump threated to impose high tariffs on Chinese products. Shipping companies saw a surge in demand as producers rushed to get products into the United States before the tariffs took effect.[47] In early 2019, Soren Skou, chief executive of Maersk, told investors "We see weaknesses, in particular, in China and Europe. We expect container demand growth to fall to 1 to 3% this year from 3.7% to 3.8% last year."[48] United Parcel Service's CEO David Abney concurred, stating "3D printing is becoming the face of manufacturing and distribution. It allows manufacturers to go from mass production to custom production."[49]

The underlying technological advances and structural changes in economies—most importantly, how one makes money—are the main drivers behind globalization, but political forces sometimes also play a central role. Political leaders sometimes facilitate a globally integrated market and resist it at other times. The devastating impact of World War I and the global tariff wars of the 1930s demonstrate how governments can create so much friction that it is impossible to make serious profits in international trade. When that happens, deglobalization follows. Similarly, government support can make overseas trade more profitable. The post–World War II wave of globalization received extensive government assistance. As noted, Bretton Woods established a rules based order for trade and finance. And the Marshall Plan provide for economic recovery in Europe even as NATO provided security.

Prominent U.S. foreign policy and national security elites still contend the United States must remain fully engaged overseas to protect its interests. Ten leading practitioners recently concluded that

> the best way to ensure the longevity of a rules-based international system favorable to U.S. interests is not to retreat behind two oceans...The proper course is to extend American power and U.S. leadership in Asia, Europe, and the Greater Middle East..."[50]

However, in the last few years, the public mood has shifted in both Europe and America. Dissatisfaction with past policies and priorities pushed by elites has led to a palpable populist narrative. Voters have focused inwardly on economic and cultural issues. Nationalist parties have been present in various nations in Europe for decades, but a confluence of factors have raised their profile and power dramatically. Perhaps the biggest political shock came when the British voted in favor of Brexit. By focusing on the anger and fear of their supporters, proponents never even had to define what the exit would look like. *The Economist* reported that the "yes" vote represented "an angry revolt by millions of British voters against their government, the leaders of the main political parties, big business and experts of all stripes."[51] Over three years later, the British government still has not defined Brexit. Whatever the outcome, a significant portion of the British population will be deeply dissatisfied with their government.

The voters in the United Kingdom were not alone in responding to the nationalist appeals of right-wing parties. In Poland, the Law and Freedom Party came to power in 2015, winning the country's first post-1989 outright majority. In Denmark, the Euro-skeptic, anti-immigrant Danish People's Party finished second in the 2015 elections and passed some of the toughest anti-immigration laws in Europe. In Finland, the True Finns Party also came in second in 2015 elections. Anti-immigrant parties are also making gains in Greece, Hungary, Italy, Netherlands, Sweden, and Switzerland.[52]

The anti-European, anti-immigration parties continued to gain strength in 2016. In May 2016 the United Kingdom's *Telegraph* noted "the toxic combination of the most prolonged period of economic stagnation and the worst refugee crisis since the end of the Second World War has seen the far-Right surging across the continent, from Athens to Amsterdam and many points in between."[53] In Austria's December 2016 presidential run-off election, where neither mainstream party was represented, Nick Hofer of the Freedom Party of Austria (FPÖ) was only narrowly defeated. However, by December 2017, the FPÖ took control of the defense, interior, and foreign ministry as part of the new coalition government. The FPÖ took a tough stance on immigration and asylum seekers, and its leader, Heinz-Christian Strache, who has warned of Austria's "Islamification," became vice-chancellor of Austria (2017–2019).[54]

In the Netherlands, Geert Wilders' Party for Freedom, which led in early 2017 polls, was turned back and finished in second place. Although falling short of expectations, the Party for Freedom's move into second place indicated significant anti-immigration feeling among the Dutch.[55] In the 2017 elections, the far-right Alternative for Germany Party entered the German parliament for the first time and is the largest opposition party.[56]

In France, the National Front, founded in 1972 as a right-wing, nation-alist, anti-immigrant party, thrived in 2016 and early 2017. High-profile terror attacks, high rates of immigration from North Africa, and declining prospects for France's working class led to a surge of support. Nationalist Party leader Marine Le Pen even stated she would become the next president as the third leg of a "global" revolution after Brexit and Amer-ican president Donald Trump's election. Although Emmanuel Macron's resounding win in final round indicated that the French had backed away from the National Front's extreme positions, the very fact that Le Pen was a serious contender to run France indicates the strong shift to the right wing in French politics.

Le Pen's second-place finish did not indicate the European movement to the right had peaked. In April 2018, Hungary's Viktor Orbán was not only reelected, but his far-right Fidesz Party also gained a supermajority in parliament.[57]

Amotz Asa-El, the former executive editor of the *Jerusalem Post* and a leading commentator on international affairs, wrote "the zeitgeist is about fear. People throughout the rich world feel insecure about their jobs, their safety, and their identity. Identity is threatened, they feel, by immigration; safety by terror; and jobs by globalization."[58]

The same anti-immigration, anti–free trade passions that drove European elections played a major role in the U.S. 2016 presidential election. As a senator, Hillary Clinton spoke out in favor of free trade; and as Secretary of State, she favored the Trans-Pacific Partnership (TPP) as a method of strengthening both the U.S. economy and alliances in Asia.[59] But in the 2016 presidential campaign, candidate Clinton was driven to modify early campaign promises and go on record as opposing the TPP trade agreement.

Throughout his campaign, Trump aggressively attacked both North American Free Trade Agreement (NAFTA), the TPP, and the Transatlantic Trade and Investment Partnership.

Both Trump and Clinton were responding to the changing voter attitudes. The assumption that global trade is good may still exist among policymakers and economists, but it is rapidly fading among voters. In 2002, Pew Research found that seventy-eight percent of Americans supported global trade. By 2008, the percentage had fallen to fifty-three percent.[60] In 2014, when Pew changed the questions from whether trade was good for the nation to whether trade improved the livelihood of Americans, favorable ratings plunged. Only seventeen percent of Americans thought trade leads to higher wages, and only twenty percent believed it created new jobs.[61] In August 2016, the *Guardian* noted "never before have both main presidential candidates broken with the orthodoxy that globalisation is always good for Americans."[62]

The election of Trump clearly indicates that many Americans share the anti-globalization, anti-immigration nationalism of their European counterparts. This is not a new attitude but one that has been steadily growing globally. Since the financial crisis of 2008, more than 3,500 protectionist measures have been instituted globally as well as numerous additional administrative requirements that have increased the difficulty of conducting international trade.[63] The trend toward protectionism does not seem to be slowing. The December 2016 meeting of the WTO's Trade Policy Review Body noted that, of the 2,978 measures recorded since 2009, only 740 had been removed.[64]

Scholars and economists can provide convincing evidence that globalization has allowed developing countries to make great gains relative to the leading economies of the United States, Japan, and the European Union. In doing so, they summarize the position of many globalists.

> The open, rules-based trading system has delivered immense benefits—for the world, for individual countries, and for average citizens in these countries...Three challenges must be met to preserve this system. Rich countries must sustain the social consensus in favor of open markets and globalization at a time of considerable economic uncertainty and weakness. China and other middle-income countries must remain open, and mega-regionalism must be prevented from leading to discrimination and trade conflicts.[65]

Unfortunately, the wealthiest nations are leading the charge for more trade restrictions. The Center for Economic Policy Research, a leading UK-based think tank, found that the richest countries passed twenty-three percent more protectionist measures in 2013 than they had in 2009.[66] As part of its efforts to grow its own industries, India established a world-leading five-hundred trade restrictions between 2008 and 2015.[67] The 2016 and 2017 election campaigns in the United States and Europe revealed a great deal of populist anger and resulted in a serious discussions over measures to protect domestic production. For its part, China has quietly but firmly done so. And, at the time of this writing, the United States–China trade wars have continued with no new treaty in sight.

Part of the problem is that economists and scholars are hard pressed to prove that globalization has benefitted specific countries, and they are even harder pressed to prove the benefit to the individuals who have seen their standards of living decline during this period. In fact, post-crisis, multinational firms "created jobs abroad but not at home. Between 2009 and 2013, only five percent or 400,000 of the net jobs created in America were created by multinational firms domiciled there. ... The profits from their hoards of intellectual property were pocketed by a wealthy shareholder elite. Political willingness to help multinationals duly lapsed."[68]

With Trump about to assume office in January 2017, the *Wall Street Journal*, not known for populist views, summarized the source of uneasiness about the political shift against globalization.

> Free trade, greater interconnectedness and rapid technological change have lifted billions out of poverty and created a burgeoning middle class in the developing world. Wealthy countries have grown richer, too. But the benefits have gone disproportionately to a minority, leaving many people left behind or alienated.[69]

One of the key drivers of the 2016 through the 2018 elections in the United States and Europe was the anger of those voters who perceive that globalization has left them behind.

This shift from globalism has not been limited to the United States and Europe. In its 2016 year-end roundup issue, *The Economist* noted:

> As globalism has become a slur, nationalism, and even authoritarianism, have flourished...Indeed for most people on Earth there has never been a better time to be alive. Large parts of the West, however, do not see it that way. For them progress happens mainly to other people. Wealth does not spread itself, new technologies destroy jobs that never come back, an underclass is beyond help

or redemption, and other cultures pose a threat—sometimes a violent one.[70]

FACTORS SLOWING DEGLOBALIZATION

Although technological convergence is driving companies towards deglobalization, there remain a number of factors that will inhibit its speed. In particular, embedded supply chains and lack of skilled labor will act as brakes. When manufacturing moved overseas, so did the supply chains that support it. When calculating the possible benefits of reshoring, CEOs must also consider the potential costs of a rebuilding the supply chain in the new location. The United Nations Conference on Trade and Development noted that "developed countries now lack the supplier networks that some developing countries have built to complement assembly activities."[71] Fortunately, advanced manufacturing, particularly 3D manufacturing, is eliminating the requirement for many of the subassemblies and assemblies. In January 2019, McKinsey Global Institute Company reported that supply value chains were already adjusting by "becoming more regional and less global."[72]

The supply-chain problem will get better over time; however, skilled labor may remain a major problem. From 2010 to 2016, the United States regained one million manufacturing jobs.[73] The job growth could have been faster, but employers have been unable to find skilled laborer to fill available jobs. Mursix Corporation, a creator of seat belt buckles and bed frames, is typical. Valued at $42 million, its average wage is over $20 an hour with a benefits package. Yet, it cannot fill its labor requirements. "In an effort to draw talent, the firm even set up an apprenticeship, paying promising employees as they learn the trade."[74] The problem is many otherwise-eligible workers are not willing or are unable to retrain. Although the number of open manufacturing jobs is at a fifteen-year high, many low-skilled former factory workers seem to be frozen out of the growing high-tech manufacturing sector.[75]

The Deloitte Manufacturing Institute projects that over the next decade "three and a half million manufacturing jobs likely need to be filled and the skills gap is expected to result in 2 million of those jobs going unfilled."[76] U.S. firms were short more than 300,000 skilled workers though 2016 and well into 2017.[77] The shortage of skilled labor will delay globalization but also speed the transition to automation.

SUMMARY

In 2007, cross-border goods, services, and financial flows made up fifty-three percent of the global economy. By 2015, that had dropped to only thirty-nine percent.[78] Since 2012, global trade has grown at only three percent, less than half the average of the last three decades.[79] Of particular concern, the slowdown was not limited to developed economies but also hit emerging economies in both goods and services. In late 2016, global finance ministers and central bankers met in Washington, D.C., to discuss the alarming indications of deglobalization."[80] Although McKinsey Global Institute (MGI) reported in 2014 "that global flows could...more than double or triple their current scale,"[81] by 2016, it changed its tone. MGI also reported that "after 20 years of rapid growth, traditional flows of goods, services, and finance have declined relative to GDP."[82]

As usual with interactively complex problems, analysts are split over whether recent reductions in trade and financial flows are a cyclical downturn or a sustained long-term shift. Some predict globalization will resume and even accelerate.[83] In contrast, I argue that the convergence of new technologies reinforced by political and social forces will dramatically alter trade patterns. Over the next decade or two, these trends will result in regionalization and even some localization of manufacturing, services, energy, and food production. Profits, politics, and social trends will all drive trade patterns toward regional trade blocks. As always, popular political moods and social movements are subject to sudden reversal. However, even if they shift back in favor of globalization, the converging technologies will still make it more profitable to produce in the target market, and that will fundamentally change the global economy. Nor is this period of deglobalization likely to be short. Political and even security factors may shift quickly. But the technological convergence that is making it more profitable to produce locally and regionally will not be short lived. To explore what is driving this shift, it is necessary to examine the new technologies whose convergence will so dramatically alter how, where, and what is made—and that leads us to chapter 2.

NOTES

1. "Definition of globalization," *Financial Times,* http://lexicon.ft.com/term? term=globalisation.
2. Alex Gray, "What is globalization anyway?" *World Economic Forum,* January 10, 2017, https://www.weforum.org/agenda/2017/01/what-is-globalization-explainer/.
3. "Turning Their Backs on the World," *Economist,* February 19–25, 2009, http://www.economist.com/node/13145370.
4. Parag Khanna, *Connectography: Mapping the Future of Global Civilization* (New York: Random House, 2016), 35.
5. *World Trade Report 2013: Factors Shaping the Future of World Trade* (Geneva: World Trade Organization, 2014), 46, https://www.wto.org/ english/res_e/booksp_e/world_trade_report13_e.pdf.
6. *World Trade Report 2008: Trade in a Globalizing World* (Geneva: World Trade Organization, 2009), 15, https://www.wto.org/english/res_e/ booksp_e/anrep_e/world_trade_report08_e.pdf.
7. Sven Beckert, *Empire of Cotton: A New History of Global Capitalism,* (London: Penguin, 2014).
8. *World Trade Report 2013,* 51.
9. Paul Krugman, "Growing World Trade: Causes and Consequences," Brookings Papers on Economic Activity, 1:1995, https://www. brookings.edu/wp-content/uploads/2016/07/1995a_bpea_krugman_ cooper_srinivasan.pdf, 331.
10. Theodore Phalan, Deema Yazigi, and Thomas Rustici, "The Smoot-Hawley Tariff and the Great Depression," Foundation for Economic Education, February 29, 2012, https://fee.org/articles/the-smoot-hawley-tariff-and-the-great-depression.
11. Buttonwood, "What Was Decided at the Bretton Woods Summit," *Economist,* July 30–August 5, 2014, http://www.economist.com/blogs/ economist-explains/2014/06/economist-explains-20.
12. *World Trade Report 2013,* 52.
13. Chart: "Merchandise Trade (% of GDP)," World Bank, http://data. worldbank.org/indicator/TG.VAL.TOTL.GD.ZS.
14. *World Trade Report 2008,* 15.
15. Chart: "Trade (% of GDP), World Bank, http://data.worldbank.org/ indicator/NE.TRD.GNFS.ZS/countries/1W-CN-US?display=graph.

16. Jayshree Bajoria, "The Dangers of 'Deglobalization,'" *Council on Foreign Relations*, March 16, 2009, http://www.cfr.org/immigration/dangers-deglobalization/p18768.

17. *The Economist*, "Turning Their Backs on the World," February 2009.

18. "GDP (Current US$)," The World Bank, https://data.worldbank.org/indicator/NY.GDP.MKTP.CD.

19. "Merchandise Trade (% of GDP)," The World Bank, https://data.worldbank.org/indicator/TG.VAL.TOTL.GD.ZS?end=2018&start=1960&view=chart.

20. United Nations World Economic Situation and Prospects 2018, viii, https://www.un.org/development/desa/dpad/wp-content/uploads/sites/45/publication/WESP2018_Full_Web-1.pdf.

21. "Global trade growth loses momentum as trade tensions persist," World Trade Organization, April 2, 2019, https://www.wto.org/english/news_e/pres19_e/pr837_e.htm.

22. Reuters, "Trump tariff war with China sends U.S. retailers on buying binge," *NBC News*, December 20, 2018, https://www.nbcnews.com/business/business-news/trump-tariff-war-china-sends-u-s-retailers-buying-binge-n950251.

23. "Trade: Merchandise Exports (Current US$)," http://data.worldbank.org/topic/trade.

24. "WTO trade indicator points to slower trade growth into first quarter of 2019," February 19, 2019, https://www.wto.org/english/news_e/news19_e/wtoi_19feb19_e.htm.

25. Ruchir Sharma, *Rise and Fall of Nations: Forces of Change in the Post Crisis World,* (New York: Norton, 2016), 172.

26. "The Trouble with GDP," *Economist*, April 30–May 6, 2016, http://www.economist.com/news/briefing/21697845-gross-domestic-product-gdp-increasingly-poor-measure-prosperity-it-not-even.

27. Ibid.

28. Matthieu Bussiere, Julia Schmidt, and Natacha Valla, "International Financial Flows in the New Normal: Key Patterns (and Why We Should Care)," *CEPII Policy Brief*, no. 10, March 2016, www.cepii.fr/PDF_PUB/pb/2016/pb2016-10.pdf.

29. Sharma, *Rise and Fall of Nations*, 5.

30. Peter McQuade and Martin Schmitz, "The Great Moderation in International Capital Flows: A Global Phenomenon?" European Central Bank, Working Paper Series, no. 1952, August 2016, 2, https://www.ecb.europa.eu/pub/pdf/scpwps/ecbwp1952.en.pdf.

31. Sharma, *Rise and Fall of Nations*, 2.
32. "World Economic Situation and Prospects 2018," United Nations, 39, https://www.un.org/development/desa/dpad/wp-content/uploads/sites/45/publication/WESP2018_Full_Web-1.pdf.
33. Susan Lund, James Manyika, and Jacques Bughin, "Globalization Is Becoming More about Data and Less about Stuff," *Harvard Business Review*, March 14, 2016, https://hbr.org/2016/03/globalization-is-becoming-more-about-data-and-less-about-stuff.
34. James Manyinka et al., "Digital Globalization: The New Era of Global Flows," McKinsey Global Institute, February 2016, http://www.mckinsey.com/business-functions/digital-mckinsey/our-insights/digital-globalization-the-new-era-of-global-flows.
35. "GDP (Current US$)," World Bank.
36. Jillian D. Onfro, "More than 70% of internet traffic during peak hours now comes from video and music streaming," *Business Insider,* December 7, 2015, http://www.businessinsider.com/sandvine-bandwidth-data-shows-70-of-internet-traffic-is-video-and-music-streaming-2015-12.
37. "The Zettabyte Era: Trends and Analysis," Cisco Systems, June 2, 2016, http://www.cisco.com/c/en/us/solutions/collateral/service-provider/visual-networking-index-vni/vni-hyperconnectivity-wp.html.
38. "In Retreat," *Economist,* January 28–February 3, 2017, 11, https://www.economist.com/news/briefing/21715653-biggest-business-idea-past-three-decades-deep-trouble-retreat-global.
39. "The Retreat of the Global Company," *Economist,* January 28–February 3, 2017, 18–19, https://www.economist.com/news/briefing/21715653-biggest-business-idea-past-three-decades-deep-trouble-retreat-global.
40. Rana Foroohar, "We've Reached the End of Global Trade," *Time*, October 12, 2016, http://time.com/4521528/2016-election-global-trade.
41. Steven A. Altman et al., "DHL Global Connectedness Index 2018," DHL, February 19, 2019, 49, https://www.dpdhl.com/content/dam/dpdhl/en/media-center/media-relations/documents/2019/dhl-gci-2018-full-study.pdf.
42. Ibid, 4–5.
43. Bruce Barnard, "Global Container Ship Fleet Soars to 20 Million TEUs," *joc.com*, January 11, 2016, http://www.joc.com/maritime-news/ships-shipbuilding/global-container-ship-fleet-soars-20-million-teus_20160111.html.
44. Marcus Hand, "Updated: Maersk Line to Cut 4,000 Staff, Cancel Triple-E Newbuild Options," *Sea Trade Maritime News*, November 4, 2015, http://

www.seatrade-maritime.com/news/americas/maersk-line-to-cut-4000-staff-cancel-triple-e-newbuild-options.html.

45. Patrick Fitzgerald, "South Korea's Hanjin Shipping Files for U.S. Bankruptcy Protection," *Wall Street Journal*, September 4, 2016, http://www.wsj.com/articles/south-koreas-hanjin-shipping-files-for-u-s-bankruptcy-protection-1473002745.

46. Richard Milne, "Maersk Conglomerate to Break Up," *Financial Times*, September 22, 2016, https://www.ft.com/content/6fe125a4-8095-11e6-8e50-8ec15fb462f4.

47. Patrik Bergland, "Container Rate Development: 2018 Year-to-Date Trans-Pacific," *Xenata*, October 24, 2018, https://www.xeneta.com/blog/container-rate-development-2018-trans-pacific.

48. Costas Paris, "A Storm is Gathering Over Container Shipping," *Wall Street Journal*, March 3, 2019, https://www.wsj.com/articles/a-storm-is-gathering-over-container-shipping-11551612600.

49. Henry Carmichael, "Combination of 3D printing and fast shipping will lead to next industrial revolution – or disrupt it," *Freight Waves*, January 14, 2019, https://www.freightwaves.com/news/technology/fast-radius-ups-3d-printing.

50. Eric S. Edelman et al., "Extending American Power: Strategies to Expand U.S. Engagement in a Competitive World Order," Center for New American Security, May 16, 2016, 2, https://s3.amazonaws.com/files.cnas.org/documents/CNASReport-EAP-FINAL-1.pdf.

51. "The Brexit Vote Reveals a Country Split Down the Middle," *Economist*, June 24–30, 2016, http://www.economist.com/news/britain/21701257-results-paint-picture-angry-country-divided-class-age-and-region-country-divided.

52. "Guide to Nationalist Parties Challenging Europe," BBC News, May 23, 2016, http://www.bbc.com/news/world-europe-36130006.

53. Peter Foster, "The Rise of the Far-Right in Europe Is Not a False Alarm," *Telegraph*, May 19, 2016, http://www.telegraph.co.uk/news/2016/05/19/the-rise-of-the-far-right-in-europe-is-not-a-false-alarm.

54. Ralph Atkins and Mehreen Khan, "Far-right Freedom party enters Austrian government," *Financial Times*, December 17, 2017, https://www.ft.com/content/4608e324-e26a-11e7-97e2-916d4fbac0da.

55. Bill Campbell, "Geert Wilders, 'Dutch Donald Trump,' Takes Second Place in Closely Watched Election," *National Public Radio News*, March 16, 2017, http://www.npr.org/sections/thetwo-way/2017/03/16/520376

715/geert-wilders-dutch-donald-trump-takes-second-place-in-closely-watched-election.

56. "Germany coalition deal: Merkel set to lead fourth government," *BBC News,* March 4, 2018, http://www.bbc.com/news/world-europe-43276732.

57. James McAuley, "After Orbán's win in Hungary, Anxiety," *Washington Post,* April 10, 2018, A9.

58. Amotz Asa-El, "Deglobalization Is Already in Full Swing," *Market Watch,* August 31, 2016, http://www.marketwatch.com/story/deglobalization-is-already-in-full-swing-2016-08-31.

59. David Nakamura, "Hillary Clinton's Hedge on Trade Leaves Obama without Political Cover," *Washington Post,* May 12, 2016, https://www. washingtonpost.com/politics/on-trade-deal-hillary-clinton-keeps-her-distance-from-obama-and-her-past/2015/05/11/bc2cc604-f7e1-11e4-9ef4 -1bb7ce3b3fb7_story.html?tid=a_inl&utm_term=.929e96f8c832.

60. "Global Public Opinion in the Bush Years (2001–2008)," Pew Research Center, December 28, 2008, http://www.pewglobal.org/2008/12/18/ global-public-opinion-in-the-bush-years-2001-2008/#enthusiasm-for-globalization.

61. Bruce Stokes, "Most of the World Supports Globalization in Theory, but Many Question It in Practice," Pew Research Center, September 16, 2014, http://www.pewresearch.org/fact-tank/2014/09/16/most-of-the-world-supports-globalization-in-theory-but-many-question-it-in-practice.

62. Dan Roberts and Ryan Felton, "Trump and Clinton's Free Trade Retreat: a Pivotal Moment for the World's Economic Future," *Guardian,* August 20, 2016, https://www.theguardian.com/us-news/2016/aug/20/trump-clinton-free-trade-policies-tpp.

63. Josh Sumbrun, "Forces That Opened up Borders Show Signs of Sputtering," *Wall Street Journal,* April 4, 2016, A2.

64. Roberto Azevedo, "Trade Policy Review Body: Annual Overview of Developments in the International Trading Environment," World Trade Organization, December 9, 2016, https://www.wto.org/english/news_e/ spra_e/spra152_e.htm.

65. Arvind Subramanian and Martin Kessler, "The Hyperglobalization of Trade and Its Future," in *Towards a Better Global Economy: Policy Implications for Citizens Worldwide in the 21st Century,* ed. Franklin Allen et al., Oxford Scholarship Online, November 2014, doi:10.1093/ acprof:oso/9780198723455.003.0004.

66. Joshua Kurlantzick, "The Great Deglobalizing," *Boston Globe,* February 1, 2015, https://www.bostonglobe.com/ideas/2015/02/01/the-great-deglobalizing/a8TNmTd7pZNNtjhcK5hBZP/story.html.
67. Simon J. Evenett and Johannes Fritz, "The Tide Turns? Trade, Protectionism, and Slowing Global Growth: The 18th Global Trade Alert Report," Center for Economic Policy Research, 2015, 22, http://voxeu.org/sites/default/files/file/GTA18_final.pdf.
68. "The Retreat of the Global Company."
69. Stephen Fidler, "The New Landscape," *Wall Street Journal,* January 17, 2017, R6.
70. "The Year of Living Dangerously," *Economist,* December 24–30, 2016, 11.
71. "Robots and Industrialization in Developing Countries," United Nations Conference on Trade and Development, Policy Brief No. 50, October 2016, 2, http://unctad.org/en/PublicationsLibrary/presspb2016d6_en.pdf.
72. Susan Lund et al., "Globalization in transition," McKinsey Global Institute, January 2019, 8, https://www.mckinsey.com/featured-insights/innovation-and-growth/globalization-in-transition-the-future-of-trade-and-value-chains.
73. U.S. Department of Labor Databases, Tables & Calculators by Subject, https://data.bls.gov/pdq/SurveyOutputServlet.
74. Danielle Paquette, "Why So Many U.S. Manufacturers Are Putting Up 'Help Wanted' Signs," *Washington Post,* December 15, 2014, https://www.washingtonpost.com/news/wonk/wp/2016/12/15/are-manufacturing-jobs-really-dying-its-complicated/?utm_term=.41685dd49c88.
75. Andrew Tangel and Patrick McGroatry, "Factories Rebound but Job Gains Lag," *Wall Street Journal,* December 19, 2016, A2.
76. "The Skills Gap in U.S. Manufacturing 2015 and Beyond," Deloitte Manufacturing Institute, http://www.themanufacturinginstitute.org/~/media/827DBC76533942679A15EF7067A704CD.ashx.
77. Mary Josephs, "U.S. Manufacturing Labor Shortage: How to Make Your Company a Happy Exception," *Forbes,* March 15, 2017, https://www.forbes.com/sites/maryjosephs/2017/03/15/u-s-manufacturing-labor-shortage-how-to-make-your-company-a-happy-exception/#2aa6f4c27e13.
78. Rana Foroohar, "We've Reached the End of Global Trade," *Time,* October 12, 2016, http://time.com/4521528/2016-election-global-trade.
79. Simon Nixon, "Risk of Deglobalization Hangs over World Economy," Wall Street Journal, October 5, 2016, http://www.wsj.com/articles/risk-of-deglobalization-hangs-over-world-economy-1475685469.

80. Ian Talley and William Mauldin, "Globalization Is on the Skids," *Wall Street Journal*, October 7, 2016, A1.
81. James Manyika et al., "Digital Globalization: The New Era of Global Flows," McKinsey Global Institute, April 2014, http://www.mckinsey.com/business-functions/strategy-and-corporate-finance/our-insights/global-flows-in-a-digital-age.
82. Manyika, "Digital Globalization: The New Era of Global Flows," 8.
83. Kishore Mahbubani and Lawrence H. Summers, "The Fusion of Civilizations: The Case for Global Optimism," *Foreign Affairs*, May/June 2016, 126.

CHAPTER 2

TECHNOLOGICAL CONVERGENCE

Like earlier industrial revolutions, this new one will emerge from the convergence of multiple technologies. Despite the shorthand sometimes used to identify previous revolutions, none of them was driven by a single technology. Each needed a convergence of numerous new technologies along with accompanying economic, social, and political changes. Still, for the purposes of this book, it is useful to review the previous industrial revolutions quickly. It is also important to note that their failure to line up precisely with corresponding globalization periods indicates that, although technology was critical to the revolutions, they also required political and social conditions to magnify their effects.

Klaus lists the first three industrial revolutions as:

—First Industrial Revolution—from about 1760 to 1840, the invention of railroads and steam engines led to mechanical production.

—Second Industrial Revolution—from the late nineteenth to early twentieth century, electrical power and the assembly line made mass production feasible.

—Third Industrial Revolution—beginning in the 1960s, the digital revolution changed information was handled with the arrival of the mainframe computer (1960s), personal computing (1970s and 1980s) and Internet connectivity (1990s to present).[1]

Historians and other economists generally agree with Schwab's outline of the first three industrial revolutions. Robert J. Gordon of Northwestern University wrote that

a useful organising principle to understand the pace of growth since 1750 is the sequence of three industrial revolutions. The first (IR1) with its main inventions between 1750 and 1830 created steam engines, cotton spinning, and railroads. The second (IR2) was the most important, with its three central inventions of electricity, the internal combustion engine, and running water...The computer and internet revolution (IR3) began around 1960 and reached its climax in the dot.com era of the late 1990s...[2]

However, Gordon feels that technologically driven growth has faltered and will not overcome inherent difficulties. In contrast, Schwab is quite optimistic about the Fourth Industrial Revolution. He encourages readers

to think about the staggering confluence of emerging technology breakthroughs, covering wide-ranging fields such as artificial intelligence (AI), robotics, the internet of things (IoT), autonomous vehicles, 3D printing, nanotechnology, biotechnology, materials science, energy storage and quantum computing, to name a few. Many of these innovations are in their infancy, but they are already reaching an inflection point in their development as they build on and amplify each other in a fusion of technologies across the physical, digital and biological worlds.[3]

Schwab is convinced the convergence of these technologies is going to revolutionize almost every aspect of our lives, mostly in a positive way. However, when discussing its impact on international security, he was concerned that the technologies will provide much greater power to nonstate actors and create instability in many regions. I agree but believe it is important to expand the argument to include the impact that this revolution will have on relations between and among nation states, as well as the major impacts it will have on the character of war.

This book will not attempt to deal with all the technologies driving the Fourth Industrial Revolution but only those that will most directly impact international trade flows and the conduct of war. It will focus on the advances in eight individual areas—robotics, artificial intelligence (AI), 3D printing, energy, food production, nanotechnology, drones, and space.

This chapter will focus on the first five—robotics, AI, 3D printing, energy, and food production—and how they will greatly enhance the productive capability of a society. In chapter 5, I will address how advances in nanotechnology, drones, task-specific artificial intelligence and space will have direct impact on the character of war. The speed with which these technologies are advancing is a major element in the power of this revolution. To compensate in a small way for this lag between research and publication, each section illustrates how developments in each field have been accelerating in the last few years to let the reader extrapolate on what the future might bring. Each has been developing for decades. Each has hit the knee of its exponential growth curve.[4] Over the next ten to twenty years, their convergence will drive deglobalization and major shifts in the character of war.

ROBOTICS

Robotics covers a vast field that will fundamentally alter how humans do things from deep sea to outer space. We will start by examining industrial robots, then move on to collaborative and social robots.

Industrial Robots

RobotWorx, a company that sells a wide range of industrial robots, defines an industrial robot as "a mechanical device that is automatically controlled, versatile enough to be programmed to perform a variety of applications, and re-programmable with a large work space, several degrees of freedom, and the ability to use an arm with different tooling."[5]

George Charles Devol, Jr. applied for the first patent for an industrial robot in 1954 and sold his first commercial models to General Motors in 1961. His intent was to relieve workers of heavy, monotonous, dangerous work and to make money doing it. Throughout the 1970s and 1980s, robots steadily evolved with improvements in degrees of freedom, range of motion, strength, speed, reliability, accuracy, and repeatability. However, as Tesla Corporation discovered in its attempt to build a fully automated automobile factory, it takes time to make automation successful.[6] From the CEO to the factory floor, people have to figure out how to integrate the tools a new industrial revolution provides. But the company did learn. In the third quarter of 2018, Tesla reached its production goal making 53,239 Model 3s in a three-month period.[7]

With focused effort, solutions are found. The increasing flexibility and effectiveness of industrial robots is resulting in rapid, steady growth in their numbers. From 2005 to 2008, global industrial robots sales averaged 115,000 per year. This increased to 294,000 units by 2016. Of those, Asia purchased sixty-six percent, Europe took twenty percent, and Americas only fourteen percent. Although China is currently the largest market for industrial robots, it still remained below the International Monetary Fund's criteria for an advanced economy's average number of robots per 10,000 manufacturing employees. In 2016, China had sixty-eight per 10,000 workers whereas advanced economies average seventy-four. The United States had 201; Japan 303; Germany, 309; Singapore, 488; and South Korea, with its heavy industries, 631. With Korea demonstrating the potential density for industrial robots, the rest of the world clearly has much room for growth. In fact, sales grew by another thirty percent in 2017.[8]

The additional capabilities provided by sensors and improved mechanics mean industrial robots are become useful and cost effective in a wide range of industries outside the automotive industry. The Changying

Precision Technology Company automated its mobile phone production lines and reduced the personnel needed from 650 employees to just sixty. Its management plans to drop that number to twenty and increase productivity by 250 percent at the same time. Although an increase of 250 percent in productivity and better quality with a ninety-seven percent reduction in labor force may be an extreme example, the fact that this is possible is driving chief executive officers to explore how industrial robots can improve their companies' competitiveness.[9]

The U.S. steel industry is a prime example. Between 1962 and 2005, the steel industry shed seventy-five percent of its workforce, but its shipment of steel products in 2005 equaled that of the early 1960s. Output per worker grew by a factor of five. Despite the massive shedding of jobs in the industry, steel has been one of the fastest growing manufacturing industries in the last three decades, behind only computer software and equipment.[10] And, of course, CEOs who have to produce growth for stockholders see the job-shedding aspect of robotics as a feature, not a bug.

Collaborative Robots

A product with potential for even greater growth—and hence greater impact on many aspects of life—are collaborative robots, or cobots. Unlike industrial robots that have to be separated from humans, cobots are specifically designed to work in collaboration with humans. And unlike industrial robots, which are expensive and have limited flexibility, cobots are cheap and flexible. Designed to be mobile, they are easy to move to a different location and assign a new task. They are already working in homes, labs, hospitals, nursing homes, warehouses, farms, and distributions centers to tend, test, carry, assemble, package, pick, place, count, and inspect.[11] And unlike most large industrial robots, collaborative robots are relatively easy to upgrade. A wide variety of companies are rapidly increasing the types of cobots available as well as their capabilities.[12]

In 2019, basic cobots cost around $24,000.[13] Assuming a forty-hour workweek and three-year lifespan, this works out to just about $4 an hour, which is not only well below U.S. labor costs but also competitive with wages in emerging economies. And if you are running a plant with two shifts, it drops to just $2 an hour; three shifts, about $1.35—well below even most emerging economy wages. In addition, robots do not need medical, retirement, or leave benefits.

Just as important, cobots are easily programmable. "A non-technical person can teach it what to do through arm movement and simple button presses, and it can master a new task in half an hour or so. There is also little assembly or setup required."[14]

Numerous companies are developing a wide range of cobots that can be configured to execute an expanding number of tasks.[15] In 2015, ABB introduced a two-armed YuMi robot that can put together car dashboards, wristwatches, and eyewear. Western manufacturers see them as essential to assist aging workforces. Goldman Sachs notes that "the average age of workers in BMW's Welt factory is rising (43 vs. 40 a few years ago) as new technologies, such as exoskeletons, are increasing the longevity of employees."[16] Of particular importance, the cobots can manage the heavy components and reach into the awkward places that are part of an assembly process.

Designboom notes that Aethon's TUG robots are already being used as couriers in University of California San Francisco's hospital, delivering everything from laboratory samples to food trays to linens. The Da Vinci robot demonstrates how the precision skills of robots can apply in a range of situations, from assisting surgeons with delicate surgery to providing tattoo artists with unparalleled precision. In 2016, Japan opened its first hotel ninety percent staffed with robots—from the velociraptor that checks guests in to the simple TUG that delivers luggage to their rooms.[17] Although it turned out the velociraptor was a bit "buggy" and personal assistants in each room were not as effective as those in new phones, half the hotels staff continues to be robotic.[18]

Cobots are also assisting with farming, warehouse operations, security, and even as exoskeletons provide strength and protection to people.[19] The low prices, minimal technical support required, and flexibility mean that thousands of small- and medium-sized businesses that would never consider purchasing industrial robots are buying cobots The small- and medium-enterprise marketplace consists of almost six million companies worldwide. Conservative owners may be reluctant to invest, but the fact that cobots continue to improve their cost advantage over human labor means they may have to.[20] In its series, Factory of the Future, Goldman Sachs notes that today's cobots have a payback period as short as six months.[21] ABI Research predicts global revenue from robots will "grow at an annual rate compound rate of 49.9 percent between 2016 and 2025 compared to 12.1 percent for industrial robots."[22]

In Japan, Ufactory is hoping inexpensive robotic arms that can be programed by the purchasers will lead to crowdsourcing of increasingly effective software. With an expected retail price of only $426 dollars, these arms will open robotics to an enormous pool of talented amateurs.[23]

Even as costs come down quickly, the capability of cobots is increasing at an exceptional rate. As recently as 2012, teaching a robot to sew was considered a "DARPA-hard" project. DARPA, the Defense Advanced Research Projects Agency, prides itself on tackling only the toughest problems—hence the slogan "DARPA-hard." In 2012, it granted a $1.3 million grant to develop a robot that could sew. Because U.S. law requires all military uniforms to be made in the United States, its success would significantly reduce the cost of uniforms.[24] Naturally nicknamed "sewbots," these systems are mastering the complex task of sewing—and thus are threatening to disrupt the global clothing industry. Sewing is a complex, highly physical job that requires cognitive skills to manipulate a variety of materials with different characteristics that must be sewn at odd angles and along curves. Given this and the fact that labor was a major cost driver, clothing manufacturing moved to low-wage areas. Until recently, machines did not have the dexterity and judgement to master these tasks.

However, Softwear Automation has brought together recent advances in robotics, sensors, and limited artificial intelligence and created Lowry, an automatic cutting and direct-sewing machine.[25] The implications for the global garment industry are enormous.

The field of robotics seems to have reached the knee of its exponential growth curve. From heavy-duty industrial robots to small personal robots, the range of capabilities is expanding rapidly even as cost drops and ease of use improves. Much like the mechanization of the first industrial revolution, robotics will result in increased output at reduced costs. Robots are eliminating the cost of labor advantage. Proximity and responsiveness to the market, higher skills of the labor that is needed, fair legal systems, strong and transparent financial markets are increasingly driving decisions on where to produce products or provide services. By eliminating any advantage to producing in low cost regions, they are, and will continue to be, central to the return of production to home markets. And, even as industry masters the mechanical aspects of robotics, key advances are being made in the field of artificial intelligence which will further enhance the advantages robots provide in production.

ARTIFICIAL INTELLIGENCE

Artificial intelligence (AI) has recently begun to make rapid, very useful advances. Unfortunately, the term "artificial intelligence" can cause much confusion. Much of current discussion concerns artificial general intelligence (AGI), which itself has a variety of different definitions. In fact, there is a great deal of disagreement in the AI research community as to when or even if this goal is achievable.

For the purposes of this book, it is important to differentiate between AGI and limited or task-specific AI. In contrast to AGI, limited or task-specific AI is about a machine operating with a set of guidelines to accomplish specific tasks. Such a system would provide great practical capabilities in its specified field but would not be capable of fully independent operation. At the 2016 O'Reilly AI Conference, Oren Etzioni noted that whereas "narrow machine learning technology that has achieved outstanding results on a series of narrow tasks like speech recognition or playing Go...Super-human performance on a narrow task does not translate to human-level performance in general."[26] However, this does not mean limited AI is not already having a massive impact on global production chains—and that impact will only expand in the future.

Andrew Ng, the lead for Baidu's AI team, agrees that AI has had major impact but notes it is still extremely limited. Most applications take data inputs and generate a simple output, such as finding a human face in a photo, evaluating the probability that a loan will be repaid, translating a sentence, determining if a mechanical system is about to fail, and other similar relatively simple but economically important tasks.[27] Although each program is tightly focused and clearly limited, the cumulative economic effect will be very high. Ng's rule of thumb is that "if a typical person can do a mental task with less than one second of thought, we can probably automate it using AI either now or in the near future."[28] This sounds rather innocuous but the amount of work that even limited AI can automate includes a vast array of human work —and threatens millions of jobs.

Numerous research centers are pushing to develop AGI, and in doing so they are rapidly advancing the capabilities of limited AI. One promising approach mimics the neurons of the brain. The JASON team noted that "starting around 2010, the field of AI has been jolted by broad and unforeseen successes of a specific, decades-old technology: multi-layer neural networks (NNs)."[29] In the human brain, connections between pairs of neurons get stronger or weaker as a person learns from life. Researchers have established artificial neural networks that operate on the same principle. Like humans in training or school, these artificial neural networks learn by guided trial-and-error using the successes to build the numerical relationships among artificial neurons. But they are nowhere near approaching human brain capacity. "Google Brain's investment [has] allowed for the creation of artificial neural networks comparable to the brains of mice."[30] However, mice can solve basic problems such as mazes.

In effect, while working to develop AGI, research teams are building limited artificial learning networks. Google has started to combine the abilities of robots and AI to learn a task and then pass that knowledge along to other systems.

In 2016, team learning by robots moved out of the lab and onto the factory floor. Fanuc, a maker of industrial robots, created robots that reprogram themselves as a team. In the past, it took days for an engineer to write code to change the task for a single industrial robot; today Fanuc has a different approach. Each robot videos itself so that after completing the task, it can evaluate how it did. The robot then tries to improve on the next trial. It repeats the process videoing, analyzing, and experimenting until it arrives at an optimized solution. Using this process, a robot on an assembly line can teach itself a new task—such as assembling a small motor when supplied with the parts—overnight. "But even with reinforcement learning and artificial intelligence, it may take a single robot hours to reprogram itself. With parallel computing, however, eight robots working together for one hour can learn just as much as a single robot working for eight hours. It is dramatically faster than hand-coding custom instructions."[31] In three to five years, this process will be widely available and thus will further reduce the cost of assigning robots to execute new tasks.[32]

Nor is AI limited to physical work. In January 2017 Fukoku Mutual Life Insurance, a Japanese insurance company, licensed software based on the famous "Watson" from International Business Machines (IBM) to replace thirty-four insurance claim workers with "IBM Watson Explorer." Watson will scan hospital records and other documents to determine insurance payouts. It will also factor in the specific injuries, each patient's medical history, and the procedures administered.

Fukoku Mutual will spend $1.7 million (200 million yen) to install the AI system, and $128,000 per year for maintenance...The company saves roughly $1.1 million per year on employee salaries by using the IBM software, meaning it hopes to see a return on the investment in less than two years.[33]

IBM and Fukoku believe they will not only reduce costs but also improve efficiency. Once again, note the very short time anticipated for return on investment. If these predictions come true, it will provide major incentives for other firms to follow suit simply to remain competitive in their industries.

A different form of AI can develop optimal designs for a wide variety of structures. Autodesk's "Dreamcatcher system allows designers to input specific design objectives, including functional requirements, material type, manufacturing method, performance criteria, and cost restrictions."[34] The system then evaluates the vast number of designs it generates in a cyber design space to satisfy the design requirements. Tasked with designing a fastener for construction, it created one that is approximately half the height and weighs seventy-five percent less than one designed for traditional production methods. This led to an overall weight reduction of the total structure of more than forty percent. This approach can be used to redesign any high-quality, metal part. But the resulting designs cannot be produced using conventional manufacturing techniques.[35] Thus, we need to explore another emerging technologies— 3D printing.

3D PRINTING

Like all the technologies in this section, 3D printing, also known as additive manufacturing, is not brand new. The first patent was granted in 1986. Due to its very slow speeds and uneven finishes, 3D printing was initially used primarily to produce prototypes and a limited number of unique low-volume products. But in the last decade, it has transformed from an industry focused on prototyping to one producing a wide range of products. In addition to increasing the speed of printing and refining the finishes, a great deal of effort has gone into expanding the number of materials that can be used. By 2017, industry information centers no longer attempted to list all the materials being printed but only those most commonly used—metals, plastics, paper, biological materials, and even food. More exciting, 3D manufacturing is rapidly creating entire new materials, "up to 140 different Digital Materials can be realized from combining the existing primary materials in different ways."[36] 3D printing is quite literally changing what can be made.

Meanwhile, researchers and 3D companies continued to pursue both versatility and speed. Multimaterial printers were one of the big steps. In 2015, MIT researchers developed the MultiFab. At a unit cost of only $7,000, it can handle up to ten materials at a time to print products from lenses to fabrics to fiber optics bundles to complex metamaterials, with applications ranging from scientific to aesthetic.[37] And its products do not require postproduction processing. Instead of printing a series of pieces that then have to be assembled, the machine prints the assembly in one go. As businesses learn to use these multimaterial printers, the range of products they will be able to print will expand exponentially. Further, 3D printing is efficient because material wastage is near zero. It may be cheaper to make a part from titanium using additive manufacturing than from steel using traditional machining.

The range of products—from medical devices to aircraft parts to buildings and bridges—and the order of magnitude increase in the speed of printing is already challenging traditional manufacturing.[38] Massive increases in printing speed mean 3D printing has moved beyond prototyping and very high value parts. In April 2016, Carbon3D released a commercial printer that was one hundred times faster than existing printers. The rapid improvements mean 3D printing captured twenty percent of the global plastics manufacturing market in 2016.[39] Not to be outdone, metal printers have combined high speed and low cost to make them a system of choice even for mass production of small parts. The fact that key patents are expiring soon will further accelerate improvements in printer capabilities and capacities.[40]

In early 2019, researchers from University of California, Berkeley, and Lawrence Livermore National Laboratory developed a new technique that allows small objects to be printed whole rather than in successive layers and is up sixty times faster depending on the object. Based on an off-the-shelf video projector and a laptop, this opens the field of printing in resins to virtually anyone with an interest.[41]

3D printing opens

> up the possibility of a totally different supply chain, run with lower costs and a lower carbon footprint. The materials and energy it takes for manufacturers to create new parts will be harnessed into electronic design files that can be printed on-demand, anywhere in the world. And countless numbers of spare parts will never physically need to trucked and flown to their destination. In these new, transformative supply chains, many spare parts might not even need to exist, which could translate to huge savings on warehousing costs.[42]

3D printing is revolutionizing manufacturing in many industries. The ability to change each product by changing the software means the era of mass customization and local production is on us. No longer will parts have to be shipped across oceans and then trucked to the user. They will be printed on site. 3D printing is clearly on the path to causing major disruptions in global trade.

ENERGY

Energy, in the form of petroleum, natural gas, and coal, has been a key component of global trade for the last half century. Yet, for most of human history, energy was essentially a local product. Post–World War II, the exhaustion of U.S. oil fields and the rapidly rising demand for energy led to the massive expansion of the global oil industry. Since then oil has been a critical factor in national security planning. However, the influence of petroleum on both the global economy and national security may be waning. Rapid advances in energy technology, to include shale (tight) oil and renewable energy sources, are changing the global energy markets —and in many cases moving energy sources from overseas companies to locally produced oil, gas, and renewables.

In its "World Energy Outlook 2017," the International Energy Agency (IEA) stated

> Four large-scale shifts in the global energy system set the scene for the World Energy Outlook 2017: the rapid deployment and falling costs of clean energy technologies, the growing electrification of energy, the shift to a more services-oriented economy and a cleaner energy mix in China, and the resilience of shale gas and tight oil in the United States.[43]

Gas and Oil
Coal, previously the dominant source of energy, has steadily been losing ground in the West and is now losing ground in China and even India. Further, the U.S. fracking revolution is resulting in a global increase in demand for natural gas even as oil use may have peaked. In November 2016, the *Wall Street Journal* ran a front-page article reporting that global oil producers such as Royal Dutch Shell and even state-owned Saudi Aramco anticipate that the world has reached peak oil usage and are preparing for a future decline in demand.[44]

Hydraulic fracturing, or "fracking," has had the biggest impact on global energy supply in the last decade. The process of fracturing or breaking up hard stone five thousand to nine thousand feet underground to free trapped shale (tight) oil has been around almost as long as the oil industry. As early as the 1860s, drillers were using explosives to free this oil. Explosive fracking was effective but highly dangerous, and drillers worked hard to find alternatives. But modern-day fracking did not begin until the 1990s, when George P. Mitchell combined hydraulic fracturing with horizontal drilling and created a process that made recovery of shale oil profitable.

Most analysts felt it would come online slowly, like traditional oil projects. In 2012, the U.S. Energy Information Administration (EIA) estimated shale oil production could reach 2.8 million barrels per day (bpd) by 2035. It did so by 2013.[45] In late November of 2014, an industry expert noted that the EIA predicted the United States would become the world's largest oil producer by 2020.[46] This was realized by June 2014.[47]

The price of West Texas Intermediate, a benchmark price, dropped from $98 a barrel in 2013 to $48 in 2015.[48] Obviously, this caused a crisis for major oil exporters. Many called for a global reduction in production, the historic approach to falling oil prices taken by the Organization of Petroleum Exporting Countries (OPEC). But Saudi Arabia, the key swing producer, decided on a much more aggressive approach. In an effort to drive shale oil producers out of business, the Saudis decided to increase production. By driving down the price, they hoped to bankrupt U.S. producers and regain control of the global oil price.[49] U.S. producers responded by consistently cutting costs. By early 2018, Permian basin oil reached the point it could be profitable at less than $30 a barrel and the basin is projected to account for one-quarter of all new oil production globally over the next decade.[50] Thus, even as oil prices fell to record lows, U.S. producers thrived.

Perhaps the most powerful aspect of U.S. shale oil operations is the speed with which fracking operations can be shut down or reopened in response to demand. Conventional oil fields take years to bring online and then have to produce for years to pay for the massive infrastructure costs. U.S. firms have become so good at fracking that they can get fields online in a matter of months. From October 2016 to January 2017, U.S. crude production increased 500,000 barrels a day in response to the price increasing from $45 to $50 a barrel.[51]

Even more important for future economic growth, U.S. gains in efficiency show that many producers are eager to open wells even with the price of oil below $60 a barrel. Although there will still be price spikes during time of crisis, U.S. oil supplies may well ensure the price of West Texas Intermediate remains near $65 a barrel (2018 dollars) for a long time.

Natural Gas

Fracking has also resulted in a natural gas boom in the United States. As recently as 2007, U.S. companies were racing to build liquid natural gas (LNG) import facilities. The demand for natural gas was growing very quickly, and U.S. production was falling. In October 2005, the Henry Hub (U.S.) spot price rose to $13.42 per million British thermal units (MBTU). Then the fracking revolution occurred, which resulted in a massive drop in price to $1.93 per MBTU by December 2015—a reduction of eighty-five percent. Suddenly companies were applying for permits to turn their LNG import facilities into LNG export facilities. Figure 4 records the shifting cost of gas in the United States compared to Europe and Asia. Clearly, U.S. LNG exports can provide a healthy profit even factoring in liquefaction and shipping costs.

There was concern among some analysts that the rapid expansion of LNG export facilities would result in significantly higher prices for American industry as companies shipped gas overseas in search of higher prices. In March 2018 the second of five planned U.S. natural gas export trains opened, and electricity production continued its rapid shift from coal to gas, yet Henry Hub spot price was $2.78 on April 6, 2018—only twenty percent of its peak price in 2008.[52]

Fracking drove the price of natural gas in the United States down as early as 2008. Figure 4 shows that, as late as 2005, those U.S. industries that made heavy use of natural gas for their products (e.g., the petrochemical industry) or to generate energy for production were at a disadvantage in global competition. U.S. companies paid significantly more for this vital input.

Figure 4. Global Natural Gas Benchmark Prices in U.S. dollars per MMbtu. [53]

Global Natural Gas Benchmark Prices
(U.S. Dollars per Mmbtu)

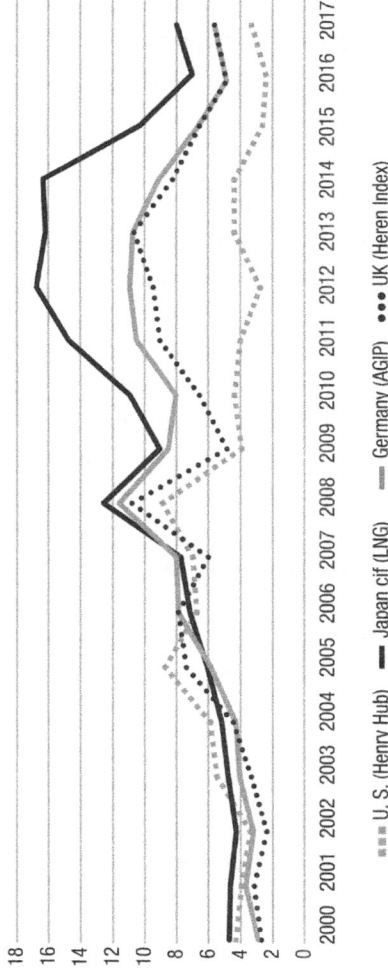

■■■ U.S. (Henry Hub)   ▬ Japan cif (LNG)   ▬ Germany (AGIP)   ●●● UK (Heren Index)

Source: British Petroleum Natural Gas, https://www.bp.com/en/global/corporate/energy-economics/statistical-review-of-world-energy/natural-gas.html#natural-gas-prices.

By 2008, fracking had completely reversed the situation, and the cost advantage to U.S. manufacturers has only increased since then. Even when a combination of falling demand in China and very low oil prices resulted in the LNG price in Japan falling to about $9 per (MBTU) in March 2018 contracts, natural gas prices in the United States remained less than half that of Europe and one-third that of Asia.[54]

During the political debate over whether to license LNG export facilities, opponents stated the United States would be giving away a huge cost advantage that was supporting the return of jobs. They were concerned that exporting large quantities of natural gas would bring the world price down to that of the United States and erode our manufacturing advantage. Although the cost differential did in fact decrease a small amount, U.S. industries that use high volumes on natural gas still maintain a significant cost advantage over foreign competitors. Gas delivered by pipeline has much lower shipping costs than liquid natural gas. To prepare natural gas for export as liquid natural gas, it must be liquefied (cooled to -260 degrees Fahrenheit), shipped by sea, and gasified. Each step adds significantly to the cost for consumers who use LNG rather than pipeline-supplied gas. The minimum cost an overseas customer can pay for U.S. LNG is the U.S. cost of natural gas, plus the liquefaction costs, plus shipping costs. It is the liquefaction and shipping costs that will maintain the U.S. price advantage.

Renewables and New Transmission Lines

In its October 2016 renewable energy market report, the IEA reported that 2015 was a record year for renewables and increased its predictions for growth over the next five years. "Generation from renewables is expected to exceed 7600 TWh [terawatt hours] by 2021—equivalent to the total electricity generation of the United States and the European Union put together today."[55]

Figure 5. Global Renewable Energy Production.

Global Renewable Energy Production as a % of Total
(does not include hydro)

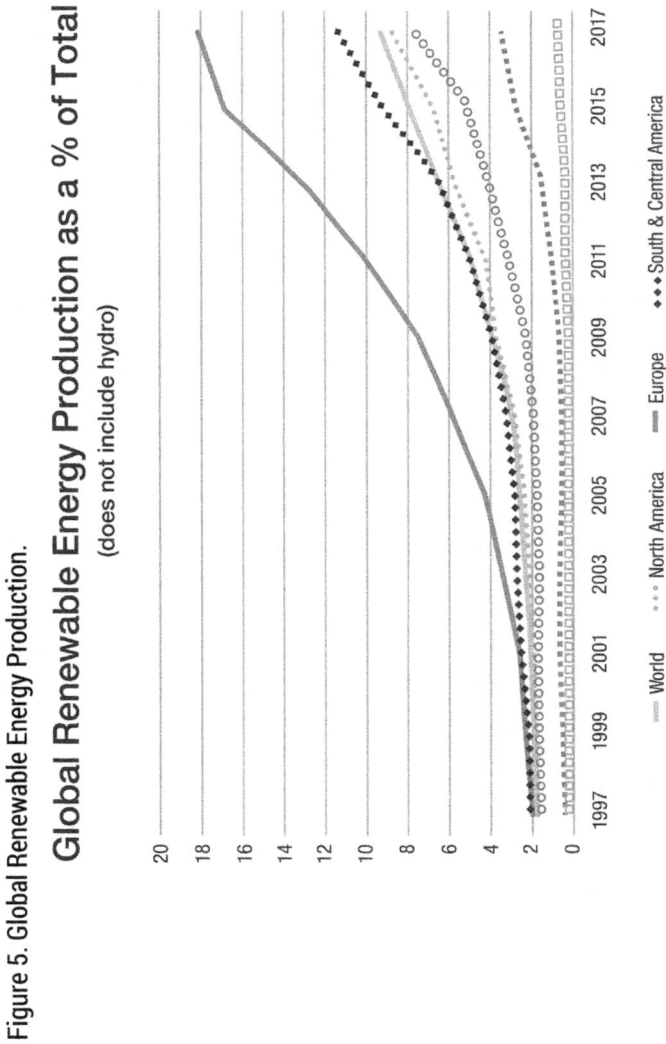

Source: British Petroleum Renewable Energy, https://www.bp.com/en/global/corporate/energy-economics/statis-tical-review-of-world-energy/renewable-energy.html.

In its 2017 report, the IEA noted new renewables installation increased to 165 gigawatts or almost two-thirds of all newly installed electrical energy production.[56] In its 2019 Global Energy Perspective, McKinsey predicted that, even as energy consumption doubles by 2050, renewables will generate over 50% of electricity by 2035.[57] Figure 5 provides an overview of the rapid global growth of renewable energy production.

China is making a big bet on renewables. China's energy agency announced in January 2017 that it will spend at least $360 billion through 2020 on renewable energy sources.[58] This is on top of its massive growth in wind energy installations in 2015 and 2016. During 2015, China installed one large wind turbine every hour to create 30,000 megawatts of new wind turbine generation in that single year.[59] Facing a ballooning subsidy deficit, the Chinese government reduced its subsidies for clean energy in early 2019. However, some analysts believe funding will increase substantially in the second half of the year as investors rush to invest in new projects.[60]

However, there are two major problems with renewables. One, they are inherently intermittent. Wind intensity varies in unpredictable ways, and solar fails every night and during bad weather. Even hydro power is subject to reduction during periods of drought. Second, the best solar exposure or steadiest winds are often far from the places people live. Thus, renewable energy and power transmission must be thought of as an integrated problem. Around the world, nations and private business are installing renewables and long-line high-voltage transmission systems.

China's plan to exploit the existing and still-building wind power as well as the hydro power in its far southeast relies on building more transmission lines. Beginning in 2010, China began installing ultra-high voltage direct current (UHVdc) lines to move the power two thousand kilometers from generators to users. The State Grid Corporation of China announced it will invest another six hundred billion yuan (about $90 billion) by 2020 to improve its power distribution systems.

Yet investment in long lines does not solve all the problems in a power network. Even with its huge investment in UHVdc lines, China will still face major distribution bottlenecks because of constraints in local grids, fluctuation of renewable power supply, and power plant performance.[61] Roughly one-fifth of the wind power generated across China, and up to half in some areas, goes undistributed due to power transmission network problems.[62] Despite these challenges, China's leadership is clearly set on increasing the use of renewables both as a way of dealing with its massive pollution problems and as insurance against the interruption of overseas oil, gas, and coal in the event of conflict.

Europe has a different situation—because it does not have a unified grid, excess power produced by renewables in one part of the continent cannot be delivered to users in another part. On sunny days, Spain produces more solar power than it can use. When the North Sea is windy, northern European countries have more wind power than they can use. As a partial response, 50Hz, which operates the grid in northern Germany, wants to build an UHVdc line linking Europe's energy producers and markets.[63] When the wind blows hard at night while Europe is asleep, the energy could be sent to Scandinavia to pump water back uphill into the hydroelectric reservoirs so power will be available during peak daytime hours. The only way to achieve this is with an integrated European wide grid. As with most Western countries, major infrastructure projects will run into numerous environmental and NIMBY (not in my back yard) protests. Beyond even these hurdles, building such a system will require great trust between nations because each will be outsourcing part of its power production to another. Given the current distrust in the European Union, this may be the most difficult hurdle of all. To avoid these difficulties, companies and individuals will install small-scale installation to take themselves partly or even entirely off the grid.

The situation is yet again different in the United States. Here, coal is rapidly being replaced by a mix of natural gas and renewables. The fracking revolution means natural gas is both cheaper and cleaner than coal. Natural gas plants are also more efficient as base load plants needed to compensate for the intermittency of renewables. Of the twenty-seven gigawatts of new electricity generation installed in the United States in 2016, more than sixty percent were renewables—primarily wind and solar—and thirty-three percent were natural gas with coal accounting for less than one gigawatt.[64] Renewables remained a major player in 2017 representing 49 percent of all new installations.[65] Further, a recent study from the Energy Institute at the University of Texas at Austin noted

> Overall, natural gas combined cycle power plants [gas generator that uses waste heat to drive a steam generator] are the lowest cost option for at least a third of US counties for most cases considered. Wind is also commonly found to be the lowest cost option.[66]

In 2006, the International Energy Agency predicted global installed photovoltaic capacity by 2013 would be twenty gigawatts. It was actually seven times larger—140 gigawatts and increased to 227 gigawatts by 2015. On cost alone, solar is clearly competitive. This was reflected by the fact that new solar installations in the United States in 2016 were ninety-five percent higher than 2015, nearly doubling from 7,493 megawatts to 14,426. Of particular interest, it was utility scale segment that grew fastest, installing 145 percent more capacity in 2016 than in 2015. [67] From 2007 to 2016, solar installation has averaged fifty-nine percent growth and has grown from 0.1 percent of electricity production to two percent.[68] Solar installation slowed in 2017 to 10,600 megawatts and similar levels in 2018. But, led by utilities, it surged again in 2019 with projected installation of over 13,000 megawatts.[69]

These statistics reflect only utility-scale generating capacity and thus do not account for the growing private installation of renewable energy. Both developing and developed countries are seeing huge growth in local production and grids.[70] In fact, Bangladesh is the world's largest market for home solar system.

During the first three quarters of 2016, more than three gigawatts or fifteen percent of additional residential and nonresidential solar generating capacity was privately installed in the United States.[71] There is also a growing business in providing renewable energy to major corporations.[72]

Like Europe and China, the United States needs to invest in transmission lines if it is to maximize the use of renewables. Fortunately, it has a successful model—Texas. For historical reasons, the U.S. power grid is divided into three major sections—the Eastern Interconnection, the Western Interconnection, and the Texas Interconnection. Because its power grid is contained within the state, Texas overcame the various forms of political resistance and built transmission lines from its very windy western plains to its energy-hungry eastern cities. At times, wind provides forty percent of Texas's power needs. Other regions have great potential for renewables—the Great Plains and offshore for wind, the Southwest for solar. In March 2017, Xcel announced plans to install eight hundred megawatts of new wind generation capability in the Dakotas and Minnesota.[73] Delayed by regulators since 2005, a three-thousand-megawatt line is finally being built to take Wyoming wind energy to southern California.[74] Other investors are seeking to link wind and solar energy to the southeastern and eastern United States. Like Europe, as individual states learn to coordinate the construction of transmission lines, renewables will be shifted across the grid and reduce the reliance on backup generation.

Batteries' Impact on Energy Sources

Whether the user is a major power company looking for a way to store power to feed back into the grid or an individual homeowner seeking to get off the grid, batteries can provide an alternative to fossil fuel backups. This is another field where many researchers—commercial, government, and university—are pursuing a variety of possibilities.

Commercial power companies need massive storage capability to take over the "peaker" function now performed by natural gas–burning plants. These plants come online only during periods of peak load to prevent brownouts or even blackouts. Unfortunately, developing battery storage has been a slow process. "It took 30 years to install enough systems to add up to a gigawatt," but an estimated "1.7 gigawatts [are] expected to go into service in 2017 alone. State regulators are a key driver, with California ordering utilities to install at least 1.3 gigawatts of storage by 2020."[75] In June 2017, Massachusetts mandated that two hundred megawatt hours of storage be installed by 2020 and committed $10 million in public funds to the goal.[76]

Driven partly by California's Public Utilities Commission, Southern California Edison plans to install a one-hundred-megawatt storage battery by 2020. Moving much more quickly, Elon Musk combined Tesla Motors and SolarCity to create a new way of supplying power. In July 2017, he signed a contract to provide one hundred megawatts of storage in Australia and had the system running and highly profitable by January 2018.[77] By October, it was on "track to make back a third of its construction costs in its first year of operation."[78]

The combination of Tesla's success, rapidly falling prices for storage, and government mandates have piqued the interest of big banks. "Lenders including Investec Plc, Mitsubishi UFJ Financial Group Inc. and Prudential Financial Inc. are looking to finance large-scale energy-storage projects from California to Germany, marking a coming-of-age moment for the fledgling industry."[79]

The convergence of fracking, renewables, energy grids, and batteries means that more and more energy production will be local or, at most, regional. Renewables can be moved vast distances via transmission lines so they can tie a region together. But there will not be a global market for renewables. Unlike oil, propane, coal, and LNG, it is impractical and unnecessary to move renewable energy across oceans. Thus, unlike the gas/oil market, which contributes to globalization, the renewables market will contribute to regionalization—and even to localization as more and more businesses and homes take advantage of improving battery capacity to move off grid.

FOOD PRODUCTION

Agriculture is another area that has seen increased global trade over the last few decades. High-value fruits, vegetables, and flowers move from nations with favorable growing conditions to those without. However, indoor farming has begun to undercut this trade by providing locally produced, fresher organic products. A facility in Tokyo produces 10,000 heads of lettuce per day in only 25,000 square feet—less than half of a football field—and is building another all-robot operation.[80] This second operation plans to produce 50,000 heads of lettuce daily and scale up to produce 500,000 heads a day within five years.[81] Now that the concept has been proven, Japanese electronics firms are putting their unused factories into food production.[82] "According to the Japanese Ministry of Economy, Trade, and Industry, Japan currently has about 211 computer-operated plant factories—hydroponic and aeroponic farms growing food in closed environments without the utilization of sunlight."[83]

The industry is not restricted to Japan. The U.S. firm AeroFarms runs one of the world's largest vertical farms and, by tuning light and environmental conditions to the specific needs of each crop, harvest up to thirty times a year. Similar urban farms are being built across Europe and Russia. They are part of a vertical farm industry that is attempting to grow produce close to where it will be eaten. The business model is to sell to high-end grocery stores with a guarantee of produce that is moved from the stalk to the shelf in only four hours year-round.

High-value vegetable crops are not a major factor in global trade, but they are very important for some economies. The movement of that production from low-wage, warm countries to high-wage countries simply adds one more element to the deglobalization process.

In addition to meeting the growing demand for fresh, local produce, these farms may gain a cost advantage. They do not require herbicides or pesticides, use ninety-nine percent less water, waste eighty percent less food, use forty percent less power, reduce shipping costs, and are not subject to weather irregularities.[84] Scaled-up, these processes will seriously reduce the market for long-range shipping of high-value agricultural products. It is less clear whether bulk products such as grain can be farmed using the same techniques. However, Japanese firms are growing rice in a number of their facilities on a test basis.

Cultured (vat-grown) meat will also have an effect on global trade. Currently in its infancy, cultured or "clean" meat remains expensive and of inferior quality. But the fact that it has been done and is steadily improving in taste and texture changes the nature of the problem. It is no longer a question of biological feasibility but of engineering and production. In the last five years, Mosa Meat, a Dutch firm, has cut the price of its vat-grown burger from $300,000 to $600 and plans to be at $11 per burger by 2020.[85] Moreover, proponents state that it takes ninety percent less water and ninety percent less land, produces ninety percent less greenhouse gases, and uses forty-five percent less energy to grow a pound of cultured meat compared to growing it on the hoof.[86] Cultured meat will not require antibiotics and will be produced in a much more sanitary environment than current processes.

Progress in cultured meat has reached the point major corporations such as Tyson Foods, Cargill, and PHW Group (the third largest poultry producer in Europe) are investing.[87] Almost all predictions show meat consumption increasing globally over the next couple of decades. The U.S. market for meat and poultry alone was $186 billion in 2014.[88] The growing global market will provide massive financial incentive to master the production of cultured meat or meat substitutes. When it succeeds, it will reduce the import/export not just of meat products but of the agricultural feed products necessary to raise animals. The top five soybean exporters shipped a total of over sixty million metric tons in 2015, most of it as animal feed.[89] One result will be the repurposing of huge tracts of land currently used to raise livestock and their feed.

CONCLUSION

The convergence of these technologies will change our societies in ways that are hard to imagine. It is already clear it will change what we make, how we make it, and where we make it. Manufacturing is moving to mass customization—production runs of one! Most important, manufacturing will be located near the market.

New technologies will also return service-industry jobs to the markets they serve. Renewable energy is inherently regional rather than global. Environmental movements will reinforce these trends by pushing to reduce the impact of manufacturing and agriculture on the environment. In the next chapter, we explore the global economic changes that might evolve from these drivers. And in the fourth chapter, we examine the military implications.

NOTES

1. Schwab, *The Fourth Industrial Revolution*, 6–7.
2. Robert J. Gordon, "Is US Economic Growth Over? Faltering Innovation Confronts the Six Headwinds?" Center for Economic Policy Research, September 2012, 1–2,http://www.cepr.org/sites/default/files/policy_ insights/PolicyInsight63.pdf.
3. Schwab, *The Fourth Industrial Revolution*, 1.
4. See Ray Kuzweil's *The Singularity is Near,* (New York: Penguin Books, 2006) for a complete discussion on exponential innovation curves.
5. "The History of Industrial Robots," RobotWorx Web site, https://www. used-robots.com/education/the-history-of-industrial-robots.
6. Kirsten Korosec, "Tesla CEO Elon Musk Admits 'Humans Are Underrated'," *Fortune,* April 13, 2018, http://fortune.com/2018/04/13/ tesla-elon-musk-robot-human-model-3/.
7. Tim Higgins, "Tesla Meets Model 3 Production Goal, but Struggles With Deliveries," *Wall Street Journal,* October 3, 2018, https://www.wsj.com/ articles/tesla-produced-80-142-vehicles-in-third-quarter-1538484764.
8. Kagan Pittman, "Industrial Robots Smashing Records in Global Sales and Installations," *engineering.com,* Oct 26, 2018, https://www. engineering.com/AdvancedManufacturing/ArticleID/17865/Industrial-Robots-Smashing-Records-in-Global-Sales-and-Installations.aspx.
9. Mihai Andrei, "Chinese Factory Replaces 90% of Human Workers with Robots. Production Rises by 250%, Defects Drop by 80%," *ZME Science,* February 3, 2017, http://www.zmescience.com/other/economics/china-factory-robots-03022017.
10. Allan Collard-Wexler and Jan De Loecker, "Reallocation and Technology: Evidence from the US Steel Industry," *American Economic Review* 105, no. 1: 131–71, doi:10.1257/aer.20130090.
11. Frank Tobe, "Why Co-Bots Will be a Huge Innovation and Growth Driver for Robotics Industry," *IEEE Spectrum,* December 30, 2016, http:// spectrum.ieee.org/automaton/robotics/industrial-robots/collaborative-robots-innovation-growth-driver.
12. Bruce Gieselman, "Upgrades to collaborative robots bring cost savings," *Plastics Machinery,* June 2017, http://plasticsmachinerymagazine.com/ technology/upgrades-to-collaborative-robots-bring-cost-savings.html.

13. Ben Halder, "How China's 'Cobot' Revolution Could Transform Automation," *OZY,* March 25, 2019, https://www.ozy.com/fast-forward/how-chinas-cobot-revolution-could-transform-automation/93044.
14. "Lightweight cobots take on heavy-duty jobs–even welding," *Universal Robots,* November 9, 2017, https://blog.universal-robots.com/lightweight-cobots-take-on-heavy-duty-jobs-even-welding.
15. Tobe, "Why Co-Bots Will Be a Huge Innovation and Growth Driver for Robotics Industry."
16. "Goldman Sachs Factory of the Future," *Robotenomics,* July 26, 2016, https://robotenomics.com/tag/goldman-sachs-factory-of-the-future.
17. Gideon Louis-Kraus, "Check in with the velociraptor at the world's first robot hotel," *Wired,* March 2, 2016, https://www.wired.com/2016/03/robot-henn-na-hotel-japan/.
18. Dan Robotzski, "Japan's Robot Hotel Just Laid Off Half Its Robots," *Futurism,* January 15, 2019, https://futurism.com/japan-robot-hotel.
19. "Designboom's TECH Predictions for 2017: Robotics," *Designboom,* http://www.designboom.com/technology/designboom-tech-predictions-robotics-12-26-2016.
20. Ibid.
21. "Goldman Sachs, "Factory of the Future: Beyond the Assembly Line, June 3, 2016, https://www.goldmansachs.com/insights/pages/factory-of-the-future.html.
22. Halder, "Cobot Revolution."
23. Michael Irving, "uArm Swift Home Robot Designed Not to Cost an Arm and a Leg," *New Atlas,* January 24, 2017, http://newatlas.com/uarm-swift-pro-robot-arm/47529/?utm_source=Gizmag+Subscribers&utm_campaign=2996e1082e-UA-2235360–4&utm_medium=email&utm_term=0_65b67362bd-2996e1082e-92283385.
24. "Made to Measure," *Economist,* May 30–June 6, 2015, http://www.economist.com/news/technology-quarterly/21651925-robotic-sewing-machine-could-throw-garment-workers-low-cost-countries-out.
25. "Sewbots," Softwear Automation, http://softwearautomation.com/tech-packs/.
26. Gil Press, "12 Observations about Artificial Intelligence from the O'Reilly AI Conference," *Forbes,* October 31, 2016, https://www.forbes.com/sites/gilpress/2016/10/31/12-observations-about-artificial-intelligence-from-the-oreilly-ai-conference/#746b284f2ea2.

27. Andrew Ng, "What Artificial Intelligence Can and Can't Do Right Now," *Harvard Business Review*, November 9, 2016, https://hbr.org/2016/11/what-artificial-intelligence-can-and-cant-do-right-now.

28. Ibid.

29. "Perspectives on Research in Artificial Intelligence and Artificial General Intelligence Relevant to DoD," JASON, The Mitre Corporation, January 2017, 1, https://fas.org/irp/agency/dod/jason/ai-dod.pdf.

30. Gideon Lewis-Kraus, "The Great A. I. Awakening," *New York Times Magazine*, December 14, 2016, http://www.nytimes.com/2016/12/14/magazine/the-great-ai-awakening.html?_r=0.

31. April Glaser, "These Industrial Robots Teach Each Other New Skills While We Sleep," *recode*, October 14, 2016, http://www.recode.net/2016/10/14/13274428/artificial-intelligence-ai-robots-auto-production-audi.

32. Amanda Schaffer, "Robots That Teach Each Other," *MIT Technology Review*, February 23, 2016, https://www.technologyreview.com/s/600768/10-breakthrough-technologies-2016-robots-that-teach-each-other.

33. David Gershgorn, "Japanese White-Collar Workers Are Already Being Replaced by Artificial Intelligence," *Quartz*, January 2, 2017, http://qz.com/875491/japanese-white-collar-workers-are-already-being-replaced-by-artificial-intelligence.

34. Carlos E. Perez, "The Alien Style of Deep Learning Generative Design," *New Atlas*, December 24, 2017, https://medium.com/intuitionmachine/the-alien-look-of-deep-learning-generative-design-5c5f871f7d10#.hp9oywmsv.

35. Ibid.

36. "The Free Beginners Guide: 3D Printing Materials," *3D Printing Industry*, https://3dprintingindustry.com/3d-printing-basics-free-beginners-guide/materials.

37. David Szondy, "MultiFab Mixes and Matches 10 Different Materials in a Single 3D Print," *Gizmag*, August 25, 2015, http://newatlas.com/multifab-3d-printer-10-materials/39074 /.

38. Bridget Butler Millsaps, "ORNL Researchers Improve 3D Printing at the Nanoscale with Simulation Guided Process," *3D Print.com*, August 16, 2016, https://3dprint.com/146101/ornl-3d-printing-nanoscale.

39. Olivier Scalabre, "The Next Manufacturing Revolution Is Here," *TED talks*, May 2016, https://www.bcgperspectives.com/ted-at-bcg/?utm_source=201701TEDTT&utm_medium=Email&utm_campaign=otr#video/AyWtIwwEgS0.

40. Jelor Gallego, "A Host of Soon-to-be-Expired Patents are Set to Revolutionize 3D Printing," *Futurism,* May 17, 2017, https://futurism.com/expiring-patents-set-to-improve-3d-world/.
41. Erin Winick, "Watch this super-speedy 3D printer make objects suddenly appear," *MIT Technology Review,* January 31, 2019, https://www.technologyreview.com/s/612869/watch-this-super-speedy-3d-printer-make-objects-suddenly-appear/.
42. Mary Ann Yule, "A Manufacturing Renaissance: How 3D Printing Can Bring Back Local," *Techvibes,* December 8, 2016, https://techvibes.com/2016/12/05/d-3d-printing-mary-ann-yule-president-of-hp-canada.
43. "World Energy Outlook 2017," International Energy Agency, December 14, 2017, http://www.iea.org/weo2017/#section-2.
44. Sarah Kent and Brian Spegele, "Oil Firms Anticipate Day of Reckoning," *Wall Street Journal,* November 28, 2016, 1.
45. Catherine Ngai, "Shale Boom Confounds Forecasts as U.S. Set to Pass Russia, Saudi Arabia," *Reuters,* July 9, 2014, http://www.reuters.com/article/us-usa-oil-shale-forecasts-analysis-idUSKBN0FE0CJ20140709.
46. Isaac Arnsdorf, Wael Mahdi, and Grant Smith, "Saudis Go Back to the Future to Take on U.S. Shale Rivals," *Bloomberg,* November 4, 2014, https://www.bloomberg.com/news/articles/2014-11-04/saudis-go-back-to-the-future-to-take-on-u-s-shale-rivals.
47. "Hydraulic Fracturing Accounts for about Half of Current U.S. Crude Oil Production," U.S. Energy Information Agency, March 15, 2015, http://www.eia.gov/todayinenergy/detail.php?id=25372.
48. "Cushing, OK WTI Spot Price FOB Annual," U.S. Energy Information Agency, http://www.eia.gov/opendata/qb.php?sdid=PET.RWTC.A.
49. Arnsdorf, "Saudis Go Back to the Future."
50. Jeffrey, Ball, "Inside America's oil boom," Brookings Institute, June 1, 2018, https://www.brookings.edu/blog/planetpolicy/2018/06/01/inside-americas-oil-boom/?utm_campaign=brookings-comm&utm_source=hs_email&utm_medium=email&utm_content=63440789.
51. Francine Lacqua and Javier Blas, "IEA Sees Significant Gains in U.S. Shale Oil as Prices Rise," *Bloomberg,* January 18, 2017, https://www.bloomberg.com/news/articles/2017-01-18/iea-sees-significant-increase-in-u-s-shale-oil-as-prices-rise.
52. "Henry Hub Natural Gas Spot Price," U.S. Energy Information Agency, March 26, 2018, https://www.eia.gov/dnav/ng/hist/rngwhhdD.htm.

53. British Petroleum Natural Gas, https://www.bp.com/en/global/corporate/energy-economics/statistical-review-of-world-energy/natural-gas.html#natural-gas-prices.
54. "Japan Liquefied Natural Gas Import Price: 9.10 USD/MMBtu for Mar 2018," *YCharts,* https://ycharts.com/indicators/japan_liquefied_natural_gas_import_price.
55. "Medium-Term Renewable Energy Market Report 2016," International Energy Agency, October 2016, https://www.iea.org/newsroom/news/2016/october/medium-term-renewable-energy-market-report-2016.html.
56. "Renewables 2017: A new era for solar power," International Energy Agency, October 4, 2017, https://www.iea.org/publications/renewables2017/.
57. "Global Energy Perspective 2019: Reference Case," McKinsey, January 2019, 3, https://www.mckinsey.com/~/media/McKinsey/Industries/Oil%20and%20Gas/Our%20Insights/Global%20Energy%20Perspective%202019/McKinsey-Energy-Insights-Global-Energy-Perspective-2019_Reference-Case-Summary.ashx.
58. Michael Forsythe, "China Aims to Spend at Least $360 Billion on Renewable Energy by 2020," *New York Times,* January 5, 2017, http://www.nytimes.com/2017/01/05/world/asia/china-renewable-energy-investment.html?src=me.
59. Lauri Myllyvirta, "China: Six little known facts about the country's solar and wind boom," *Unearthed,* July 9, 2016, http://www.nytimes.com/2017/01/05/world/asia/china-renewable-energy-investment.html?src=me.
60. Leslie Hook, "Global investment in clean energy slides as China pulls back," *Financial Times,* July 10, 2019, https://www.ft.com/content/f415c010-a305-11e9-974c-ad1c6ab5efd1.
61. Eric Ng, "China's Under-Utilized Ultra-High-Voltage Power Lines No Silver Bullet to Rid Grid of Bottlenecks," *South China Morning Post,* February 14, 2016, http://www.scmp.com/business/article/1912878/chinas-under-utilised-ultra-high-voltage-power-lines-no-silver-bullet-rid.
62. Brian Spengele, "China to Put a Little Less Energy into Clean Power," *Wall Street Journal,* December 5, 2016, A9.
63. "Electricity now flows across continents, courtesy of direct current," *The Economist,* January 14–20, 2017, https://www.economist.com/news/science-and-technology/21714325-transmitting-power-over-thousands-kilometres-requires-new-electricity.

64. "U.S. electric generating capacity increase in 2016 was largest net change since 2011," U.S. Energy Information Administration, February 27, 2017, https://www.eia.gov/todayinenergy/detail.php?id=30112.
65. Cara Marcy, "Nearly half of utility-scale capacity installed in 2017 came from renewables," U.S. Energy Information Administration, January 10, 2018, https://www.eia.gov/todayinenergy/detail.php?id=34472.
66. Joshua D. Rhodes et al., "New U.S. Power Costs: by County, with Environmental Externalities," University of Texas at Austin White Paper, July 2016, 2, https://energy.utexas.edu/sites/default/files/UTAustin_FCe_LCOE_2016.pdf.
67. Mike Munsell, "US Solar Market Grows 95% in 2016, Smashes Records," *gtm*, February 15, 2017, https://www.greentechmedia.com/articles/read/us-solar-market-grows-95-in-2016-smashes-records.
68. "U.S. Solar Market Through 2017: Key Takeaways," Solar Energy Industry Association, 2018, https://www.seia.org/solar-industry-research-data.
69. "U.S. Solar Market Insight," Solar Energy Industries Association, June 18, 2019, https://www.seia.org/us-solar-market-insight.
70. "Renewables 2016: Global Status Report," REN21, http://www.ren21.net/wp-content/uploads/2016/06/GSR_2016_Full_Report.pdf.
71. "Solar Market Insight Report 2016 Q4," Solar Energy Industries Association, http://www.seia.org/research-resources/solar-market-insight-report-2016-q4.
72. Michael Holder, "Solar Panel Researchers Investigate Powering Trains by Bypassing Grid," *Guardian*, January 10, 2017, https://www.theguardian.com/environment/2017/jan/10/solar-panel-research-power-trains-imperial-college-london-1010.
73. Mike Hughlett, "Xcel unveils new phase of wind power construction, with huge plant in South Dakota," *Star Tribune*, March 16, 2017, http://www.startribune.com/xcel-unveils-new-phase-of-wind-power-construction-with-huge-plant-in-south-dakota/416340794.
74. James Temple, "How to Get Wyoming Wind to California, and Cut 80% of U.S. Carbon Emissions," *MIT Technology Review*, December 28, 2017, https://www.technologyreview.com/s/609766/how-to-get-wyoming-wind-to-california-and-cut-80-of-us-carbon-emissions/.
75. Joe Ryan and Brian Eckhouse, "The Age of the Giant Battery Is Almost upon Us," *Bloomberg*, February 20, 2017, https://www.bloomberg.com/news/articles/2017-02-21/big-batteries-coming-of-age-prompt-bankers-to-place-their-bets.

76. "Baker-Polito Administration Sets 200 Megawatt-Hour Energy Storage Target," Press Release, June 20, 2017, https://www.mass.gov/news/baker-polito-administration-sets-200-megawatt-hour-energy-storage-target.

77. Fred Lambert, "Tesla's giant battery in Australia made around $1 million in just a few days," *electrek,* January 23, 2018, https://electrek.co/2018/01/23/tesla-giant-battery-australia-1-million/.

78. Calla Wahlquist, "South Australia's Tesla battery on track to make back a third of cost in a year," *The Guardian,* September 27, 2018, https://www.theguardian.com/technology/2018/sep/27/south-australias-tesla-battery-on-track-to-make-back-a-third-of-cost-in-a-year.

79. Eckhouse, "The Age of the Giant Battery Is Almost upon Us."

80. Kurt, "World's Largest Indoor Farm Is 100 Times More Productive," *Urbanist Web,* http://weburbanist.com/2015/01/11/worlds-largest-indoor-farm-is-100-times-more-productive.

81. Jonathan Vanian, "A Nearly All-Robot Farm To Sprout In 2017," *Fortune,* February 1, 2016, http://fortune.com/2016/02/01/robot-farm-lettuce-japan-2017/.

82. Jun Hongo, "Fully Automated Lettuce Factory to Open in Japan," *Wall Street Journal,* August 21, 2015, http://blogs.wsj.com/japanrealtime/2015/08/21/fully-automated-lettuce-factory-to-open-in-japan.

83. Robin Plaskoff Horton, "Indoor & Underground Urban Farms Growing in Size and Number," *Urban Gardens,* October 18, 2015, http://www.urbangardensweb.com/2015/10/18/indoor-underground-urban-farms-growing-in-size-and-number.

84. Kurt, "World's Largest Indoor Farm."

85. G. Owen Shaefer, "Lab-Grown Meat," *Scientific American,* September 14, 2018, https://www.scientificamerican.com/article/lab-grown-meat/. .

86. Brian Kateman, "Mosa Meat: All Beef and No Butcher," *Good Food Institute,* June 17, 2016, https://www.impossiblefoods.com/burger.

87. Chase Purdy, "The world's biggest meat companies are betting on cell-cultured meat," *Quartz,* January 30, 2018, https://qz.com/1193161/tyson-foods-is-investing-in-lab-grown-meat/.

88. "The United States Meat Industry at a Glance," North American Meat Institute, https://www.meatinstitute.org/index.php?ht=d/sp/i/47465/pid/47465.

89. Index Mundi, "Soybean Meal Exports by Country in one hundred MT," http://www.indexmundi.com/agriculture/?commodity=soybean-meal&graph=exports.

Chapter 3

Economic Impact

The history of international trade is active; it is a dynamic story of expansion and contraction. Improvements in transportation, financial systems, preventive medicine, and political stability have consistently led to global trade expansion. These improvements let regions produce and trade globally, making use of their competitive advantages.

There are numerous models that attempt to explain why particular nations thrive economically. And, as with all things economic, there is a great deal of disagreement as to which model is best or even what factors are critical. If President Harry Truman were alive today, he would still be searching for his one-handed economist.

Lacking this mythical economist, I will use Michael Porter's Diamond Model to examine how the fourth industrial revolution is changing competitive advantages in global trade. It describes four major elements required for successful businesses—firm strategy, structure and rivalry; factor conditions; demand conditions; and related supporting industries. While not a formal part of his model, it also includes discussion of the impact of government and chance on business. Firm strategy, structure, and rivalry expresses how firms are organized and plan as well as how they are improved if they have to compete against other local firms. Factors address the natural, capital, and human resources available to the company. Demand conditions provide the underlying base for the company as well as providing feedback on its products that drives improvement and innovation. Finally, related supporting industries provide not only a base of suppliers but also an innovation incubator.

The convergence of technologies in the fourth industrial revolution is shifting the balance among these factors. Unless a nation has very high tariffs to protect its industries, all must still compete hard to continually improve or face bankruptcy. In fact, globalization forced many companies to compete against aggressive, foreign firms. Those that survived did so by improving their products. The U.S. auto industry is a good example.

This will not change, but U.S. companies will gain significant advantages from the other elements. Advanced manufacturing is reducing and even eliminating the cost of labor as a factor while simultaneously increasing the value of access to capital and a well-educated labor force. And U.S. firms will continue to benefit from lower energy costs than most of their competitors. One of its greatest advantage are the world-class research and educational institutions of the United States. U.S. firms are also favored by being in the world's largest economy and a market that demands frequent product cycles which increases the value of proximity. Finally, while the U.S. has suffered from the loss of supply chains as traditional manufacturing moved overseas, advanced manufacturing is creating entirely new and very different supply chains that are being built in home markets.

Rather than new technology making it more efficient to exploit Ricard's traditional comparative advantages (cheap labor, proximity to raw materials, etc.) of making something in one location and then shipping it to market, this industrial revolution will make local production better and cheaper. It will change how, what, and where we manufacture—as well as how we provide services and financing—for a broad spectrum of businesses.

How We Make Things

The combination of robotics, artificial intelligence, and 3D printing is rapidly changing how we make things. The trend is accelerating, and there is no end in sight.

Industrial Robots

Even though it requires major capital investment, Foxconn, the Taiwanese chip manufacturer, has decided it can increase profits by replacing most of its mainland Chinese workforce with industrial robots.[1] In order to maintain high-quality, high-volume production, Foxconn carefully studied each task and wrote precise rules for each. One worker reported that, to achieve production targets, she "had to adopt a particular posture, her stool had to stay within yellow and black lines; every movement was studied, rationalized and standardized for maximum efficiency." Adaption, ingenuity, creativity, innovation, and judgment were not only not required but were proscribed. The job description sounds like it was written for a robot. In fact, Foxconn has already developed its own line of robots, installed more than 40,000, and is manufacturing an additional 10,000 a year.[2]

Foxconn sees robots as both cheaper and easier to work with. Robots will not strike, require vacations, get sick, or slow down. Although they do require human assistance, there will be a vastly smaller workforce, and that workforce will be more highly educated and better paid. This is clearly desirable for an individual firm, but the implications for the economy as a whole are extraordinary.

According to Boston Consulting Group, about ten percent of all manufacturing is currently automated, and this number will rise to twenty-five percent by 2025. Driving the trend is the dramatic decrease in the operating cost of robots. An electronics-manufacturing robot costs only about $4 per hour for routine assembly tasks.[3] In contrast, the cost of labor in China averaged $14.60 per hour plus benefits in 2016. In 2000, labor represented only thirty percent of China's manufacturing costs.

By 2015, it was sixty-four percent.[4] With China's total labor force now declining, the robots cost advantage will only increase. And China's "Made in China 2025" program provides subsidies for upgrading plants from human to robot labor.

The potential savings are enormous. Foxconn reduced its labor force in a single factory in Kunshan China from 110,000 to 50,000 by installing robots guided by artificial intelligence. As many as six hundred other major Chinese companies have similar plans.[5] In 2016, Dongguan City created a plan to replace human workers with robots at 1,000 to 1,500 factories to strengthen its role as a manufacturing hub.[6] As a nation, China plans to produce 100,000 industrial robots for domestic use per year by 2020.[7]

Collaborative Robots

Collaborative robots or cobots, which represented less than five percent of global sales in 2015, will soon have an even greater impact than industrial robots. At a current average cost globally of only $24,000 they are appealing strongly to the smaller companies that account for seventy percent of global manufacturing.[8] In addition to being affordable,

> they can be placed alongside humans in small-spaced electronics assembly lines, because they are affordable and easily trainable, and because they are flexible to handle short runs, repetitive and boring jobs, and ergonomically challenging tasks...teams made of humans and robots collaborating efficiently can be more productive than teams made of either humans or robots alone. Also, the cooperative process reduced human idle time by 85 percent."[9]

Once again, whether you consider that a bug or a feature depends on whether you represent management or labor.

In 2014, total cobot sales were $116 million but growing explosively.[10] Barclays predicts cobot sales increasing to $12 billion by 2025, an increase of over one hundred times in just ten years.[11]

Accelerating the drive to robotics is the fact that those CEOs who have already used robots are the most enthusiastic about buying more. Ninety-four percent of those CEOs who had already adopted robots say the robots increased productivity.[12] Increased productivity combined with reduced labor cost makes the rapid adoption of these robots very attractive even to small businesses.

Sewbots

As mentioned in chapter 2, sewbots are a new category of cobots that is maturing rapidly and will have a massive impact on the global clothing industry. Starting in the late 1960s, textiles, clothing, and footwear (TCF) moved their operations to low-wage countries simply to remain competitive. The insoluble problem for the industry was the difficult, labor-intensive nature of sewing. When robots began moving into heavy industry in the early 1960s, no robot could sew. TCF companies could only move overseas.

It was not until the early 2010s that automation first began to take over the complex process of actually making clothing. By June 2016, Softwear had twenty robots working in the field, one assembling thirty separate pieces of fabric to create the final product.[13] At the same time, Henderson Sewing Machine Company demonstrated a machine that fed a two-headed sewing machine and cost only $25,000. Moreover, as Henderson stated, "it doesn't get sick, doesn't take vacation."[14]

Using robotics, clothing manufacturers have found they can get better quality much faster and produce near their markets. Henderson Sewing Machine Company signed a customer who previously ordered customized logos from China—9.5 million units a year. The time from order to arrival could take nine months; and if the colors were not quite right, the customer was stuck. Henderson established a system in the United States where the final customer orders online, machines cut, screen, dry, sew, pack, and ship the product the following day.[15] And only one worker per shift is needed to run the machine. Although the technology is only a few years old, sewbots have also mastered making T-shirts and jeans.

Today sewbots can provide low cost labor in proximity to the customer in order to provide "socially conscious," individually customized clothing and shoes near the customers—and at a higher profit margin.

3D Printing

3D printing is creating entirely new ways to manufacture a rapidly expanding range of products from medical devices to aircraft parts to buildings and bridges. The recent orders of magnitude increase in the speed of printing is challenging traditional manufacturing. United Parcel Service (UPS) established a new initiative called "Direct Digital Manufacturing" focused on providing very rapid 3D printing of any customer's design. The

> facility will house a staggering 100 3D printers which can be used to manufacturing one-off parts, or mass manufacture 1,000 of the same part...[the printers] run 24 hours a day, 7 days a week, and require just three employees total; one per 8 hour shift.[16]

The building was designed to expand easily to 1,000 printers. UPS also offers 3D printing in over one hundred stores nationwide and opened a 3D-printing facility in Singapore.[17]

> The concept is simple, local production of a vast number of components will hit the international shipping market hard... UPS wants to stop shipping your parts long distance. It wants to make them locally and then deliver them to your door as fast as possible.[18]

Staples has followed suit and put 3D printers in one hundred of its stores.

This new method of manufacturing has four major advantages: it largely eliminates labor-cost advantages through the elimination of humans in the process, it reduces shipping time for finished products, it eliminates most inventory and warehousing costs, and it eliminates most shipping costs.

In sum, automation driven by improved robotics and task-specific artificial intelligence combined with 3D printing is changing how we make a wide range of products from an expanding range of materials—to include many which cannot be created any other way.

WHAT WE MAKE

As the technology improved, 3D printing rapidly moved from prototyping to production. General Electric uses 3D printed nozzles on its new LEAP jet engines. Rather than being assembled from eighteen smaller parts, the new nozzle is printed as a single piece that is lighter, stronger, longer lasting, more efficient, and cheaper.[19] More recently, it used 3D printing for over one-third of the parts in its new Advanced Turboprop engine. The most amazing result was consolidating 855 separate parts per engine to just twelve.[20] At the other end of the complexity spectrum, after ten years of development and hundreds of prototypes, Chanel began printing mascara brushes—at the rate of one million per month in a single facility.[21]

Perhaps more revolutionary is the fact that, for the first time, designers can design for purpose. Current manufacturing techniques often require that optimal design be subordinated to manufacturing limitations. In the past, the designer may have envisioned the most efficient form for a product, but that form might be impossible to machine or build. Compromising design to account for manufacturing limitations results in lower operational efficiency and higher manufacturing costs. 3D printing frees the designer to create virtually any form and see it printed to specification.

3D printing also allows designers and engineers to experiment with new techniques to increase strength and functionality. Honeycombed structures, like those in bird bones, maximize strength for a given weight, but such structures have been very expensive and difficult to make with traditional manufacturing. 3D printing can make them with relative ease. Further, 3D printing expands the possibility of using new alloys, including gradient alloys. These are alloys where the percentage of each type of metal in the alloy changes over the length or breadth of the part. This expands the material properties of the product and increases the precision in production.

Thus, 3D printing is having a major impact on manufacturing by bringing two other changes—mass customization and design for purpose. Because each print is guided by software, each individual product can be customized at no extra cost simply by selecting different options in the software.

3D printing will also let us make things that have never been made before. 3D laser lithography "enables the rapid fabrication of nano-, micro- and mesostructures with feature sizes starting from about hundred nanometers up to several micrometers."[22] The ability to print at this scale means entirely new products including micro-optics and photonics, integrated wafer-level optics, micro-fluidics, cell scaffolds and tissue engineering as well as biomimetics. A team of researchers has a miniature 3D-printed lens that uses two pairs of lenses to achieve the visual acuity of an eagle with obvious application for surveillance drones.[23]

Just as remarkable, 3D printing can actually improve the performance of existing materials. For instance, 3D-printed ceramics can have ten times the compressive strength of commercially available ceramics, tolerate higher temperatures, and be printed in complex lattices further increasing the strength to weight ratio.[24] Not only will 3D printing allow faster, better production but it will allow the production of entirely new products made of entirely new materials.

WHERE WE MAKE THINGS

Boston Consulting expects that manufacturers will "no longer simply chase cheap labor." Factories will employ fewer people, and those that remain are more likely to be highly skilled. That could lure more manufacturers back to the United States from lower-wage emerging market countries.[25]

Automated sewing and 3D printing mean custom clothing and shoes are moving from high-end individualized fashion houses to the mass market. As the software is perfected and material base widens, all clothing may be made to individual order because there is virtually no additive cost to customizing each product. Today, companies are even exploring using bio-printed leather to create belts and shoes.[26] Instead of making mass-produced clothing, companies will mass produce clothing made specifically to each customer's personal measurements.

The move to automation in TCF industry will cause major disruptions in the nations currently producing these products. The International Labor Organization reports that sewbots are

> more likely to be deployed in destination markets such as China, Europe, and the United States. The disruptive impact on the sector in Association of South East Asian Nations (ASEAN) could be very substantial, as robotic automation poses a significant threat of job displacement.[27]

A modern automated sewing machine can produce twice as many T-shirts per shift as a ten-person sewing line. This threatens sixty to seventy-five million jobs in the clothing industry.[28]

Because robot labor costs roughly the same anywhere, the response is to move the manufacturing facility to the market. Moving close to the market has three great benefits for manufacturers. It reduces transportation costs, increases efficiency and quality control, and is more responsive to customers' requests for changes and customization. Further, 3D printing reduces the need for existing supply chains will make reshoring easier and cheaper.

General Electric recently opened a 125,000 square foot, $40-million plant in Pittsburg dedicated to 3D printing. It allows GE to more effectively and less expensively produce complete components for its aircraft engines. GE is not alone. Boeing, Rolls Royce, and Airbus are just some of the companies in the aircraft industry that are establishing 3D-printing facilities. They are entering new markets such as fabricating custom-fit medical hip joints even as they improve their old processes by speeding the design cycle with rapid prototyping.[29]

POWER PRODUCTION

Most people get their power from a local power company so they may not think changes in power production will have much impact on international trade. The reality is that a great deal of energy in the form of gas, oil, and coal have been traded internationally. However, the explosion in fracking in the United States is dramatically shifting that trade. From a peak import demand of over five billion barrels of oil in 2005, U.S. demand dropped to 3.7 billion barrels in 2017.[30] This figure alone does not capture the magnitude of the shift. Since 2005, U.S. petroleum and other petroleum-based liquids exports have increased from 425 million barrels a year to over 2.4 billion barrels a year.[31] Thus the net effect on global oil trade is a reduction of U.S. import demand from five billion barrels a year to only 1.3 billion barrels. With the projected global demand increasing only 2.6 billion barrels a year by 2040, demand from the rest of the world will not make up for the decline in U.S. imports.[32] By shifting a huge part of its demand from imports to national production, the United States is reducing the global trade in oil.

Fracking has also dramatically reduced U.S. demand for imported chemicals. It provides the United States with plentiful supplies of cheap natural gas—the critical feedstock for many chemical-industry products. The result has been heavy investment in new U.S. petrochemical plants, with 310 new projects underway that will satisfy most U.S. demand and increase U.S. exports from $17 billion in 2016 to $110 billion by 2027.[33] This unplanned advantage for America's chemical subsector will have spillover benefits as the expansion stimulates local development of directly related service and manufacturing businesses.

Fossil fuel is not the only industry changing dramatically. Renewable energy production remains on a steep upward curve as cost per kilowatt hour steadily decreases. Unlike oil, coal, and LNG, which are in forms suitable for storage and global transport, renewable energy is distributed locally or regionally rather than globally. In addition, the rising use of "distributed generation" will further localize energy production and distribution. Distributed generation uses small-scale technologies to produce electricity close to the end users. Further, solar and wind energy are increasingly being installed behind the meter so that the energy is consumed where it is produced. Moreover, not all distributed-power schemes involve renewable sources or batteries.

> Wesleyan University in Connecticut has installed a system based around an efficient engine running on natural gas (which fracking has made cheap in America). Besides generating about 95 % of the electricity that the university needs, the set-up captures much of the engine's waste heat to provide heating and hot water, cutting the institution's net energy consumption by thirty percent."[34]

Clearly this trend reduces both demand for and trade in energy.

Joshua Pearce, a solar expert at the Michigan Tech Open Sustainability Technology Lab, believes that "we're just a few years away from affordable batteries, which—along with a backup generator—will allow existing and new solar customers to disconnect from the grid entirely."[35] The possibility that large numbers of consumers will move off grid cannot be discarded.

INTERNET FRAGMENTATION

Almost since its creation, the internet has been seen as a technology that would drive globalization. By eliminating time and distance, it brings people closer together. Unfortunately, this benign vision is not completely accurate. Although most states see open use of the internet as critical to economic growth, authoritarian states, particularly China and Russia, are Balkanizing the internet to restrict access to information.

Initially considered an impossible goal, China has steadily improved its ability to control what people can access inside its territory. As early as 1997, *Wired* magazine coined the phrase "The Great Firewall" to cover the wide range of efforts China had undertaken to restrict its citizens access to information. China's position is clear.

> A network that allows individuals to do as they please, lets them go brazenly wherever they wish, is a hegemonistic network that harms the rights of others...Our ideal is to create an exclusively Chinese-language network. It will be a Net that has Chinese characteristics, one that is an information superhighway for the masses.[36]

China continues to improve its technical ability to control what its people can see online. By 2017, what "China calls the 'Golden Shield' had evolved into giant mechanism of censorship and surveillance that blocked tens of thousands of sites deemed inimical to the Communist Party's narrative and control."[37] On January 23, 2017, the Ministry of Industry and Information Technology announced internet service providers (ISP) are now "forbidden to create or rent communication channels, including VPNs [virtual private networks], without governmental approval, to run cross-border operations."[38] Chinese citizens previously used VPNs to get around China's internet censorship. China has also demanded that Western technology companies share their codes to provide China better control of data concerning not only the Western companies but also Chinese companies and China's economy.[39] Finally, China augments its technology with two million human monitors.[40]

In addition to controlling what users inside China can access, Chinese authorities collect financial, social, political, legal, and credit data on each of its citizens. Using this daily record of activity, Chinese authorities plan to assign a personal social credit score. Although they have not clearly stated what they will use the score for, it is likely it will be used for evaluating loans, school admission, and permission to travel.[41] Not supposed to operate nationwide until 2020, reports indicate that China has already banned nine million citizens from buying domestic airline tickets and three million from buying business-class train tickets. Not yet officially announced as policy, many Chinese already believe low scores will reduce chances for state industry jobs, block enrollment in the best schools, and restrict vacation choices.[42] As a result, many people will self-censor by avoiding any websites they feel might affect their social credit score. This is a powerful tool to reduce the contact Chinese citizens have with content from providers outside China.

The opportunities for totalitarian states to tighten control over their populations are obvious. They can literally monitor an individual's activities through every single purchase, phone call, and text. Any contact with the digital world will be recorded and available to security forces. Through the increasing use of facial-recognition technology, cell-phone tracking, the massive increases in the number of surveillance cameras deployed, and computerized surveillance of social-media sites, Chinese security services have proven they can track and arrest individuals even in huge crowds.[43] They will also have data on the movements of the individual and can use software to see with whom he or she has come in proximity.

In April 2016,

> the U.S. government officially classified the Great Firewall as a barrier to trade, noting that eight of the twenty-five most trafficked sites globally were now blocked in China. The American Chamber of Commerce in China says that 4 out of 5 of its members companies report a negative impact on their business from Internet censorship.[44]

Yet there is no indication that China will turn back.

Fearing an internet-driven color revolution, Russia wanted to track activity online and to be able to switch off connections in times of crisis. Knowing it lacked the technological prowess and equipment to do so, Russia turned to China. In April 2016, top Russian and Chinese officials met in Moscow to discuss cooperation.[45] By November 2016, it was clear that Russia was importing aspects of the Great Firewall. During the same month, Russia demonstrated its improved capability when it blocked LinkedIn's networking site—a clear signal of its intent to control the internet within its borders.[46] In March 2019, Russia announced that it would test its ability to disconnect its internet from the rest of the world —even though the test may cost $304 million.[47] And, like China, Russia is reinforcing its technology with legal measures requiring local telecoms companies to not only retain all user's data for six months but also provide the encryption keys to the government.[48]

Both China and Russia have made it clear that they consider "internet sovereignty" a legitimate aspect of a state's control of its own territory. Other authoritarian states are attempting to replicate China's success. In early January 2017, Iran, in an attempt to block pornography sites within its country, actually affected web servers worldwide.[49]

These states know restricted access to the internet will inevitably reduce their nations' participation in the global economy, but they have decided the costs of connectivity exceed the benefits of globalization. In addition, the revelations by Edward Snowden that the United States was exploiting the connectivity for intelligence provided additional incentive.

Even democracies are placing limits on the internet. Based on a ruling by the European Court of Justice, the European Union instituted its controversial "right to be forgotten." According to the European Commission, "Individuals have the right—under certain conditions—to ask search engines to remove links with personal information about them."[50]

Well-intentioned efforts to protect their citizens mean some democratic states go even farther. France's data protection authority, the Commission

Nationale de l'Informatique et des Libertés (CNIL), whose stated mission is to "to protect personal data, support innovation, preserve individual liberties,"[51]

> wants Google to delete search links everywhere. Europe's much-contested right to be forgotten would thus be given global reach... Courts and governments have embarked on what some call a "legal arms race" to impose a maze of national or regional rules, often conflicting, in the digital realm.[52]

In India, local authorities use the justification of national security or prevention of communal violence to suspend "broadband or mobile Internet services across districts for hours or even days at a stretch."[53] As unrest continued in Kashmir, India shut down internet service 154 times between January 2016 and May 2018. The country with the next most shutdowns was Pakistan—at only nineteen times.[54]

The measures to restrict access to the internet are in fact working. The 2018 Freedom on the Net report by Freedom House, a nonprofit that monitors economic, social, and political freedom worldwide, reported that freedom on the internet had declined for the eighth year in a row.[55] In its 2018 "Health of the Internet" report, Mozilla noted that "Two-thirds of the world's Internet users live in countries where Internet and media censorship are common."[56]

Nor are states the only driver of fragmentation on the internet. Social media has created "closed loop" networks where people of similar views can meet online for discussions and "news" without the danger of hearing or seeing anything that does not agree with their preconceived views. The 2016, 2017, and 2018 elections in the United States and Europe provided stark illustrations how people on both the left and the right can isolate themselves from the views of others, thereby strongly reinforcing both their own views and the rejection of others.

The profit motive has driven software developers to exploit this trend. "The success of Toutiao [a very popular Chinese news aggregation app] has been achieved, in large part, by using machine learning to figure out users' interests and tastes, and tailoring its offerings accordingly to get more clicks."[57] The payoff for confirming and reinforcing its customers' tastes has been remarkable. Toutiao's parent company, Beijing Bytedance Technology, was valued at $500 million in 2014. In 2016, investors were considering valuation in excess of $10 billion.[58]

Of course, other social-media firms will have to modify their software to compete and the net affect will be further social fragmentation as various viewpoints are reinforced and hardened—often with incorrect information.

RESHORING

With labor costs essentially equal across the globe for tasks done by robots, manufacturing in the United States is seeing a resurgence. Thomas Roehmer, MIT Sloan School of Management, stated there are five good reasons to reshore manufacturing jobs: 1) U.S. workers are ten to twelve times more productive than Chinese and the wage gap is narrowing quickly, 2) more customers want both immediate gratification and made-to-order products, 3) the learning curve within the company is much faster if all employees are located close together, 4) the maker movement (3D printing) is changing the competitive field, and 5) energy costs are much lower in the United States.[59]

American firms are not the only ones that recognize U.S. economic advantages emerging with the Fourth Industrial Revolution. "Average annual foreign direct investment (FDI) into American manufacturing has more than tripled since 2004 (contemporaneous with the start of the shale oil boom) to over $250 billion and has consistently grown faster than domestic investments."[60] Cho Tak Wong, the billionaire chairman of Fuyao Group, bought the largest auto-glass plant in the United States. His investment reflects a major change in globalization.

Now it is China that experts fear is losing steam, forcing the country's wealthy investors and corporations to seek out profits overseas. They are snapping up U.S. businesses at a record rate and employing tens of thousands of U.S. workers.[61]

This was reflected in the flow of foreign direct investment into the United States through 2016. However, uncertainty created by the Trump administration's trade and tariff policies has resulted in a major decrease in FDI since.

Further reducing the influence which labor costs have on the decision to return manufacturing to the United States is the massive increase in productivity of U.S. manufacturing. In 2015, researchers from Ball University's Center for Economic and Business Research studied manufacturing productivity from 2000 to 2010. They noted "had we kept 2000-levels of productivity and applied them to 2010-level of production, we would have required 20.9 million manufacturing workers. Instead, we employed only 12.1 million."[62] Boston Consulting Group noted

> "job intensity" of America's manufacturing industries is only going to decline. In 1980, it took 25 jobs to generate $1 million in manufacturing output in the U.S. Today it takes five jobs.[63]

Another factor accelerating the shift of manufacturing back to the United States is the reduction in risk to intellectual property. Despite efforts by major brands to protect their intellectual property, the problem persists. China's share of global manufacturing is seventeen percent, but it is the origin of eighty-four percent of counterfeit or pirated goods.[64] Taking production out of China will not stop counterfeiting, but it will make it much more difficult and thus reduce the profit margin.

Hal Sirkin, an analyst with Boston Consulting, predicts that "you're going to see more localization rather than more scale...I can put up a plant, change the software and manufacture all sorts of things, not in the hundreds of millions but runs of five million or 10 million units."[65] In addition, the plant does not have to be product or even industry specific. Easily reprogrammable, flexible robots and cobots could be working on cars one month and washing machines the next.

Robots, paired with 3D printers, artificial intelligence, and scanners, are even beginning to produce shoes in high-wage countries. In September 2016, Adidas proudly displayed the first shoes produced in Germany in three decades. Its Speedfactory

> will employ just 160 people: one robotic production line will make soles, the other production line the upper part of shoes...Currently an Adidas shoe takes 18 months to move from idea to store shelf. The aim is to reduce this to five hours, with customers able to customize their order in stores.[66]

A number of additional footwear-makers are also seeking to use sewbots combined with 3D printing technology, names like Nike, New Balance, and Under Armor among them. The goal is to create shoes customized for each consumer's foot based on his or her personal preferences.[67]

This is not just happening in the United States. Numerous companies are building smaller, high-technology plants to be near major markets around the world. These companies understand colocation has significant benefits—particularly when technology eliminates the labor-cost advantage of large, distant factories. Colocation reduces shipping costs, and in some cases reduces or even eliminates inventory altogether. "Just in time" local production means no finished items in stock—only a supply of input materials. A greater benefit of onshoring manufacturing is that it allows closer interaction between design and manufacturing. In a world used to frequent hardware upgrades, colocation accelerates those upgrades by speeding up the design, test, build, employ, and improve cycle.

In 2017, Foxconn announced it was building a new flat-screen factory in Wisconsin.[68] Although it required a $3 billion incentive package, the very fact the Taiwan-based company would choose the United States rather than a location in Asia to build a new factory is an indicator of major changes in the economics of production.

China is reshoring too. As the cost of Chinese labor has increased over the last few years, firms were moving out of China to lower-cost areas in Southeast Asia. To maintain its economic growth, China's leaders are fighting back with a concerted effort to maintain current industries and return others to China. As early as 2009, the Chinese Ministry of Commerce initiated a "Made in China" campaign in an attempt to capture its internal market and retain its export markets. Chinese firms had caused a series of scandals with unsafe food and toys, and this advertising campaign stressed that China made high-quality products in partnership with Western firms. By 2014, the tone of "Made in China" campaign shifted. In response to Prime Minister Narendra Modi's "Made in India" campaign, China's government offered tax breaks and other incentives to encourage Chinese companies to invest in research and development as well as the manufacturing equipment upgrades needed to produce higher quality products in China.[69] Because both nation's programs focus on encouraging their populations to purchase local products, they are inherently anti-globalization.

This trend will not be limited to developed economies. The costs of 3D printers, robotics, and artificial intelligence are dropping drastically. Printers vary from massive building-size gantry units to microwave-unit size, but all have decreased in cost by a factor of ten in the last five years. Some firms are even producing small, solar-powered printers, thus eliminating the requirement for a power grid and dramatically expanding the number and location of potential producers.

Boston Consulting Group envisioned the factory of the future as including smart robots that allow a single production line to produce variations of a product; collaborative robots to assist production-line workers with tasks requiring strength, reaching difficult places, and precision; additive manufacturing (noting that BMW already produces more than 10,000 parts with 3D printers), and other advanced technologies. Of automotive executives surveyed, thirteen percent think these technologies are important today but seventy percent say they will be highly relevant by 2030.[70] In short, converging technologies are changing corporate calculations on where products are made. In its analysis of why global corporations are in retreat, *The Economist* noted

> Many industries that tried to globalise seem to work best when national or regional. For some, the penny has dropped. Retailers, such as Britain's Tesco and France's Casino have abandoned many of their foreign adventures. American's telecoms giants, AT&T and Verizon, have put away their passports. Financial firms are focusing on their "core" markets. ... General Electric is localizing its production, supply chains and management. Emerson, a conglomerate that has over one hundred factories outside America, sources about 80% of its production in the region where it is sold...Siemens, a German industrial giant, employs 50,000 in American and has 60 factories there.[71]

The bottom line is that more and more products will be produced locally which will steadily reduce the need for international trade in manufactured goods. This will cut out entire segments of the global supply chain. Without the requirement to build sub-assemblies, then ship them to final assembly, and then on to the customer eliminated, the supply chain will be greatly simplified. Raw materials will be shipped to facilities that turn them into materials suitable for printers. Those will be shipped to local production centers where the product is printed and then delivered locally.

SERVICE INDUSTRIES ARE COMING HOME TOO

Service industries are reshoring too as task-specific artificial intelligence takes over more high-order tasks. Back-office jobs as varied as call-center attendants, teaching assistants, computer programmers, accountants, radiologists, oncologists, loan officers, associate lawyers, IT support, and insurance-claims clerks are all being mastered by task-specific artificial intelligence.

Early adopters of AI-driven customer-service centers like United Services Automobile Association have achieved very positive results.[72] Pairing AI with humans has resulted in lower costs and higher customer satisfaction. In May 2017, Infosys, an Indian tech outsourcing firm, announced it was hiring 10,000 Americans so it could open four US-based hubs. Although it was built by providing services using inexpensive Indian labor, the CEO realized the world is changing and he plans to hire from U.S. universities and community colleges. "We want to create a culture of close proximity."[73] Even as Infosys is hiring Americans to staff service centers, it is laying off personnel in India which is causing some uncertainty in a profession which had been seen as a certain path to the middle class.[74]

The impact of artificial intelligence has not been limited to routine call-center tasks. Indian information-technology (IT) companies laid off 56,000 workers in 2017. This is the first time Tata Consulting and Infosys, two major companies, have ever reduced their number of IT employees. Hiring for entry-level positions plummeted across the industry, and analysts are concerned this may just be the beginning of IT job losses to artificial intelligence.[75] "It seems that workers in India's vast code-writing centres are as much at risk of being made obsolescent by automation as those in factories making cars or shoes."[76]

The sophistication of artificial intelligence is growing so quickly that in 2016 the Georgia Institute of Technology employed a software program they named "Jill Watson" as a teaching assistant for an online course. The university did not tell the students until after they had submitted end-of-course critiques. All of the students thought Ms. Watson was a very effective and helpful teaching assistant. None guessed she was not human.[77] Baker & Hostetler, a law firm, announced it has hired her "brother," Ross, also based on Watson, as a lawyer for its bankruptcy practice.[78]

Watson-based AI is continually pushing into new areas. In 2015, it demonstrated a truly remarkable ninety-percent accuracy in diagnosing lung cancer at a time human doctors were averaging fifty percent.[79] In 2016, it correctly diagnosed leukemia in a Japanese patient. The team of doctors had been baffled for months and thus called in IBM's Watson to consult. The machine spent ten minutes comparing the patient's symptoms against twenty million oncological records previously uploaded by the University of Tokyo's Institute of Medical Science, and then gave the diagnosis and recommended a treatment.[80]

Although improving services is a major goal, cost savings are likely to be the primary driver in the shift of services from people to task-specific AI. In June 2016, J.P. Morgan deployed software that sifts through 12,000 commercial-loan contracts in seconds. Lawyers and accountants working together used to take 360,000 hours to accomplish the same task.[81]

Even as AI moves into sophisticated tasks, robotics will also take over mundane tasks like delivery, stocking, and cleaning. Not surprisingly, Amazon is pioneering this effort. Its entire shipping process is orchestrated down to the second by task-specific artificial intelligence, with much of the work done by robots. The average time a human spends on each order has decreased from an hour and a half with only people to one minute with the addition of robots.[82] Amazon's efforts have paid off. Despite expecting increased demand for the 2018 holiday season, it cut its temporary workforce from 120,000 to 100,000.[83]

An interesting new development in AI is robotic process automation (RPA). RPA is a type of software that assumes the routine aspects of a person's job. Many of the back-office tasks performed in a wide variety of business consist of essentially mechanical tasks such as collecting data from various forms, organizing it, and putting it in the correct block of another document. The software cannot do the entire job, but it can relieve the human of many mundane and time-consuming tasks. In sixteen case studies done by the London School of Economics, the return on investment for shifting from human labor to AI was between thirty and two hundred percent in a single year.[84] Not only did it save the firms a great deal of money, it allowed workers to focus on the human tasks requiring emotional intelligence, judgement, and customer service. It markedly improved customer service and brought some back-office functions back to the home country. The firms who applied AI had an opportunity to grow—and add new employees. However, the firm that previously delivered the service, often in India or the Philippines, inevitably suffered from the loss of business and had to lay people off.

The offshoring consultancy firm Everest Group has observed a rapid and significant shift of call-center operations back to home countries. It notes that improving technology has allowed a shift in emphasis from cost containment to customer service. Its recent research showed that "in 2015, the percentage of contact center contracts with significant onshore delivery climbed to 53 percent, up from 49 percent in 2013 and just over a third (35 percent) in 2010."[85]

Human-machine teaming appears to be the most productive approach. The machine will do the predictable parts of the job as the human takes care of the unpredictable parts. Both machine and human will be more effective. The result will be more interesting jobs with better pay but fewer of us will be needed to maintain productivity.

SHIFTS IN EMPLOYMENT

This represents the front end of a global shift of labor to automation. Frey and Osborne's now-famous 2014 report, "The Future of Employment: How susceptible are jobs to computerisation?" suggested that forty-seven percent of current jobs are at risk.[86] The Gowdner report, "The Future of Jobs, 2025: Working Side By Side With Robots," is much less pessimistic but still sees a sixteen percent loss of jobs to automation.[87] In March 2017, PwC, a research firm, reported that up to thirty-eight percent of U.S. jobs will be automated in the next fifteen years with heavy losses for high-school graduates working in retail-oriented financial-service jobs.[88]

Despite the range of estimates, all agree automation will have significant impact on who makes things and how.

This has interesting implications for deglobalization. Unpredictable work—forestry, onsite construction, landscaping—involves local labor. Those jobs cannot be exported overseas. In contrast, the predictable jobs are exactly those jobs that have already either been exported overseas or automated to include many of the routine tasks of assembly-line workers, lawyers, accountants, radiologists, and reporters. As robots and AI take over these jobs, there will no longer be a labor advantage to exporting them.

In short, non-routine tasks—whether manual or cognitive—will still be done by humans even as routine tasks, even cognitive ones, are taken over by machines. And this is not a new phenomenon; computer technology has been eating jobs since 1990.

Examining the Federal Reserve data in figure 6, you see a divergence between the growth of non-routine and routine jobs starting about 1990. Prior to this time, routine and non-routine jobs, whether cognitive or manual, increased at roughly at the same rate in response to growth in the U.S. economy. However, as computers began to move into the workplace, the growth curves diverged. Although non-routine manual and non-routine cognitive jobs continued to grow along with the economy, routine job growth slowed and then declined. At first glance, the decline does not appear dramatic, but the cumulative impact certainly is. If routine work had paralleled the growth of non-routine cognitive, the United States would have over fifty million more jobs available. Even if routine jobs had grown at the slower rate of non-routine manual labor, the United States would have over thirty million more jobs available. Although it is unlikely the U.S. population of 330 million could have filled those jobs, the U.S. labor situation would be dramatically different.

Figure 6. Routine vs. Non-Routine Jobs.

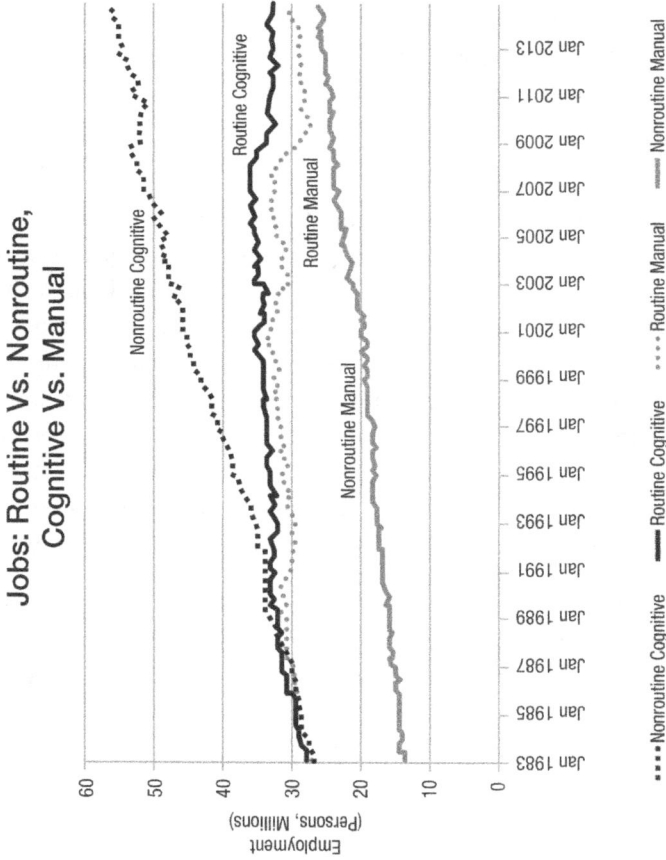

Jobs: Routine Vs. Nonroutine, Cognitive Vs. Manual

Source: Maximiliano Dvorkin, "Jobs Involving Routine Tasks Aren't Growing," Federal Reserve Bank of St. Louis, https://www.stlouisfed.org/on-the-economy/2016/january/jobs-involving-routine-tasks-arent-growing?utm_source=OTEBlog&utm_medium=PopularPosts&utm_campaign=position1.

The ability to manufacture greater wealth with fewer people is not new to manufacturing. Figure 7 shows the relationship between the manufacturing sector's growing productivity and its reduced demand for labor per unit of production. In is important to understand that the value of U.S. manufacturing output has been improving steadily since 1947. Except for short downturns for recessions and a much larger one for the Great Recession, manufacturing value has increased even as manufacturing employment decreased. Of particular note is the fact that although manufacturing employment had a steep decline from 2000 to 2010 it began to recover in 2011, although not as quickly as it declined.[89]

Unfortunately, the trend of eliminating routine work seems to be accelerating. Routine activities make up fifty-one percent of the labor activities in the U.S. economy accounting for almost $2.7 trillion in annual wages. These jobs are most prevalent in manufacturing, accommodation, food service, and retail which are exactly the areas cobots are penetrating fastest.[90] In addition to the economic impact, the loss of jobs and fear of loss to automation had a major impact on the 2016 U.S. presidential election. "Specifically, counties with the most 'routine' jobs—those in manufacturing, sales, clerical work and related occupations that are easier to automate or send offshore—were far more likely to vote for Trump."[91]

Automation will be common across countries, with China, India, Japan, and the United States accounting for just over half the wages and two-thirds of the jobs which McKinsey projects will be at least partially automated.[92]

Figure 7. Manufacturing Output vs. Employment 1997 to 2017.

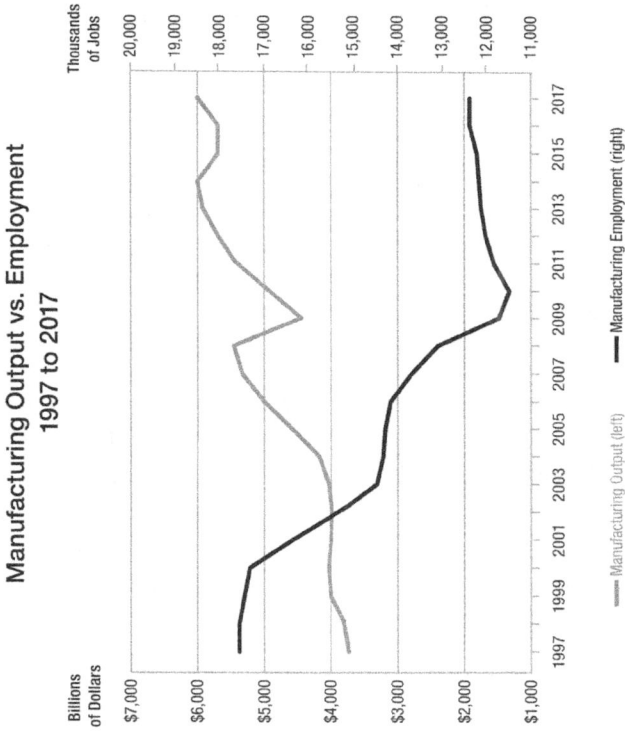

Manufacturing Output vs. Employment
1997 to 2017

Source: "All Employees: Manufacturing," FRED Economic Research, https://fred.stlouisfed.org/series/MANEMP. "Manufacturing Sector: Real Output," FRED Economic Research, https://fred.stlouisfed.org/series/OUTMS.

FUTURE OF WORK IN THE UNITED STATES

Although reshoring will bring jobs back to developed nations, automation means fewer jobs per factory and they will require more training and education. The U.S. auto industry is an example of how old industries have shifted to automation. "In 1950, GM employed nearly 600,000 workers. Today it has a workforce of 200,000 and recently announced record earnings and revenue for Q3 [the third quarter] of 2016."[93] But the problem for workers is much wider than just old industries. Services, particularly information services, use massively fewer workers to create greater value.

> Compare Detroit in 1990 and Silicon Valley in 2014. The three top companies in Detroit produced revenues of $250bn [billion] with 1.2m [million] employees and a combined market capitalisation of $36bn [billion]. The top three companies in Silicon Valley in 2014 had revenues of $247bn [billion], only 137,000 employees, but a market capitalisation of $1.09tn [trillion].[94]

At the same time, artificial intelligence plus robotics will soon replace numerous non-manufacturing jobs that have sustained U.S. workers for generations. Uber and Google are both working on self-driving taxis. Uber, Volvo, Mercedes, and Scania all road-tested self-driving trucks during 2016. Although it may be a decade or more before these self-driving vehicles are on the road in significant numbers, they will have major impacts on American workers.

Trucking firms are very interested in self-driving vehicles because thirty-five percent of their operating costs are drivers' wages and benefits. Necessity will reinforce cost reduction. In 2015, the American Trucking Association reported a shortage of 30,000 drivers with projections that the shortage could increase to 239,000 by 2020. It is particularly acute because the workforce is aging rapidly. In 2015, fifty-five percent of drivers were over forty-five years old and only five percent were under twenty-four years old.[95] The combination of costs and labor shortages will ensure trucking firms shift to self-driving vehicles as soon as they are legal.

Nor will the industry have to wait for its older trucks to wear out, Otto is working on a $30,000 kit to convert existing trucks into self-driving vehicles.[96] Given that drivers are limited to eleven hours of driving a day (which is much more easily monitored with GPS-equipped trucks than with the old paper logs), the new kits could literally double the productivity of the capital invested in commercial trucks. If early road test results hold, there should be a significant reduction in vehicle accidents.

Self-driving vehicles will not only put the 5.7 million Commercial Drivers Licensed (CDL) jobs at risk but also the millions of driving jobs that do not require a CDL—taxis, airport shuttles, and delivery vans.[97] In addition, self-driving vehicles will also threaten those who work in areas that support professional drivers; these include truck stop restaurants, drivers' license bureau staff, truck wash employees, and taxi dispatchers.

DARPA is also pursuing autonomous flight technology to replace pilots. Undoubtedly, the public will resist pilotless passenger airliners, but the very large air-freight business is intensely interested the savings and potentially improved safety record of robotic aircraft.[98] Due to automation, pilots average as little as four minutes per flight at the controls of an Airbus and only seven minutes for a Boeing jet.[99] It is no wonder that air-freight operators are investigating whether one pilot could remotely supervise several jets.

Even as fast-food chains are deploying self-ordering kiosks to eliminate counter workers, startups are working on robots to produce pizzas, sandwiches, sushi, noodles, and more. Café X in San Francisco has robotic baristas.[100] In short, the food industry is striving to replace a huge number of human workers with robots. Food manufacturing is also finding it can cut personnel by seventy-three percent by investing in automation.[101] When building a new plant, adding robots is just an extension of the already-heavy capital costs but its return on investment has been repeatedly verified in production metrics. Investment in machinery pays off in much higher production per man hour.

Wall Street jobs are also being taken by AI. Key parts of the finance industry have already been automated.

> In 2000, there were 5,500 traders on the New York Stock Exchange; now there are fewer than 400...more than ten thousand "front office producer" jobs have been lost within the top 10 banks since 2011.[102]

Whereas these changes are all observable, the creation of new jobs is less so. Techno-optimists admit the fourth industrial revolution will alter many aspects of work. But they note that previous revolutions had the same impact including the uncertainty about jobs. At the start of the industrial revolution, seventy percent of Americans worked on farms. Today fewer than two percent do, but there is not massive unemployment. Instead people are doing jobs no one could possibly have conceived of during the nineteenth century. Optimists note that technological improvements have consistently improved productivity and wealth— if not always evenly.

> Well-paid tasks could increase in number as services related to manufacturing grow...Capital-intensive high-tech manufacturing is often better done amid the designers and engineers who thought up the product...3D printing, though more expensive than tradi-tional mass manufacturing, is being used to make more luxurious and pricier wares, such as motorbikes, in the heart of cities like London and New York, close to both designers and consumers.[103]

As noted, these developments provide better, higher-paying jobs for those workers who develop the needed skills. Unskilled labor will not fare as well.

Another development, the "gig economy" is further altering the job market. The gig economy consists of part-time workers who have no contract but work individual "gigs." They are contractors with no benefits or promise of additional employment. Each gig worker has to string together jobs for himself or herself. The advantage is each worker selects how much and what kind of work to accept. The downside is the high level of uncertainty involved. For workers with certain skills like plumbers, copywriters, or website designers, the connectivity provided by the internet has greatly eased their ability to find work. Unfortunately for less-skilled workers it means that an increasing number of jobs provide no security. For instance, Five Guys, a fast-food chain, typically has twenty-five workers per store but twenty of them are part-time. Rather than paying current employees to work extra shifts (and having them qualifying for benefits and legal protections, which would mean additional costs), the managers hire gig workers to cover shifts as needed.[104]

Intuit, the owner of Turbo Tax, stated that the gig economy represented thirty-four percent of the U.S. workforce in 2016 and projects it to be forty-three percent by 2020.[105] The increasing availability of workers who can be hired for a single shift is reducing the bargaining power of both full-time and part-time workers in some retail businesses. Further, the internet means some gig workers compete in a global market. Jobs such as transcription, photo editing, data entry, and even personal-assistant tasks are being outsourced to Africa and Asia. An Oxford University study showed the global surplus of labor has resulted in "deflated wages, disempowered workers, and scant labor protections for many."[106]

This reality, together with advances in technology and robotics, creates a recipe for challenges. As figure 6 shows, despite significant job economic growth in the United States, there has been virtually no growth in routine labor since 1990.

PROFIT IS THE PRIMARY DRIVER

The two largest economies in the world—the United States and China —are working hard to reshore manufacturing. In the United States, the decision to do so is made based on how each CEO thinks it will impact profits and market share. With robots eroding the labor cost advantage, a key factor is that CEOs think they can make more money by localizing production to better respond to market demands. In competitive fields, failure to do so will yield market share to more agile competitors.

In China, there is a much larger government component to the drive to both retain and reshore manufacturing. China is spending heavily to keep its exports competitive in the global market, and it is working hard to convince its citizens to consume Chinese goods rather than imports. This drive to shift from an export-driven economy to one driven by domestic consumption is seen as essential to the future of the Communist Party —large-scale unemployment will cause unrest. And it is showing some success. Ten years ago exports made up thirty-seven percent of China's GDP. Today it is just twenty-two percent and continues to drop.[107] Chinese firms are dominating its domestic market. Local champions like Baidu, Alibaba, and Tencent have driven off Western competition by adapting their products to Chinese needs and desires. And the Chinese government is assisting its local champions by using formal and informal rules to restrict foreign firms' ability to compete.

Other manufacturing powers, particularly Germany, are also working to reshore the industries they can and distributing factories globally to ensure they can be responsive enough to sell in those markets. The worldwide shift to local, responsive, mass customization has started in high-income, high-wage nations but will spread globally as the cost of robots comes down and factory owners face the issues of adapting or going out of business.

Both domestic and international manufacturing and service firms are realizing that the ways that things are made and services provided are changing rapidly. Advanced manufacturing techniques are eliminating the cost of labor advantage at the same time that consumers are demanding more responsive and more customized products. The growing understanding of the advantages of having decision makers, designers, engineers, and manufacturing teams collocated is reinforcing these drivers. For the West, firm rule of law and respect for intellectual property as well as an educated work force are becoming key drivers in the decisions concerning where to locate facilities. The trend, even for multinational companies, is to locate manufacturing and services in the market they serve rather than trying to consolidate these functions in low-cost labor areas. The net result is a further shift of trade from global to regional and even national.

Notes

1. Catalin Cimpanu, "iPhone Chipmaker Foxconn Set to Replace Most Human Workers with Robots," *bleepingComputer*, December 31, 2016, https://www.bleepingcomputer.com/news/apple/iphone-chipmaker-foxconn-set-to-replace-most-human-workers-with-robots/.
2. Ibid.
3. Paul Davidson, "More Robots Coming to U.S. Factories," *USA Today*, February 10, 2015, http://www.usatoday.com/story/money/2015/02/09/bcg-report-on-factory-robots/23143259.
4. Robbie Whelan and Ester Fung, "China's Factories Turn to Robots," *Wall Street Journal*, August 17, 2016, B1–B2.
5. Mandy Zuo, "Rise of the Robots: 60,000 Workers Culled from Just One Factory As China's Struggling Electronics Hub Turns to Artificial Intelligence," *South China Morning Post*, May 21, 2016, http://www.scmp.com/news/china/economy/article/1949918/rise-robots-60000-workers-culled-just-one-factory-chinas.
6. Conner Forrest, "Chinese Factory Replaces 90% of Humans with Robots, Production Soars," *TechRepublic*, July 30, 2015, http://www.techrepublic.com/article/chinese-factory-replaces-90-of-humans-with-robots-production-soars/.
7. "Robot density rises globally," International Federation of Robotic, February 7, 2018, https://ifr.org/ifr-press-releases/news/robot-density-rises-globally.
8. Peggy Hollinger, "Meet the cobots: humans and robots together on the factory floor," *Financial Times*, May 5, 2016, https://www.ft.com/content/6d5d609e-02e2-11e6-af1d-c47326021344.
9. Frank Tobe, "Why Co-Bots Will Be a Huge Innovation and Growth Driver for Robotics Industry," *IEEE Spectrum*, December 30, 2015, http://spectrum.ieee.org/automaton/robotics/industrial-robots/collaborative-robots-innovation-growth-driver.
10. Andrew Zaleski, "Man and machine: The new collaborative workplace of the future," *NBR*, October 31, 2016, http://nbr.com/2016/10/31/man-and-machine-the-new-collaborative-workplace-of-the-future/.
11. "Cobots – The Game-Changer of Industrial Automation," *Industrial Automation Asia*, July 23, 2017, http://www.iaasiaonline.com/issues-insights/cobots-game-changer-industrial-automation/.

12. Lamont Wood, "Service Robots: the Next Big Productivity Platform," *PwC*, September 8, 2016, http://usblogs.pwc.com/emerging-technology/service-robots-the-next-big-productivity-platform.

13. Matt LaWell, "A Common Thread from the First Industrial Revolution to the Fourth," *Industry Week*, June 6, 2016, http://www.industryweek.com/manufacturing-leader-week/common-thread-first-industrial-revolution-fourth?page=1.

14. Virginia Postrel, "Robots Are the New Seamstresses," *Bloomberg View*, June 2, 2016, https://www.businessoffashion.com/articles/news-analysis/robots-are-the-new-low-wage-seamstresses.

15. Ibid.

16. Eddie Krassenstein, "CloudDDM—Factory with 100 (Eventually 1,000) 3D Printers & Just 3 Employees Opens at UPS's Worldwide Hub," *3D PrintBoard*, May 4, 2015, https://3dprint.com/62642/cloudddm-ups.

17. Nick Hall, "UPS and SAP Do a Deal to Expand 3D Print Capability," *3d PrintBoard*, May 18, 2016, https://3dprintingindustry.com/news/79207-79207.

18. Ibid.

19. "3D Printing Creates New Parts for Aircraft Engines," *GE Global Research*, http://www.geglobalresearch.com/innovation/3d-printing-creates-new-parts-aircraft-engines.

20. Matthew Van Dusen, "GE's 3D-Printed Airplane Engine Will Run This Year," *GE Reports*,https://www.ge.com/reports/mad-props-3d-printed-airplane-engine-will-run-year/.

21. Eric Lai, "Chanel announces plan to mass-produce a 3D-printed mascara brush," *3D Printing Industry*, March 20, 2018, https://3dprintingindustry.com/news/chanel-announces-plan-mass-GEproduce-3d-printed-mascara-brush-130715/.

22. "Spectrum of Applications," Nanoscribe GmbH, http://www.nanoscribe.de/files/9214/9701/0780/ApplicationFlyer_V07_2017_web.pdf.

23. Simon Thiele et al., "3d-Printed Eagle Eye: Compound Microlens System for Foveated Imaging," *Science Advances* 3, no. 2 (February 15, 2017), doi:10.1126/sciadv.1602655.

24. Katherine Bourzac, "3-D-Printed Ceramics," *MIT Technology Review* 119, no. 3, May–June 2016, 92.

25. Associated Press, "Robots Replacing Human Factory Workers at Faster Pace," *Los Angeles Times*, February 10, 2015, http://www.latimes.com/business/la-fi-robots-jobs-20150211-story.html.

26. Andras Forgacs, "Bio-Printing of Leather and Meat," TEDx Talk, November 7, 2013, https://www.youtube.com/watch?v=x1Q2oLxEOF8.

27. Jae-Hee Chang, Gary Rynhart, and Phu Huynh, "ASEAN in Transformation Textiles, Clothing, and Footwear: Refashioning the Future," International Labour Organization, July 2016, http://www.ilo.org/public/english/dialogue/actemp/downloads/publications/2016/asean_in_transf_2016_r6_textil.pdf.

28. "'Sewbot' makes T-shirts," *Tech Asia,* https://www.youtube.com/watch?v=qXFUqCijkUs.

29. Mills, "The Coming Revolution in American Manufacturing."

30. "Petroleum & Other Liquids," U.S. Energy Information Administration, https://www.eia.gov/dnav/pet/hist/LeafHandler.ashx?n=PET&s=MCRNTUS2&f=A.

31. Ibid.

32. "World Energy Outlook 2016," International Energy Agency, 2016, https://www.iea.org/publications/freepublications/publication/WorldEnergyOutlook2016ExecutiveSummaryEnglish.pdf.

33. Christopher Matthews, "Abundant Shale Reshapes the Plastics Industry," *Australian,* June 27, 2017, 28.

34. "Devolving Power," *Economist,* March 8–14, 2014, https://www.economist.com/news/business/21598668-big-batteries-threaten-big-power-stationsand-utilities-profits-devolving-power.

35. John Garskof, "How Utilities Are Fighting Back on Solar Power," *Consumer Reports,* June 30, 2016, http://www.consumerreports.org/energy-saving/how-utilities-are-fighting-back-on-solar-power.

36. Geremie R. Barme and Sang Ye, "The Great Firewall of China," *Wired,* June 1, 1997, https://www.wired.com/1997/06/china-3.

37. Simon Denyer, "China's scary lesson to the world: Censoring the Internet works," *Washington Post,* May 23, 2016, https://www.washingtonpost.com/world/asia_pacific/chinas-scary-lesson-to-the-world-censoring-the-internet-works/2016/05/23/413afe78-fff3-11e5-8bb1-f124a43f84dc_story.html?utm_term=.e854acc320c3.

38. Sijia Jiang, "China Cracks Down on Unauthorized Internet Connections," *Reuters,* January 23, 2017, http://www.reuters.com/article/us-china-internet-idUSKBN15715U?il=0.

39. "China's New Cyber-Security Law Is Worryingly Vague," *Economist,* June 1–7, 2017, http://www.economist.com/news/business/21722873-its-rules-are-broad-ambiguous-and-bothersome-international-firms-chinas-new-cyber-security.

40. Katie Hunt and Cy Xu, "China employs 2 million to police internet," *CNN*, October 7, 2013, https://www.cnn.com/2013/10/07/world/asia/china-internet-monitors/index.html.
41. Kevin Lui, "China's New Way of Controlling Society Will Grade You on Behavior," *Fortune*, November 29, 2016, http://fortune.com/2016/11/29/china-social-control-credit-rating.
42. Alexandra Ma, "China has started ranking citizens with a creepy 'social credit' system—here's what you can do wrong, and the embarrassing, demeaning ways they can punish you," *Business Insider,* http://www.businessinsider.com/china-social-credit-system-punishments-and-rewards-explained-2018-4.
43. Amy B. Wang, "A suspect tried to blend in with 60,000 concertgoers. China's facial-recognition cameras caught him," *Washington Post,* April 13, 2018, https://www.washingtonpost.com/news/worldviews/wp/2018/04/13/china-crime-facial-recognition-cameras-catch-suspect-at-concert-with-60000-people/?noredirect=on&utm_term=.d17301ca48e5.
44. Denyer, "China's Scary Lesson to the World: Censoring the Internet Works."
45. Andrei Soldatov and Irina Borogan, "Putin Brings China's Great Firewall to Russia in Cybersecurity Pact," *Guardian*, November 29, 2016, https://www.theguardian.com/world/2016/nov/29/putin-china-internet-great-firewall-russia-cybersecurity-pact.
46. Ibid.
47. Charlotte Jee, "Russia wants to cut itself off from the global internet. Here's what that really means," *MIT Technology Review,* March 21, 2019, https://www.technologyreview.com/s/613138/russia-wants-to-cut-itself-off-from-the-global-internet-heres-what-that-really-means/.
48. Michael Reilly, "Russia Turns to China for Help Building Its Own 'Great Firewall' of Censorship," *MIT Technology Review*, November 29, 2016, https://www.technologyreview.com/s/602986/russia-turns-to-china-for-help-building-its-own-great-firewall-of-censorship.
49. Russell Brandom, "Iran's Porn Censorship Broke Browsers As Far Away As Hong Kong," *Verge*, January 7, 2017, http://www.theverge.com/2017/1/7/14195118/iran-porn-block-censorship-overflow-bgp-hijack.
50. "Factsheet on the 'Right to Be Forgotten' Ruling," European Commission, http://ec.europa.eu/justice/data-protection/files/factsheets/factsheet_data_protection_en.pdf.
51. Official website of CNIL, https://www.cnil.fr/en/home.
52. "Lost in the Splinternet," *Economist*, November 5–11, 2016, 51.

53. Editorial Board, "While Modi Promises a 'Digital India,' Local Authorities shut down the Internet," *Washington Post*, June 24, 2017, https://www.washingtonpost.com/opinions/while-modi-promises-a-digital-india-local-authorities-shut-down-the-internet/2017/06/24/358ade0c-583c-11e7-ba90-f5875b7d1876_story.html?utm_term=.7dff420b3b4d.
54. Niall McCarthy, "The Countries Shutting Down The Internet The Most [Infographic]," *Forbes,* August 28, 2018, https://www.forbes.com/sites/niallmccarthy/2018/08/28/the-countries-shutting-down-the-internet-the-most-infographic/#143d954e1294.
55. "Freedom on the Net," Freedom House, https://freedomhouse.org/report/freedom-net/freedom-net-2018.
56. "Where social media and messaging apps were silenced," *Mozilla Health of the Internet,* April 2018, https://internethealthreport.org/2018/where-social-media-and-messaging-apps-were-silenced/.
57. Will Knight, "The Chinese News App with 600 Million Users That You've Never Heard Of," *MIT Technology Review*, January 25, 2017, https://www.technologyreview.com/s/603351/the-chinese-news-app-with-600-million-users-that-youve-never-heard-of.
58. Alec MacFarlane, Kane Wu, and Liza Lin, "Parent of News-Aggregation App Toutiao Seeks $10 Billion Valuation," *Wall Street Journal*, November 8, 2016, https://www.wsj.com/articles/parent-of-news-aggregation-app-toutiao-seeks-10-billion-valuation-1478601544.
59. Thomas Roemer, "Why It's Time to Bring Manufacturing Back Home to the U.S." February 2, 2015, *Forbes,* http://www.forbes.com/sites/forbesleadershipforum/2015/02/02/why-its-time-to-bring-manufacturing-back-home-to-the-u-s/#2e2b3a577026.
60. Mills, "The Coming Revolution in American Manufacturing."
61. Ylan Q. Mui, "A Chinese Billionaire Is Staking His Legacy—and Thousands of American Jobs—on This Factory in Ohio," *Washington Post,* October 26, 2016, https://www.washingtonpost.com/news/wonk/wp/2016/10/26/a-chinese-billionaire-is-staking-his-legacy-and-thousands-of-american-jobs-on-this-factory-in-ohio/?utm_term=.1a5a6975e005.
62. Michael J. Hicks and Srikant Devarja, "The Myth and Reality of Manufacturing in America," Center for Economic and Business Research, June 2015, 5, http://www.conexus.cberdata.org/files/MfgReality.pdf?_ga=1.30467831.930003858.1485886669.
63. Mark Juro, "Manufacturing: It's the Jobs, Stupid," *MIT Technology Review*, January–February 2017, 10.
64. "Stamping It Out," *Economist*, April 23–29, 2016, 51.

65. Ben Bland, "China's Robot Revolution," *Financial Times*, April 28, 2016, 13, https://www.ft.com/content/1dbd8c60-0cc6-11e6-ad80-67655613c2d6.

66. Tansy Hoskins, "Robot Factories Could Threaten Jobs of Millions of Garment Workers," *Guardian*, July 16, 2016, https://www.theguardian.com/sustainable-business/2016/jul/16/robot-factories-threaten-jobs-millions-garment-workers-south-east-asia-women.

67. Nick Lavars, "Adidas Launches Its First 3D-Printed Shoes," *New Atlas*, December 13, 2016, http://newatlas.com/3d-printed-adidas-public/46929.

68. Chris Isidore and Julia Horowitz, "Foxconn got a really good deal from Wisconsin. And it's getting better," *CNN Money*, December 28, 2017, http://money.cnn.com/2017/12/28/news/companies/foxconn-wisconsin-incentive-package/index.html.

69. Press Trust of India, "China Hits Back at India with 'Made in China' Campaign," *Business Standard*, September 26, 2014, http://www.business-standard.com/article/pti-stories/made-in-china-campaign-launched-with-make-in-india-114092500331_1.html.

70. Daniel Küpper et al., "The Factory of the Future," *BCG*, December 2016, 5, https://www.bcg.com/en-us/publications/2016/leaning-manufacturing-operations-factory-of-future.aspx.

71. "The Retreat of the Global Company," *Economist*, January 28–February 3, 2017, 20.

72. "AI Hits the Mainstream," *MIT Technology Review* 119, May/June 2016, 62.

73. Tracy Jan, "As Trump Targets Visas, India Firm Set to Hire in U.S.," *Washington Post*, May 3, 2017, A13.

74. Vihdi Doshi, "The High-Tech Jobs That Created India's Gilded Generation Are Disappearing," *Washington Post*, June 24, 2017, https://www.washingtonpost.com/world/asia_pacific/the-high-tech-jobs-that-created-indias-gilded-generation-are-disappearing/2017/06/22/815f1d0e-5588-11e7-9e18-968f6ad1e1d3_story.html?utm_term=.abe0c4b995d7.

75. Ananya Bhattacharya, "56,000 layoffs and counting: India's IT bloodbath this year may just be the start," *Quartz India*, December 26, 2017, https://qz.com/1152683/indian-it-layoffs-in-2017-top-56000-led-by-tcs-infosys-cognizant/.

76. "Reboot," *Economist*, January 21–27, 2017, 57.

77. Melissa Korn, "There's a Reason the Teaching Assistant Seems Robotic," *Wall Street Journal*, May 7–8, 2016, 1.

78. Susan Beck, "AI Pioneer ROSS Intelligence Lands Its First Big Law Clients," *American Lawyer*, May 6, 2016, http://www.americanlawyer.com/id=

1202757054564/AI-Pioneer-ROSS-Intelligence-Lands-Its-First-Big-Law-Clients?slreturn=20160412132159.

79. Erik Sherman, "5 White-Collar Jobs Robots Already Have Taken," *Fortune*, February 25, 2105, http://fortune.com/2015/02/25/5-jobs-that-robots-already-are-taking.

80. James Billington, "IBM's Watson Cracks Medical Mystery with Life-Saving Diagnosis for Patient Who Baffled Doctors," *International Business Times*, August 8, 2016, http://www.ibtimes.co.uk/ibms-watson-cracks-medical-mystery-life-saving-diagnosis-patient-who-baffled-doctors-15 74963.

81. "Unshackled Algorithms," *Economist*, May 27–Jun 2, 2017, 68.

82. Will Knight, "Inside Amazon's Warehouse, Human-Robot Symbiosis," *MIT Technology Review*, July 7, 2015, https://www.technologyreview.com/s/538601/inside-amazons-warehouse-human-robot-symbiosis.

83. Tyler Clifford, "Reduced holiday temp hiring is a sign Amazon is turning to more automation and robots: Citi," *CNBC*, November 2, 2018, https://www.cnbc.com/2018/11/02/citi-mark-may-amazon-relies-on-robots-less-temporary-holiday-hires.html.

84. Xavier Lhuer, "The next acronym you need to know about: RPA (robotic process automation)," McKinsey & Company, December 2016, http://www.mckinsey.com/business-functions/digital-mckinsey/our-insights/the-next-acronym-you-need-to-know-about-rpa.

85. Stephanie Overby, "Why Outsourced Call Center Roles Are Coming Back Onshore," *CIO*, August 12, 2016, http://www.cio.com/article/310 6821/outsourcing/why-outsourced-call-center-roles-are-coming-back-onshore.html.

86. Carl Benedikt Frey and Michael A. Osborne, "The Future of Employment: How Susceptible Are Jobs to Computerization?" Oxford Martin School, September 17, 2013, http://www.oxfordmartin.ox.ac.uk/downloads/academic/The_Future_of_Employment.pdf.

87. J. P. Gownder, "Robots Won't Steal All the Jobs—But They'll Transform The Way We Work," *Forrester*, August 24, 2015, https://www.forrester.com/report/The+Future+Of+Jobs+2027+Working+Side+By+Side+With+Robots/-/E-RES119861.

88. "UK Economic Outlook," PwC, March 2017, 30, https://www.pwc.co.uk/economic-services/ukeo/pwc-uk-economic-outlook-full-report-march-2017-v2.pdf.

89. Rob Traciniski, "The Paradox of Productivity," *RealClear Future.* Jul 25, 2016, http://www.realclearfuture.com/articles/2016/07/25/the_paradox_of_productivity_111930.html

90. Manyika, "A Future That Works."

91. Jed Kolko, "Trump Was Stronger Where the Economy Is Weaker," *FiveThirtyEight*, November 10, 2016, https://fivethirtyeight.com/features/trump-was-stronger-where-the-economy-is-weaker.

92. Manyika, "A Future That Works."

93. Brooks Rainwater, "Robots: The Missing Piece In Trump's Job Equation," *Fortune*, January 18, 2017, http://www.forbes.com/sites/realspin/2017/01/18/robots-the-missing-piece-in-trumps-job-equation/#6bb9e7595096.

94. James Manyika and Michael Chui, "Digital Era Brings Hyperscale Challenges," *Financial Times*, August 13, 2014, https://www.ft.com/content/f30051b2-1e36-11e4-bb68-00144feabdc0.

95. W. Ford Torrey and Dan Murray, "An Analysis of the Operational Costs of Trucking: 2015 Update," American Transportation Research Institute, September 2015, 17, http://atri-online.org/wp-content/uploads/2015/09/ATRI-Operational-Costs-of-Trucking-2015-FINAL-09-2015.pdf.

96. Jack Stewart, "$30K Retrofit Turns Dumb Semis into Self-driving Robots," *Wired*, May 17, 2016, https://www.wired.com/2016/05/otto-retrofit-autonomous-self-driving-trucks.

97. "2015 Pocket Guide to Large Truck and Bus Statistics," U.S. Department of Transportation, April 2015, 7, http://ntl.bts.gov/lib/54000/54800/54841/2015_Pocket_Guide_-_March_30_2015__For_Web_Publishing_-508c.pdf.

98. "New study shows passengers are not ready for pilotless flying, while cargo planes have much to gain from it. Safety concerns arise," *Boss Magazine*, August 17, 2017, https://thebossmagazine.com/pilotless-cargo-planes/.

99. Robyn Ironsides, "How pilots spend as little as four minutes flying some modern planes," *news.com.au*, August 8, 2016, http://www.news.com.au/travel/travel-updates/how-pilots-spend-as-little-as-four-minutes-flying-some-modern-planes/news-story/86d3260a247cab8df02563af0f66d11d.

100. Geoffrey A. Fowler, "Robot Baristas Serve Up the Future of Coffee at Cafe X," *Wall Street Journal*, January 30, 2017, https://www.wsj.com/articles/robot-baristas-serve-up-the-future-of-coffee-at-cafe-x-1485781201.

101. Eric Rosenbaum, "An egg-handling robot touches a delicate question about jobs of the future," *CNBC*, November 2, 2016, https://www.cnbc.com/2016/11/02/robot-takeover-in-food-manufacturing-extends-to-a-delicate-job-egg-handling.html.

102. Thomas H. Davenport, "Wall Street Jobs Won't Be Spared from Automation," *Harvard Business Review*, December 14, 2016, https://hbr.org/2016/12/wall-street-jobs-wont-be-spared-from-automation.

103. "They Don't Make Them Like That Anymore," *Economist*, January 14–20, 2017, 20.

104. Abha Bhattarai, "Now hiring for one day: Gig economy hits retail," *Washington Post*, May 6, 2018, G1.

105. Patrick Gillespie "Intuit: Gig economy is 34% of US workforce," *CNNMoney*, May 24, 2017, http://money.cnn.com/2017/05/24/news/economy/gig-economy-intuit/index.html.

106. Annie Lowrey, "What the Gig Economy Looks Like Around the World," *The Atlantic*, April 13, 2017, https://www.theatlantic.com/business/archive/2017/04/gig-economy-global/522954/.

107. Fareed Zakaria, "Why China May Welcome Trump," *Washington Post*, January 13, 2017, A17.

CHAPTER 4

INTERNATIONAL TRADE AND DEVELOPMENT IMPLICATIONS

Kenneth Rapoza of *Forbes* magazine writes that "globalization is in intensive care. The supply chain is moving out of China…causing some to refer to that shift as a deglobalization wave."[1] The fourth industrial revolution is collapsing supply chains by shifting their focus from global to regional and, in some cases, even to local levels. 3D printing is eliminating many of the sub-assemble steps in the chain. Services, a different form of supply chain, are also returning to home markets. Energy flows have been drastically altered in just a decade as the U.S. fracking industry has dramatically changed the international market for gas and oil. Renewable energy derived from local and regional sources is growing rapidly providing.

Financial flows have also shifted from the developing world to the developed world. These investments will increasingly go to those nations that provide the critically important rule of law, security, large internal markets, and opportunity for talented immigrants. All of this is driven by the fundamental fact that companies must enhance their productivity and profit in order to survive.

Historically, economic and political trends have moved in unpredictable cycles of varied lengths and will continue to do so. What is different about the ongoing downturn in global trade and financial flows is that this one is developing because regional and even local flows are creating more profit than long-distance flows. In the past, retreats were usually driven by degraded international security environments or political conditions that raised the costs associated with long-distance trade. However, today's retraction is not being driven by the loss of security but from the fact that investment in regional and local production brings higher returns. The fourth industrial revolution is making it more profitable to produce and consume locally for a very large number of products and services. Rather than driving globalization, the profit motive is driving deglobalization. With labor costs equalizing, nations with rule of law, honest means of adjudicating disputes, and large domestic markets have great advantages—that translate directly into competitive advantages for their industries.

The impact of deglobalization will vary greatly by country and even by city. Delineating the potential outcome for each is beyond the capacity of one researcher. Here one can only speculate on a broad level using developed, developing, and underdeveloped nations as general groupings. The extent of the change for each country will be affected by numerous factors, including how quickly political and economic leaders grasp what is happening and position their communities to take advantage of opportunities.

IMPACT ON DEVELOPED COUNTRIES

The fourth industrial revolution is already returning some manufacturing to developed countries, and rapidly advancing technology is accelerating this trend. More of the profit will remain in the developed world. Because the technological benefits can only be achieved via major capital investments in automation to replace labor, most of the benefits of the increased productivity will flow primarily to capital with a much smaller portion to higher skilled workers. Unfortunately, as noted previously, automation of factories has resulted in the elimination of jobs, ranging from a few to ninety percent, in a modern factory. Technology pessimists note that, depending on the industry, as few as ten percent of the laborers will see raises. The others, who will be mostly those with less education or lower technical skills, will have to seek other employment and may well require extensive retraining or education. In contrast, techno-optimists are confident this industrial revolution, like the previous ones, will create entirely new industries with more and better-paying jobs that will outweigh those that have been destroyed. Although it is difficult to see what those jobs might be because automation is rapidly mastering so many fields, a massive increase in jobs is one possible outcome. In the 1800s, no one predicted the need for millions of car mechanics, electricians, or data-entry staff.

But if one uses the first industrial revolution as an example to show that new jobs will be created, it is important not to overlook the decades of declining health, wages, and security that urban laborers and their families experienced. At the start of the Industrial Revolution, large numbers of agricultural laborers had to migrate to the cities because the only jobs available were in the new factories. The British Medical Bulletin noted that urban life expectancies dropped dramatically during the 1830s and 1840s. These rates did not rise above those of the early 1800s until the 1870s. By then Britain was primarily an urban society. Thus, despite the techno-optimists' beliefs that industrialization improved the lives of all people

> the only abundantly documented historical case, Britain, shows that industrialization had a powerfully negative impact on population health, concentrated particularly among the families of the relatively disempowered, displaced migrants who provided a large part of the workforce in the fast-growing industrial towns and cities.[2]

In short, the long-term health and welfare results of the Industrial Revolution were positive, but the displaced who moved to the cities to work in the factories suffered significant declines in their health and welfare—and it took over forty years to recover from this. In the abstract for the article, the author noted that "all documented developed nations endured the 'four Ds' of disruption, deprivation, disease, and death during their historic industrializations."[3]

The United States has recently seen some of the same problems with housing insecurity, rising healthcare costs, and a spike in opioid addiction. Like all major economic disruptions, there have been winners and losers. One major difference is the fact that today those dispossessed in the developed world generally have the right to vote. It was not until the 1884 Act that the percentage of British males with the right to vote increased from thirty to sixty percent—still only eighteen percent of the total population.[4] In contrast to the 1800s, today's voters can demand political leaders increase resources devoted to social welfare programs.

The United Nations has also reported that reshoring to developed nations is being accomplished by capital investment in new plants, AI, and robotics. Unfortunately, to date, the jobs being are created are concentrated in high-skill fields and this is sharpening income polarization even as national productivity increases in developed nations.[5] From 1992 to 2016, the United States' income Gini coefficient has increased from .43 to .48. The Gini coefficient measures inequality. The higher the number, the more concentrated the income among the wealthy.[6] According to the Organisation for Economic Co-Operation and Development, the United States was the fourth most unequal country in the world in terms of income. If total wealth inequality is measured rather than just current income, the United States is both the wealthiest and the most unequal of fifty-five countries studied.[7]

The populist political backlash unfolding across the United States and Europe is at least partially driven by the massive gains of the wealthy in those societies at a time of stagnant or declining wealth for the majority of their populations. The Congressional Research Service reported that even as income for the bottom quintile of the U.S. population remained stagnant from 1967 to 2015, income for the top quintile almost doubled. Figure 8 reveals the diverging increasing separation between the incomes of the top and bottom quintiles.

Figure 8. Income Distribution by Quintile.

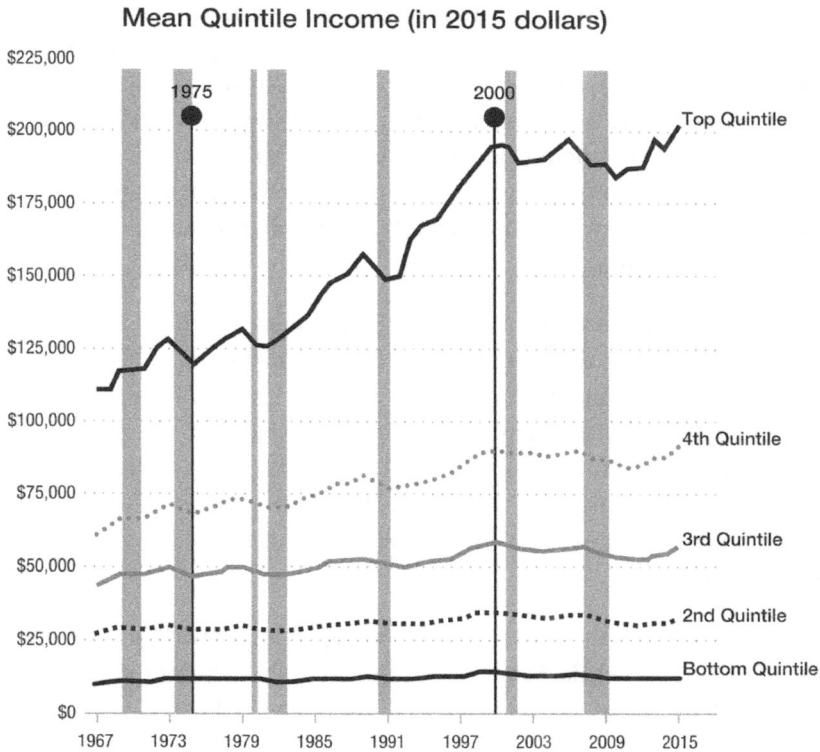

Mean Quintile Income (in 2015 dollars)

Source: Sarah A. Donovan and Marc Labonte, "The U.S. Income Distribution: Trends and Issues," Congressional Research Service, December 8, 2016, 7, https://fas.org/sgp/crs/misc/R44705.pdf.

Even more worrying is the fact that it is not just income but accumulated wealth that is flowing to the top. In its Global Wealth Report 2015, Credit Suisse reported that the top one percent of people in the world own fifty percent of the wealth and the bottom fifty percent own only one percent.[8] The growing anger is exacerbated because tax dollars actually increased the concentration of wealth at the top. During the fiscal crisis of 2008, to prevent a much worse global crash, the U.S. Treasury bailed out major banks and investment firms. Then the central banks of the United States, Japan, and Europe sustained the effort with quantitative easing —government purchase of bonds and mortgages—to promote economic growth. The U.S. government has spent over $2 trillion on quantitative easing to stimulate the economy.[9] Even though government intervention prevented a more serious crash, most of the benefits accrued in the stock and real estate markets—investments dominated by the wealthy. Thus, massive government spending actually resulted in further concentration of wealth at the top.

The Tax Cuts and Jobs Act of 2017 has exacerbated the inequality. According to Congress' Joint Committee on Taxation, in 2019 "the top 1 percent get an estimated 23.4 percent of the tax law's benefits—similar to the Tax Policy Center's estimate of the early impact of the tax law. By 2027, the 1 percent would actually get more than one hundred percent of the tax law's benefits."[10] Households with an income below $70,000 will face a tax increase. Households above those thresholds will continue to pay less tax.[11]

Not only are most Americans facing higher tax bills, they are also facing serious potential job losses as the economy adjusts to the fourth industrial revolution. Robotics and AI in particular are likely to eliminate a lot of jobs before the economy creates the new ones that have historically evolved from industrial revolutions. With a worldwide industrial labor force of about 785 million[12] and only about 2.1 million industrial robots currently deployed in 2017,[13] there is plenty of opportunity for them to replace humans.

Although collaborative robots, or cobots, have just begun to hit the market, the fact that new models reach payback point in under two years means the six million small- and medium-sized businesses worldwide will be buying millions of cobots. Currently, sales are increasing over fifty percent each year.[14] At that rate, sales double in only eighteen months and increase by a factor of almost six in four years. For service industries, IBM's Watson family of products is proving that limited artificial intelligence scales very well so it too will expand very rapidly.

As the fourth industrial revolution matures, developed nations can expect to produce much greater wealth but most of the benefits will flow to the owners of capital. Labor's share will continue its decades' long decline as automation continues to replace people. Although many of those people will find jobs in newly created industries, older, less-educated, and unhealthy individuals will struggle to transition to the new economy.

Trade restrictions will continue to be employed by developed nations to protect threatened industries. Developed countries will also continue to tighten immigration controls. This tendency will increase if underdeveloped and developing nations are unable to provide improved economies for their growing populations. As the United States and Europe have already seen, there will be popular calls to prevent immigrants from entering and to remove those who have succeeded in entering illegally.

Finally, the increased demands for border security may in fact reduce the funds available for other forms of national security. In the case of Europe, disputes over immigration policy may well reduce the cohesion of both the European Union and NATO. Today EU and NATO members from southern Europe see immigration as the key security risk. Those nations in the north and east see Russia as the primary threat.

IMPACT ON DEVELOPING COUNTRIES

As robots substitute for cheap labor, the changed global supply chain will block the traditional path of developing countries, which is moving from agricultural to light industry to heavy industry in their path to development.

This is already having an impact in developing countries. The Center for Global Development noted that profit-driven reshoring of light industry from developing countries back to developed countries may block further development. "Manufacturing has historically offered the fastest path out of poverty, but there is mounting evidence that this path may be all but closed to developing countries today."[15]

This is a major concern in international development circles. The United Nations dedicated a conference to exploring the impact of robotics on developing countries. It concluded with a grim prognosis. "Reshoring could turn global value chains on their head, and lead to their decline as a potential industrialization strategy for developing countries."[16]

Losing the opportunity to use cheap labor to move up the manufacturing value chain could be devastating for these nations. Emerging Advisors Group, a Hong Kong-based economic research firm, looked back fifty years and determined that exports were the primary driver of success for emerging nations.[17] Deglobalization will slow growth among developing nations—particularly those in Asia that were using light manufacturing and call-center service industries as their engines of growth. The collapse of financial flows to emerging markets is already hurting these countries. Ruchir Sharma observed that "after attracting positive flows of capital every year since recordkeeping began in 1978, the emerging world saw an outflow of capital for the first time in 2014 and in 2015 the dam burst, with a massive outflow of $700 billion."[18]

Developing countries dream of repeating China's success but face four major hurdles the Chinese did not. First, China had access to massive amounts of foreign direct investment. The failure of international financial flows to recover from the 2008 crisis means these financial resources are not currently available for the next wave of developing countries. Despite the passage of almost ten years since the crisis, financial flows to developing nations still have not recovered. According to the United Nations Conference on Trade and Development, foreign direct investment (FDI) fell by about two percent globally in 2016. However, flows to developing Asia fell by fifteen percent and to developing Latin America dropped by over fourteen percent.[19] The Organization for Economic and Cooperative Development noted that some developing nations like Indonesia and Vietnam continue to attract foreign direct investment and sustain healthy growth rates but even they are not achieving the rates sustained by the Asian tigers during the same phase of their development.[20]

Second, the technological transformation now under way appears to be permanently changing the economics of development because low-wage labor is less important than proximity to the market in deciding where to build new factories. As a result, investors are seeking opportunities in wealthier nations leaving fewer investment dollars available for developing nations. This shift seems to be reflected in recent FDI flows.

Third, the growing populist anger against globalization is leading to increasing tariffs that will make it more difficult to follow China's path to industrialization. China may be one of the last countries to achieve middle-income status as an export-based economy. At the time of writing, the United States and Chinese trade disputes that started with the Trump administration's tariffs had not been resolved enough to determine the actions each nation was taking. However, the dispute itself indicates the growing impetus for trade tariffs.

Fourth, many developing nations are facing "premature deindustrial-ization."[21] Deindustrialization is the point where manufacturing's share of a developing economy begins to decline. For nation's that succeeded in industrializing, the decline of manufacturing's share actually reflected the rapid growth in service industries as these nations made the shift from export-based economies to consumption-based ones. For the Asian tigers this was a sign their economies had acquired the wealth and skills necessary to move up the production value chain. Japan, Korea, Taiwan, Thailand, Malaysia, and Singapore succeeded, and China is in the process. Unfortunately, for today's developing economies, deglobalization is happening earlier in their development processes. In 1988, for the world as a whole, the peak share of manufacturing in gross domestic product (GDP) was 30.5 percent on average and attained at a per capita GDP level of $21,700. By 2010, the peak share of manufacturing was twenty-one percent (a drop of nearly a third) and attained at a level of $12,200 (a drop of nearly forty-five percent).[22]

Deindustrialization began before these nations moved from light manufacturing to heavy manufacturing—the route the Asian tigers took to prosperity. Of even more concern, the early transition away from manufacturing means these nations have not developed the skills and infrastructure to move into higher-value products. Finally, transition at a lower per capita GDP growth means the population will simply lack the income to sustain a consumption-based economy. This may block their path to further development.

The current mix of high output from mass production and low output for customized products formed the basis for today's global trade and supply chain networks. The shift to mass customization of low-volume manufacturing near the consumer will force extensive changes across the globe. This means that many large-scale assembly plants in low-wage nations will either scale down for local production only or close. In their place small- and medium-sized heavily automated manufacturing facilities will be built. But they will not replace the economic growth of the large plants, and the profits will flow to capital rather than labor. Infrastructure such as roads, railroads, plants, and port facilities, as well as zoning laws and tax structures, will all have to change to reflect the change in trade flows. Foreign direct investment flows will increasingly shift from developing to developed nations as businesses seek to build their production facilities near their customers.

For instance, China, India, Vietnam, Bangladesh, Malaysia, Turkey, and other developing nations currently produce the bulk of the world's clothing. It makes up over half of the exports for Haiti (eighty-eight percent), Bangladesh (seventy-nine percent), Lesotho (fifty-nine percent) and Cambodia (fifty-two percent).[23] This and light manufacturing should be the first step on the ladder to development. But, as noted early in this volume, the technical revolution is making garment-production facilities in the developed world profitable again. As the payoff time for robots steadily decreases, not only will developed nations produce their own clothing but robots will begin to displace labor in developing nations too. To survive, businesses in those nations will have to adopt automation when it costs less than human workers. China is clearly leading the way with major investments in automation in its factories. Chinese businesses have shed increasingly costly labor for technology that cuts costs even as it increases productivity. If other developing countries follow suit, it will increase inequality in those nations as the benefits from increased production flow to the owners of capital and laborers lose jobs.

The return of services to home countries is having similar impacts in some developing nations. India took advantage of the globalization of services and created many companies that performed back-office tasks such as bookkeeping, IT support, computer programing, and call center functions for the West. The Philippines followed in India's wake. However, as noted in chapter 3, AI-based call and service centers are bringing these services back to the host nations. Thus, even as the route to industrialization is blocked, the prospects for service-industry growth are also fading. India may not be able to grow by providing services to foreign markets. And as automation destroys the labor cost advantage, India may not be able to manufacture for the world either. It may only be able to produce for its domestic market and perhaps those of underdeveloped nations. India's problems are magnified by its huge youth bulge. For more than a decade, Indian officials and businessmen have predicted that their nation will be able to use the surging number of young people entering the labor force to industrialize by following the path of the Asian tigers. Just as this becomes possible, new technology is undercutting that labor advantage.

The developing world is seeing the path to prosperity blocked by the shift of manufacturing and services back to the developed world even as much of the developed world is further restricting immigration. These shifts are coming about just as many of these nation's youth bulges are entering the job market. Clearly this is a recipe for dissatisfaction and instability. Industrialization in low-wage countries has already led to increased economic inequality there. In 1980, before industrialization, China's Gini coefficient was 0.3. By 2012, it had risen to .49, the third highest in the world.[24]

As grim as this picture is the technologies of the fourth industrial revolution do offer these nations opportunities to develop local manufacturing and services for much less than the cost of developing factories and supply chains to support a major exporting effort. As the tools of advanced manufacturing such as 3D printers, collaborative robots, and task-specific AI continue to decrease in price, businesses in developing countries will be better able to establish facilities to produce for the local market. Thus, the GDP of most developing nations should continue to grow—but not nearly as fast as the Asian tigers did. If these nations can take advantage of the increased resources generated by local production, they can mitigate the impact of the revolution. But it will be a delicate balancing act requiring levels of trust and cooperation not seen in many societies.

Impact on underdeveloped countries

The path to industrialization taken by the Asian tigers will be firmly blocked for underdeveloped nations. Even now underdeveloped countries are losing that opportunity as companies that previously chased low-wage labor are turning to robots for both manufacturing and services. Compounding the impact of building new manufacturing plants back in the home markets, those new plants could be able to produce better products more cheaply than the infant industries of underdeveloped countries. So even domestic industries established to sell to internal markets in underdeveloped countries could be driven out of business unless protected. As early as the first industrial revolution, this was the fate of the extensive Indian cotton industry when industrialized Britain exported cheaper, better cotton cloth. The Indian industry collapsed, causing widespread hardship. The United States responded by imposing tariffs to protect its infant industries. The probable response today will be heavy tariffs to protect domestic industries which will further reduce underdeveloped nations' participation in globalization.

Deglobalization may also reduce remittances from overseas labor to many developing and underdeveloped nations. Remittances made up ten percent of the Philippines' GDP in 2016. For Nepal and Liberia, it was over thirty percent in 2015.[25] However, to date that has not been an issue. According to the World Bank, global remittances to low- and middle-income countries decreased in 2016 (-1.5 percent) but increased in 2017 (7.8 percent) and 2017 (10.8 percent). They are projected to continue to increase for the next few years.[26]

Perhaps this is because there has been less progress in automating non-routine, manual labor than routine, manual laborer. These non-routine jobs in fields like agriculture, food service, meat processing, and construction have traditionally been filled by immigrant and non-citizens workers. Unfortunately, a number of firms are making rapid progress in automating some of the most labor-intensive agricultural tasks such as picking and sorting fruits and vegetables.[27] Other firms are working to automate elements of food service and meat processing using robots.[28] Construction firms are learning to 3D print small buildings, and Saudi Arabia, one of the major sources of remittance payments, is moving quickly to exploit this new capability.[29] Fast growth in 3D-printed and factory-built homes will dramatically reduce the need for low-skill labor.[30]

In addition, the reduced demand for raw materials—even as manufacturing output increases—will exacerbate the problem for some underdeveloped countries. Because 3D printers build objects from the bottom up, they only use material where it is needed. (Traditional or subtractive manufacturing starts with a block of material and carves it to create the object—and a lot of waste.) 3D manufacturing means a lot less raw material will have to be extracted and processed for each finished product.

The fourth industrial revolution will block the twentieth-century path to development but may offer opportunities to leap forward in some fields. For instance, in Africa, telephone service mostly skipped the centralized, hard-wired model and went straight to cell phones. In some areas today, power production is making the same leap, skipping centralized power companies for local co-ops that produce and share power. Small 3D printers powered by locally produced, renewable power may provide a path for local manufacturing to develop. Once again, the challenge to political leaders will be to set the conditions for this kind of development. Unfortunately, many underdeveloped nations have been captured by an upper-class, rent-seeking elite that will see this kind of development as a threat to their rule. They are likely to use their dominant positions to control or block it.

INSTABILITY POTENTIAL

Although Schwab is mostly optimistic about the fourth industrial revolution, he is deeply concerned about the potential for increased inequality even in the developed nations. The great beneficiaries of the fourth industrial revolution are the providers of intellectual or physical capital —the innovators, the investors, and the shareholders, which explains the rising gap in wealth between those who depend on labor and those who own capital. It also accounts for the disillusionment among so many workers, convinced that their real income may not increase over their lifetime and that the children may not have a better life than theirs.[31]

Underdeveloped nations will face real challenges to stability. With the path to industrialization blocked and youth bulges maturing in many of these nations, they will face frustrated populations with little hope. One of the important traditional outlets—migration—will be increasingly difficult as developed nations institute more restrictions on immigration. In the United States and Europe, fear that mass migration is causing domestic instability is a growing political issue.

All nations will grapple with the challenges of protecting their populations, or at least some of the politically favored stakeholders, from the negative effects of the fourth industrial revolution even as they try to reap some of it benefits. The potential for national, regional, and global inequalities to cause instability will rise. These conditions will create fertile grounds for today's terror organizations which will seek not only to control the area they are in but also export terrorism to the West. Nor will developed countries be exempted as the angst and anger displayed in the recent elections demonstrated.

INCREASING REGIONALIZATION OF TRADE

The changes in manufacturing, services, energy, and internet connectivity are shifting trade toward regionalization and even some localization. Three major trade regions—North America, Asia, and Europe—(based on the three big economies of the United States, China, and the European Union) are evolving.

North America

> North American companies remain the most innovative in the world by virtually any measure. They attract top talent, earn the most patents, and command most of the world's venture capital. ... This is reinforced by the fact that North America remains at

the cutting edge of four synergistic technology revolutions: new forms of energy production, advanced and digital manufacturing, life sciences, and information technology.[32]

The Boston Consulting Group Global Manufacturing Cost-Competitiveness Index examined the costs of productivity-adjusted labor, natural gas, and electricity from 2004 to 2014 for manufacturers in twenty-five economies. BCG found that by 2014, "Mexico and the United States had improved their competitiveness against all other economies in the index. We call these two nations the 'rising global stars' of manufacturing."[33] By 2016, the Deloitte Global Manufacturing Competitiveness Index noted that although China remains ranked first, the United States climbed from fourth in 2010 to second in 2016. The executives surveyed projected the United States will rank number one in 2020 and Canada and Mexico will remain in the top ten.[34]

In short, North America is a great location to manufacture. It has a large, wealthy consumer market which will thrive as industry moves to mass customization of goods with rapid delivery. Global air freight might still allow lighter products like computer chips, small electronics, and tailored clothing made overseas to compete. However, the speed of delivery between some nations has been markedly slowed by recently imposed tariffs and procedural restrictions—and remain a risk that must be considered when planning a business location. This is another case where new technology's local-production advantages are being reinforced by political pressure.

All of the aforementioned factors are reinforced by social pressures to "buy local" and the desire to reduce the environmental impact of production. The local food movement has grown fast enough to attract the interest of investors who see a well-to-do market that is willing to pay a bit more for locally produced food.[35] In addition, indoor farming virtually eliminates the environmental impact of farming on land and waterways. The growing movements to restrict fertilizer use in major drainages (e.g., the Chesapeake Bay) will add to pressure to change how food is grown. Cultured meats will not only greatly reduce the environmental footprint of the meat industry but also appeal to the growing animal-rights movement. The net effect of "local" and environmentalist movements will be to reinforce the technological drive toward local or regional production and consumption.

Today, the United States ranks sixty-seventh out of one hundred nations in the DHL 2018 Global Connectedness Index which measures "cross-border flows of trade, capital, information and people."[36] And thirty percent of America's import and exports go to/from Canada and Mexico. They are consistently the United States' second and third largest trading partners with 15.0 and 14.3 percent of U.S. trade in 2017.[37] Thus, about eighty-six percent of the U.S. economy is actually generated within North America.

The level of regional integration of the North American market is also indicated by the percentage of Canada and Mexico's trade that is with the United States. In 2016, the United States took 75.3 percent of Canada's exports and provided 65.1 percent of its imports.[38] During the same year, Mexico sent eighty-one percent of its exports to the United States and received 46.5 percent of its imports from the United States.[39]

Asia

East Asia and Southeast Asia are also integrating. In March 2018, twelve nations signed the Comprehensive and Progressive Agreement for Trans-Pacific Partnership, a revised TPP. The participants—Australia, Brunei, Chile, New Zealand, Peru, Singapore, Vietnam, Japan, Malaysia, Canada and Mexico—represent fourteen percent of the global economy.[40] Asia ranks second on the DHL Globalization Index for intraregional trade, and the treaty will reinforce the already-strong regional networks.[41] Currently about fifty percent of all exports from East Asian nations go to other East Asian nations.[42] In 2016, 49.8 percent of China's total exports went to Asian trading partners as North America purchased only twenty one percent, Europe 18.5 percent, and Africa a mere 4.4 percent. From 2009 to 2016, China's trade grew fastest with Vietnam, Thailand, Russia, India, Taiwan, and Malaysia.[43] The fourth industrial revolution is increasing its percentage of intraregional trade.

EUROPE

The DHL 2018 Globalization Index rates the European Union (EU) as the most globally integrated region in the globe. However, this is a bit deceptive. Over seventy percent of European exports go to their neighbors on the same continent but count towards globalization.[44] In fact, they represent regionalization. Europe's most successful exporters have begun adopting the localized production model by opening more plants in the markets they serve. From running shoes to luxury autos, European firms are moving production to the markets.

LATIN AMERICA

Latin American economies have historical been tied heavily to that of the United States. But in 2011, China surpassed the United States as the region's leading trade partner (excluding U.S. trade with Mexico). From 2014 to 2017, Latin American trade with both the United States and China has decreased fifteen percent.[45] Latin America's economy contracted in 2015 and 2016 but recovered slightly 2017 and grew one percent.[46] The steep decline in trade with U.S. and China despite very strong growth in commodity exports could be an indicator that intraregional trade is increasing in Latin America. In addition, in July 2019, two decades of trade negotiation culminated in a trade agreement between the European Union and Mercosur, the trade alliance that includes Argentina, Brazil, Paraguay, and Uruguay. Leaders expressed hope that this would reverse the global trend of protectionism.[47]

SOUTH AND CENTRAL ASIA

South and Central Asia are poorly positioned geographical and politically for international or even regional trade. The two biggest economies—India and Pakistan—are openly hostile and severely restrict cross-border trade. This impacts Central Asian nations because of the extremely difficult terrain that lies between them and lack of any easily accessible seaport. It also restricts their access to the large and growing Indian market. It is not surprising that DHL ranks this region second to last in global connectedness.

AFRICA

Africa, dead last in the DHL rating, lacks many of the fundamentals necessary to integrate more fully into the global economy.[48] However, there are bright spots. Since the 2008 crash, intra–East African Community trade has increased sixty percent.[49] Unfortunately, global onshoring efforts mean that the Asian tigers' path to export-driven growth is blocked. Most of the manufactured products which these nations could produce will increasingly be made better and cheaper in the developed world.

SUMMARY

The fourth industrial revolution will bring massive improvements in productivity to manufacturing and service industries for those nations that can exploit it. With automation rapidly eliminating the advantage of low-cost labor, global manufacturing is shifting from massive plants in low-cost-labor areas producing for the entire world to regional production facilities that are closer to their consumers. The service industry is following suit. In addition, energy production and food production are becoming regional or even local. It is essential to understand that previous periods of deglobalization were driven primarily by political instability that raised the risk of international trade. Traders simply could not cover the risk and still make money. When political and social stability returned, so did globalization because the opportunity to make money did too. Today's deglobalization is different. It is being driven by business decisions more than current political, security, or social issues. Due to the combination of rising labor costs globally and improvements in automation, the overall manufacturing favorability of the United States is rising. It is "further enhanced when one includes advantages in sophisticated supply-chain logistics, ease of doing business, and low corruption. Dramatically lower energy costs have handed firms located in the U.S. an enormous competitive advantage in energy-intensive production."[50]

North America is very well situated to benefit from these changes and seems to be doing so already. "By 2015, the top ten companies in terms of stock market value were based in the United States—the first time this has happened since 2002."[51] These companies, led by Facebook, Amazon, Netflix, and Google, show that America is doing well in the newest parts of the economy.

In short, North America's reliance on the world is decreasing. It will still need raw materials, but we must keep in mind the rapid development of new materials that are replacing some imported ones. North America even has a supply of most "rare" earths. Although China currently has over ninety percent of the global market in rare earths, it is not because they are rare.[52] The United States has several sites where the concentration of the metals is high enough to mine.[53] It simply chose not to pay the costs —economic and environmental—to refine them as long as this can be done cheaply and reliably in China. After China slowed supply to Japan, the Mountain Pass California mine reopened in January of 2019 and is estimated to supply one-tenth of the world's unprocessed rare earth.[54]

Along with energy and food security, North America (and the United States in particular) is gaining greater independence in manufacturing and services. At the same time, North America's leadership in the technological race to the fourth industrial revolution means it will likely increase its exports of manufactured products to the rest of the world. Today, manufactured goods make up two-thirds of U.S. exports, with commercial aircraft, industrial machines, and telecommunications exports being particularly strong—all items that will be made cheaper and better as the fourth industrial revolution progresses. The next largest area of U.S. exports are industrial supplies—primarily chemical and petroleum products. Its huge advantage in natural gas costs means its exports of those products are likely to increase too. Consumer goods represent the smallest export market for the United States. The United States imports $594 billion in consumer goods but exports only $194 billion so it stands to gain overall as consumer goods production becomes localized. It imports $123 billion in footwear and apparel alone. If this industry moves to mass customization, that number will fall sharply. In fact, the United States' need to import should decrease overall because other large categories of imports are petroleum products ($144 billion) and automotive vehicles, parts, and engines ($350 billion).[55]

Clearly the fourth industrial revolution is changing the global economy rapidly and in unexpected ways. It is having an even more dramatic effect on military power—the subject of the next chapter.

NOTES

1. Kenneth Rapoza, "China and U.S. Pushing A Deglobalization Wave," *Forbes*, October 16, 2018, https://www.forbes.com/sites/kenrapoza/2018/10/16/china-and-u-s-pushing-a-de-globalization-wave/#195631d06a7d.

2. Simon Szreter, "Industrialization and health," *British Medical Bulletin*, June 1, 2004, 80, https://academic.oup.com/bmb/article/69/1/75/523332/Industrialization-and-health.

3. Ibid, 75.

4. "Growth of democracy: The need for change," *BBC Bitesize*, http://www.bbc.co.uk/bitesize/higher/history/democracy/changes/revision/1.

5. "Robots and Industrialization in Developing Countries."

6. "U.S. household income distribution from 1990 to 2016 (by Gini-coefficient)," *Statista*, https://www.statista.com/statistics/219643/gini-coefficient-for-us-individuals-families-and-households/.

7. Erik Sherman, "America is the richest, and most unequal, country," *Fortune*, September 30, 2015, http://fortune.com/2015/09/30/america-wealth-inequality.

8. "Global Wealth Report 2015," Credit Suisse, October 2015, 13, https://publications.credit-suisse.com/tasks/render/file/?fileID=F2425415-DCA7-80B8-EAD989AF9341D47E.

9. Trefis Team, "Quantitative Easing In Focus: The U.S. Experience," *Forbes*, November 15, 2015, http://www.forbes.com/sites/greatspeculations/2015/11/16/quantitative-easing-in-focus-the-u-s-experience/#772a58013013.

10. Tom Kertscher, "Do 70% of the benefits from Trump's tax law benefit the wealthiest 1%, as Sen. Sherrod Brown Says?" *Politifact*, March 5, 2019, https://www.politifact.com/truth-o-meter/statements/2019/mar/05/sherrod-brown/do-70-benefits-trumps-tax-law-benefit-wealthiest-1/.

11. Chye-Ching Huang, Gullermo Herrera and Brendan Duke, "JCT Estimates: Final GOP Tax Bill Skewed to Top, Hurts Many Low- and Middle-Income Americans," Center on Budget and Policy Priorities, December 19, 2017, https://www.cbpp.org/research/federal-tax/jct-estimates-final-gop-tax-bill-skewed-to-top-hurts-many-low-and-middle-income.

12. "Employment by Sector," International Labour Organization, November 2018, https://www.ilo.org/ilostat/faces/oracle/webcenter/portalapp/pagehierarchy/Page3.jspx?MBI_ID=33&_afrLoop=208834911

3751674&_afrWindowMode=0&_afrWindowId=y22ns99d3_1#!%40%40
%3F_afrWindowId%3Dy22ns99d3_1%26_afrLoop%3D2088349113751674
%26MBI_ID%3D33%26_afrWindowMode%3D0%26_adf.ctrl-state%3Dy2
2ns99d3_57.

13. "Executive Summary World Robotics 2018 Industrial Robots," https://ifr.
    org/downloads/press2018/Executive_Summary_WR_2018_Industrial_
    Robots.pdf.

14. Stephen Crowe, "Universal Robots Sees Strong Growth in Asia," *The
    Robot Report,* March 12, 2018, https://www.therobotreport.com/universal-
    robots-strong-growth-asia/.

15. Amrit Amirapu and Arvind Subramanian, "Manufacturing or Services?
    An Indian Illustration of a Development Dilemma—Working Paper 409,"
    Center for Global Development, June 10, 2015, http://www.cgdev.org/
    publication/manufacturing-or-services-indian-illustration-development-
    dilemma-working-paper-409.

16. "Robots and Industrialization in Developing Countries."

17. Sharma, *The Rise and Fall of Nations,* 207.

18. Sharma, *The Rise and Fall of Nations,* 5.

19. "World Investment Report 2017," UNCTAD, http://unctad.org/en/
    PublicationsLibrary/wir2017_en.pdf.

20. "FDI flows," OECD Data, https://data.oecd.org/fdi/fdi-flows.htm
    #indicator-chart; "FDI in Figures," OECD, https://www.oecd.org/daf/inv/
    investment-policy/FDI-in-Figures-October-2016.pdf.

21. "Arrested development," *Economist,* October 4–10, 2014, http://www.
    economist.com/news/special-report/21621158-model-development-
    through-industrialisation-its-way-out-arrested-development.

22. Amrit Amirapu and Arvind Subramanian, "India Must Reverse Its
    Deindustrialization," Peterson Institute for International Economics,
    May 9, 2014, https://piie.com/commentary/op-eds/india-must-reverse-
    its-deindustrialization.

23. Michele Petruzziello, "5 things you probably didn't know about the
    fashion industry," World Economic Forum, July 15, 2016, https://www.
    weforum.org/agenda/2015/07/5-things-you-probably-didnt-know-about-
    the-fashion-industry.

24. Gabriel Wildau and Tom Mitchell, "China's inequality among world's
    worst," *Financial Times,* January 14, 2016, https://www.ft.com/content/
    3c521faa-baa6-11e5-a7cc-280dfe875e28.

25. Dilip Ratha, "Trends in Remittances, 2016: A New Normal of Slow Growth," World Bank, October 6, 2016, http://blogs.worldbank.org/peoplemove/trends-remittances-2016-new-normal-slow-growth.
26. "Migration and Remittances: Recent Developments and Outlook, World Bank Group, December 2018, 2, https://www.knomad.org/sites/default/files/2018-12/Migration%20and%20Development%20Brief%2030.pdf.
27. Danielle Paquette, "So the machines can defeat us at chess. We have them beat at picking berries. For now," *Chicago Tribune,* February 18, 2019, https://www.chicagotribune.com/business/ct-biz-farmworker-automation-robot-fruit-picker-20190218-story.html.
28. "Meat Processing Robots," *Robotworx,* https://www.robots.com/applications/meat-processing-automation.
29. Thomas, "World's largest 3D construction printer is coming to Saudi Arabia in 2019," March 19, 2019, http://www.3ders.org/articles/20190319-worlds-largest-3d-construction-printer-is-coming-to-saudi-arabia-in-2019.html.
30. Sheri Koones, "Prefab 101: Defining The Many Forms Of Factory-Built Homes," *Forbes,* February 4 2019, https://www.forbes.com/sites/sherikoones/2019/02/04/prefab-101-defining-the-many-forms-of-factory-built-homes/#4ddba3e85bd0.
31. Schwab, *The Fourth Industrial Revolution,* 12–13.
32. Schwab, *The Fourth Industrial Revolution,"* 75.
33. "The BCG Global Manufacturing Cost-Competitiveness Index," Boston Consulting Group, August 19, 2014, https://www.bcgperspectives.com/content/interactive/lean_manufacturing_globalization_bcg_global_manufacturing_cost_competitiveness_index.
34. "Deloitte Global Manufacturing Competitiveness Index, 2016, Executive Summary," https://www2.deloitte.com/global/en/pages/manufacturing/articles/global-manufacturing-competitiveness-index.html.
35. Oran B. Hesterman, PhD, and Daniel Horan, "The demand for 'local' food is growing — here's why investors should pay attention," *Business Insider,* April 25, 2017, http://www.businessinsider.com/the-demand-for-local-food-is-growing-2017-4.
36. "DHL Global Connectedness Index 8 The State of Globalization in an Age of Ambiguity," DHL, 246, https://www.logistics.dhl/content/dam/dhl/global/core/documents/pdf/glo-core-gci-2018-full-study.pdf.
37. U.S. Census Bureau Foreign Trade 2017 Year-to-Date Total Trade, https://www.census.gov/foreign-trade/statistics/highlights/top/top1712yr.html.

38. "Canada's State of Trade," Global Affairs Canada, http://www. international.gc.ca/economist-economiste/performance/state-point/ state_2017_point/index.aspx?lang=eng#4.
39. "World Integrated Trade Solution," World Bank, http://wits.worldbank. org/CountrySnapshot/en/MEX.
40. Patrick Gillespie, "11 countries sign TPP trade pact without the United States," *CNN Money,* March 8 2018, http://money.cnn.com/2018/03/08/ news/economy/tpp-trump-tariffs/index.html.
41. Pankaj Ghemawat and Steven. A. Altman, "DHL Global Connectedness Index 2016," *DHL,* 44, http://www.dhl.com/content/dam/downloads/g0/ about_us/logistics_insights/gci_2016/DHL_GCI_2016_full_study.pdf.
42. Sharma, *Rise and Fall of Nations,* 179.
43. Daniel Workman, "China's Top Trading Partners," *World's Top Trading Partners,* March 24, 2018, http://www.worldstopexports.com/chinas-top-import-partners/.
44. Ibid, 43.
45. Carlos Torres and Randy Woods, "China Is Boosting Ties in Latin America. Trump Should Be Worried," *Bloomberg,* January 3, 2018, https:// www.bloomberg.com/news/articles/2018-01-03/china-is-boosting-ties-in-latin-america-trump-should-be-worried.
46. "Global Economic Prospects: Latin America and the Caribbean," The World Bank, January 9, 2018, http://www.worldbank.org/en/region/lac/ brief/global-economic-prospects-latin-america-and-the-caribbean.
47. Shasta Darlington, "E.U. and Four Latin American Nations Reach a Trade Deal," *New York Times,* June 28, 2019, https://www.nytimes.com/2019/0 6/28/world/americas/eu-four-latin-american-nations-trade-deal.html.
48. Ghemawat and Altman, "DHL Global Connectedness Index 2016," 44.
49. "Worth celebrating," *Economist,* June 9–16, 2016, https://www.economist. com/news/middle-east-and-africa/21700398-regional-co-operation-has-been-good-least-part-continent-worth?zid=295&ah=0bca374e65f2354d5 53956ea65f756e0.
50. Mills, "The Coming Revolution in American Manufacturing," 15.
51. Sharma, *Rise and Fall of Nations,* 361.
52. "Rare Earth Elements: What Are They? Who Has Them?" Institute for Energy Research, July 27, 2016, http://instituteforenergyresearch.org/ analysis/rare-earth-elements/.
53. "Rare Earth Elements Discovered in American Coal," *Environmental News Service,* January 30, 2018, http://ens-newswire.com/2018/01/30/rare-earth-elements-discovered-in-american-coal/; "The Future of Strategic

Natural Resources," Massachusetts Institute of Technology, http://web.
mit.edu/12.000/www/m2016/finalwebsite/solutions/deposits.html.

54. James Vincent, "Rare earth elements aren't the secret weapon China
    thinks they are," *The Verge*, May 23, 2019, https://www.theverge.com/2
    019/5/23/18637071/rare-earth-china-production-america-demand-trade-
    war-tariffs.

55. Kimberly Amadeo, "U.S. Imports and Exports: Components and Statistics,"
    Balance, February 15, 2017, https://www.thebalance.com/u-s-imports-
    and-exports-components-and-statistics-3306270.

CHAPTER 5

MILITARY IMPACT

The technologies of the fourth industrial revolution are also dramatically changing the character of conflict. The convergence of these ever-improving technologies is providing sharply increased capabilities to smaller and smaller political entities—extending even to the individual. This chapter will discuss the implications this diffusion of power has for the character of warfare and then explore how selected technologies are changing conflict.

However, it is essential to understand that the fundamental nature of war (what it is) will not change even as its character (how it is fought) changes dramatically. The nature of war will remain rooted in Clausewitz's primary trinity of passion, chance, and reason. After the Gulf War, the U.S. Department of Defense claimed that technology was changing the nature of war. It would allow U.S. leaders to see and understand everything that was happening on the battlefield while preventing the enemy from doing so. Technology would create a revolution in military affairs.

To make it work, the Department of Defense stated it needed to explore organizations and procedures along with the new technologies.[1]

Unfortunately, throughout the 1990s, the department focused primarily on technology. It was convinced technology would allow U.S. forces to "lock out" all enemy courses of action.[2] The reality fell far short of these expectations.

Despite decades of development and experimentation, technology has not allowed U.S. forces to dominate a wide range of insurgent and terrorist movements. The successes U.S. forces enjoyed have consistently been based on operational and tactical adaption rather than on technological prowess. It is critical to remember this fact. Human adaptation in the operational and tactical sphere are more important than superior technology. History is full of examples of technologically superior forces being defeated by superior ingenuity and adaptability on the part of their enemies.

As U.S. forces drew down in Iraq and Afghanistan, the Department of Defense shifted its focus to potential conflicts with near-peer competitors—and once again turned to technology. In 2014, Secretary of Defense Chuck Hagel announced the Defense Innovation Initiative or, as it is more commonly known, the Third Offset Strategy. Clearly, this was a vital effort on the part of the department and, if successful, will pay significant dividends.

However, the fourth industrial revolution will not just change how nations fight but will change the framework of conflict as it recasts society, the state, and military organizations. A key point is that the warfare changes discussed in this chapter will be happening simultaneously with and driven by economic, social, and political changes. As was the case with the previous industrial revolutions, this one will restructure the global economy, international trade patterns, and the ways and means which militaries use to achieve strategic goals.

This chapter will address how creative operational concepts can use emerging technologies—nano, drones, artificial intelligence, and space in particular—to change conflict in all domains. In addition, it will also explore hypervelocity weapons. In contrast to the small, smart, and cheap weapons the other technologies are allowing, hypervelocity will be expensive but, if it succeeds, will have a massive impact on the character of war.

NANOTECHNOLOGY

The most immediate military application of nanotechnology is nanoenergetics, or nanoexplosives. In 2002, nanoexplosives demonstrated an explosive power twice that of conventional explosives.[3] More recently, a writer asserted that the Department of Defense is using "nanoaluminum to create ultrahigh burn rate chemical explosives, with ten times greater explosive punch than conventional explosives."[4] Because there were no footnotes or references cited, it is not possible for the reader to determine why there was an exceptional increase in explosive power between 2002 and 2017. With research in this field closely held, it is difficult to say if the assertion is true. But even if two times is as good as it gets, a one-hundred-percent increase in destructive power for a weapon of the same size is a massive increase. The key is that much greater conventional explosive power is available to states—and when these explosives move into the commercial sector, they will be available to nonstate actors too.

The second area of interest is that of nanomaterials. Carbon nanotubes (created from graphene) are over one hundred times stronger than steel and are exceptional conductors. Currently, they are being used to dramatically reduce the weight needed for structural strength in a wide range of products—from electronics to vehicles to medical devices to water purification. Although the graphene that is the basis of carbon nanotubes currently remains difficult and expensive to mass produce, a number of promising methods to speed production are being explored.[5] When these or other methods under development make graphene available cheaply in large quantities, they will free designers to explore radically new designs to improve performance for products across the spectrum, from bicycles to very high-end military applications.

In a related field, numerous firms are applying nanomaterials to batteries and increasing their storage capacity.[6] Graphene is being used in supercapacitors to create batteries that can recharge almost instantly—although mass production and deployment of these supercapacitors will take a few more years. Another area of particular interest to militaries is use of nanomaterials for camouflage and stealth. A number of companies are working on smart, adaptive fabric that will change to match the background. But more importantly, many companies are working to develop nano-based paints to make it very difficult to electronically or visually detect any coated objects. At the University of California San Diego, researchers have found a cheap way to coat products with a super-thin, nonmetallic material that manipulates radar waves. German, Israeli, Indian, and U.S. firms are all testing coatings that reduce radar as well as visual and near-infrared signatures.[7]

Potentially some of the most valuable nano-products are radiation-hardened circuits. These circuits have a much higher resistance to electromagnetic pulses and microwave weapons.[8] In essence, it will be possible to create drones and missiles with electronics that are resistant to the high-power microwave weapons designed to overload electronic circuits. During the Cold War, most U.S. military electronic systems were hardened to protect them from the electromagnetic/microware pulse generated by a nuclear blast. As the U.S. military is shifting its focus back to major power competition, it is once again working to harden its electronic systems. Because they can be projected as a wave and do not require the dwell time of laser systems, microwave-energy weapons hold great promise for defense against drone swarms. Hardened circuits will make such a defense more difficult and costly.

In short, improvements in materials, circuitry, energy storage, and explosives based on nanotechnology will lead to major increases in range, payload, and stealth for a wide variety of vehicles—from high-performance aircraft to armored vehicles to cheap drones.

AERIAL DRONES

Even with the long history and recent proliferation of civilian drones, most discussions still center on the military use of large, sophisticated drones. In the past, it was military needs that drove the development of drones. Today, drone companies around the world are responding to the demand from industries as varied as "real estate, oil and gas, manufacturing, construction and engineering, infrastructure, travel and tourism, sports and events, mapping and surveying, golf courses, high rises and condos, and weddings."[9] It is essential to understand the rapid improvement in many drone capabilities is being driven by commercial uses, not military ones. As a result, most of these new capabilities will be available to anyone who wishes to purchase them—and in large numbers. Titomic, an Australian firm, has 3D printed an entire titanium drone that measure 1.8 meters in diameter.[10]

For the purpose of our discussion, it is convenient to break aerial drones into the functions they execute—surveillance, reconnaissance, communications, and strike—to see how each segment of the technology is and will be used to create military advantage.

Surveillance Drones

Surveillance drones have received a great deal of attention. It is also an area of rapidly increasing capability. The U.S. military led the way with its high-end Global Hawk, Triton, Scan Eagle, and Grey Eagle platforms which have been invaluable in counterterrorism operations. These long-endurance, remotely piloted UAVs provide the steady, uninterrupted surveillance necessary to really understand the "pattern of life" in the target area. Numerous online videos attest to their effectiveness.

Unfortunately, they are also quite expensive and require extensive support structures, as well as numerous analysts to maximize their effectiveness. A long-endurance remotely piloted drone requires a ground control station, satellite links from the ground control station or pilot (often in the United States) to where the aircraft is operating, and local launch and recovery teams at the overseas operating base. They are anything but "unmanned systems." Lieutenant General Dave Deptula, USAF (ret.) notes

> Reaper's [a larger version of the Predator] infrastructure necessitates at least 171 personnel for each CAP [Combat Air Patrol]: these include 43 mission control personnel, including seven pilots and seven sensor operators, 59 launch, recovery and maintenance personnel (including six more pilots and sensor operators), 66 Processing Exploitation Dissemination personnel for intelligence and its support (including 14 more maintenance personnel) and three 'other equipment' personnel.[11]

A CAP represents a single aircraft orbit that keeps the drone over the area it is supposed to surveil. Because a theater may request multiple CAPs on a daily basis, drone surveillance of target is a very manpower intensive operation.

Increasing the demand for personnel, the sheer volume of video produced by U.S. drones exceeds human capacity to interpret. The vast majority of the live video recorded is never even looked at by a human. The problem is exacerbated by the huge quantities of data also being acquired by both optical and electronic surveillance satellites. In response, the Pentagon expanded its intelligence analysis contracts by orders of magnitude. Both the Pentagon and those contractors are working hard to develop artificial intelligence algorithms such as Project Maven that will mine the flood of data. However, the purchase and operating costs of high-end systems put them out of reach for most organizations and even nations.

That said, there is an increasing commercial demand for long-endurance surveillance systems for everything from monitoring fisheries to exploring for oil in remote areas. As expected, commercial solutions are much less expensive and require only a few personnel. A Canadian firm, Defiant Labs, just introduced the DX-3 as a potential surveillance, mapping, or communications platform. It can remain aloft for twenty-four hours with a 6.6-pound payload and has a mission range of nine hundred miles. It can be configured with light detection and ranging (LIDAR) technology to conduct precision mapping or integrated optical or thermal cameras with high-resolution zoom. It takes off and lands vertically but then transitions to fixed-wing flight.[12] With a wingspan of only ten feet, it can easily be transported by a light vehicle.

As impressive as the DX-3's capabilities are, they have already been surpassed by even more capable commercial drones. Aerovel's Flexrotor is being purchased by fishing companies and fishing regulators alike to provide long-term (thirty hours) and long-range (1,500 miles) observation to locate fish and to monitor fishing vessels. It navigates autonomously using GPS, launches and recovers vertically. It can collect both visual and infrared video and stills.[13]

In October 2017, supervised by DARPA/NASA, Vanilla Aircraft's VA001 unmanned aircraft system conducted a nonstop, unrefueled 121-hour flight with a thirty-pound payload.[14] These drones offer commercial firms capabilities that used to be the preserve of governments.

All three systems are autonomous. This eliminates the needs for pilots or system operators. Flexrotor and DX-3 also have vertical takeoff and recovery functions, so they do not even require an airfield. VA-1 can be launched and recovered by very small crews from short runways or roads.

The rapid advances in commercial, autonomous surveillance drones and machine interpretation is dramatically lowering the cost of operating long-range, multispectral surveillance missions.

Reconnaissance Drones

Smaller, cheaper drones are not particularly effective at the surveillance mission due to their relatively short endurance. Although similar to the surveillance function, the reconnaissance function tends to focus on a specific mission or requirement. It may be as simple as getting a look over a wall or as complex as entering a denied area hundreds of miles from the drone's launch point. Here the full family of drones from small, hobbyist to long-range, extended endurance drones fulfil different aspects of the reconnaissance mission.

At the small end, quadcopters are being used by hobbyists and professionals to provide aerial images for everything from real-estate listings to movie-background roll. Both still and video camera quality is rapidly improving, and some hobbyist drones like the DJI Phantom can be equipped with both visual and infrared cameras on the same mission. And commercial competition is rapidly improving the sensors small drones can carry. Aerialtronics just put a new AI-driven camera on sale that is four inches by four inches by three inches and weighs only 1.5 pounds but has a 30x-magnification HD camera with an integrated forward-looking infrared camera.[15] It can integrate the two images to provide better target identification. In March 2018, researchers demonstrated a $700 3D-printed, hyperspectral imager light enough to mount on a small drone.[16] And Google has released its MobileNets family of lightweight computer vision models that can identify objects, faces, and landmarks.[17]

Obstacle avoidance and various types of limited autonomous flight are also available. For a few thousand dollars, a business can conduct many of the same tasks that used to require a helicopter or light plane costing hundreds of thousands to millions of dollars.

Some fire departments have adopted tethered drones to give the on-scene fire chief a long endurance overhead view of the incident. With power supplied through a tether, endurance is limited only by the mechanical reliability of the drone. Not surprisingly, criminals have also adopted drones. In May 2018, criminals used small drones to aggressively "buzz" an FBI observation post and fed the video to YouTube so other members of the group could see it.[18]

The U.S. Marine Corps is experimenting with providing an inexpensive commercial drone to each infantry squad leader to provide short-term but immediate feedback. Emergency responders in many nations are adopting longer endurance small drones to assist with search and rescue operations.

And of course, America's special operations forces make extensive use of high-end, remotely piloted drones. It is clear that terrorists, insurgents and small states will also make use of the commercial drones available in each of these categories up to and including the long-endurance drones with multispectral and electronic sensors.

Communications Relay Drones

The primary role of drones in communications is to provide temporary nodes either to extend the range of existing systems or to provide rapid replacement for a node that has sustained damage. Clearly, long endurance or tethered drones are the best suited for this mission. However, one can see how even a limited-endurance drone could be useful to small units in raid-type missions to provide extended communications during a critical window.

Airbus, the European aircraft manufacturer, has entered the drone business with a focus at the high end, both literally and figuratively. It has developed the Zephyr S and its larger stablemate, the Zephyr T (twin), both solar-powered. They can be tailored with payloads that offer voice and data communication beyond line of sight, or line of sight high-resolution optical imagery. It also has an active radar package that can be used for real-time mapping. Airbus believes Zephyr can provide persistent Internet coverage in remote areas—and has tested the endurance by keeping it aloft for fourteen days without refueling.[19] Because it operates at 70,000–90,000 feet, the Zephyr does not require coordination with either commercial air corridors or space orbits except when going on or off station.

CACI International, has also entered the field. To provide for civilian communications relay, they built the SunSpark solar drone. Only thirty-two-feet long, it has a one hundred-foot wingspan.[20]

Strike Drones

Large, long-endurance drones like the Predator have repeatedly demonstrated the ability to deliver timely precision fires in low-threat environments. Today, the Pentagon is seeking low-cost, high-performance unmanned aircraft to accompany manned aircraft into combat. Kratos Defense and Security Systems Inc. has designed the XQ-222 and aims to sell it for about two million dollars a copy, if bought in volume. The aircraft features a 1,500-mile combat radius (over two times the F-35) with a five-hundred-pound payload and can fly three thousand miles if sent on a one-way mission. It also has low-observable features as well as no requirement for an airfield to launch or recover. It takes off with a rocket assist from a stand and lands using a parachute.[21] Kratos promoted the XQ-222 at the 2017 Paris Airshow suggesting that the drones could fly in tandem with F-16 or F-35 fighters to increase the capabilities of existing aircraft dramatically.[22] And, of course, their presence at the Paris Airshow indicates America will not be the only nation with this capability. Although the XQ-222 is its most capable drone, Kratos produces an entire family of unmanned jet aircraft to include the *Mako* which has already partnered with various manned aircraft.[23]

But strike is not limited to million-dollar systems. The U.S. Army and Marine Corps have been using the $15,000 Switchblade drone as an observation and strike platform in Afghanistan since 2011. The Switchblade comes in a small tube two feet long and about three inches across. It weighs only six pounds, yet it can fly for ten kilometers providing live video to the operator. And because it is armed, the operator can use it to suicide into any targets he finds. By 2015, more than four thousand were shipped to Afghanistan to support U.S. forces.[24]

Nor do states have a monopoly on the strike mission. Starting in 2015, the Islamic State of Iraq and Syria (ISIS) began to employ drones to support its forces. These drones, costing only a few hundred dollars apiece, were either purchased as commercial products or built from scratch in local weapons facilities. ISIS had established a workshop in Ramadi to build their own drones as early as February 2016. Initially, it used drones primarily for reconnaissance and to guide suicide car bombers to their targets. By early 2017, Iraqi forces reported ISIS' first use of drones to deliver bombs—in the form of grenades—against Iraqi forces.[25] The same month ISIS began uploading videos to online websites that appear to show a small fixed-wing drone dropping two small bombs with remarkable accuracy. The videos recorded numerous attacks against a variety of personnel and vehicle targets. The bombs were not particularly powerful, but they still killed or wounded a number of people and damaged some vehicles.] In one video, the drone is used to support a complex ambush. It distracted the local Iraqi forces so that a suicide car bomber could close in and detonate his vehicle.[26]

This was not a minor effort for ISIS. In January 2017, documents detailing ISIS drone operations were seized. They revealed that as early as 2015, ISIS was conducting a well-organized effort to analyze each mission, learn from it, and improve both its equipment and operational techniques. Their efforts paid off for them. A U.S. spokesman noted more than eighty ISIS drone attacks between October 2016 and January 2017 that resulted in about a dozen dead and fifty injured government soldiers.[27] ISIS took advantage of the fact that commercial drone usage is expanding at an exceptional rate.

In addition to their use for a variety of communications, mapping, and videography, commercial drones have begun delivering packages. A key factor in how quickly drones can be deployed as delivery platforms is the regulatory environment. U.S. regulators are taking a very cautious, deliberate approach, but other nations are providing more room for experimentation. In 2016, Amazon established a nascent delivery service in the United Kingdom.[28] Dominos' delivered it first pizza on August 2016—in New Zealand. Maersk Line had a drone deliver supplies to a ship near Denmark in March. Zipline, a California-based firm, regularly delivers blood supplies to remote clinics in Rwanda. Even the United

Nations is experimenting with drone delivery in partnership with the government of Malawi for humanitarian uses.[29]

Small payloads have been a problem, but entrepreneurs are moving to solve that. In 2018, Volans-I launched an autonomous drone that can carry 20 pounds across five hundred miles at speeds of up to two hundred miles per hour.[30] TAKOF, a Canadian firm, has a helicopter drone that delivers four hundred pounds over 120 miles.[31]

In May 2018, the U.S. Department of Transportation announced it had selected ten state, local, and tribal governments within the United States to participate in the Unmanned Aircraft Systems (UAS) Integration Pilot Program. The selected governments will be able to request permission to conduct a wide variety of drone tests out of sight of the operator over wide areas (perhaps even the whole state) and will be able to fly at night.[32] More than two hundred companies have partnered with the selected governments to conduct experiments in the United States that previously had to be conducted in countries with friendlier regulatory environments.

Commercial firms have mastered the basics of drone delivery. However, to really expand the commercial delivery market, drones will have to be truly autonomous. How they are accomplishing this will be discussed in the artificial intelligence section of this chapter.

Maritime Drones

The commercial shipping industry also has much to gain from using unmanned ships, and a number of companies are experimenting with a range of vessels, from North Sea ferries to electric coastal cargo vessels to full-size container ships and tankers. However, due to administrative, legal, and safety issues, most analysts think it will be a decade or more before truly unmanned ships are sailing the open ocean. Inland waters may be different. Rolls-Royce believes it can have up to five autonomous ferries operating by 2020.[33]

Like most of the applications of innovative technology, the ones behind unmanned ships will be profit driven. The U.S. Department of Transportation estimates crew cost for foreign-flagged vessels at thirty-five percent of the total operating cost; for U.S.-flagged vessels it is sixty-eight percent.[34] Clearly, no commercial manned ship will be able to compete on cost against an unmanned ship.

In 2010, Rutgers University developed an underwater "glider" drone as part of an ongoing oceanographic effort that now has hundreds of gliders operating around the world.[35] The newer versions dive to four thousand feet and can be purchased for about $100,000 each, but commercial firms are striving to reduce the cost by ninety percent.[36] These drones have demonstrated the ability to deliver a small payload at transoceanic ranges autonomously. Michigan Tech has already produced low cost versions that can work together.[37]

In addition to oceanographic survey, military and commercial organizations are experimenting with using autonomous ships to conduct a wide variety of tasks. In 2016, the U.S. Navy commissioned the *Sea Hunter*, a 103-foot-long, unmanned trimaran designed as a long-range, independent submarine hunter.[38] The Royal Navy and French Navy are working together to develop an unmanned mine hunter. The U.S. Navy is planning to spend $2.7 billion to buy

> 10 large USVs [unmanned surface vehicles] over the next five years, as part of an overall plan to buy 232 unmanned surface, underwater and aerial vehicles of all sizes in the next five years.[39]

It is also pursuing smart swarming technology with the Low-Cost Unmanned Aerial Vehicle Swarming Technology (LOCUST)[40] as well as small watercraft.[41]

The U.S. Navy, which has also been working on unmanned underwater vehicles (UUVs) since at least 2004, is pursuing high-end versions. In December 2016, the Department of Defense announced it was planning to spend up to $3 billion on UUVs ranging from oceanographic survey to stealth reconnaissance platforms.[42] Boeing has developed the Echo Voyager, a 51-foot-long submersible designed to stay submerged for months.[43] Some will operate independently; others will operate in coordination with submarines and surface ships. Innocorp announced it has produced a drone that transitions from an unmanned underwater vehicle to an unmanned aerial vehicle that operates autonomously as a surveillance drone.[44] Although still experimental, it shows the remarkable potential of drones to span warfare domains.

By 2018, the U.S. Navy was developing unmanned vehicles to:

1. Detect and strike enemy combatants remotely and discretely, neutralizing enemy threats without putting sailors at risk.
2. Clear a mined strait within hours, quickly and cheaply, with a swarm of hundreds, if not thousands, of small unmanned mine-hunting vehicles.
3. Assign a drone to follow an adversary's submarine at safe distance from the moment it leaves port to the time it returns.
4. Assign an unmanned surface vessel constant guard of a critical port or infrastructure.[45]

UUVs can be launched from a variety of surface and subsurface platforms or remain ashore in friendly territory until needed, and then launched from a port or even the beach. Imaginatively employed, they could be a relatively inexpensive substitute for a submarine force for a small nation.

The U.S. Navy's 2020 budget requested $359 million for UUVs, $400 million for two large unmanned surface vessels, with plans to buy eight more over the next four years, and funds for eight unmanned MQ-25 Stingray aerial refuelers.[46] The United States is not alone in pursuing unmanned seapower. In June 2016, China displayed a wide range of unmanned underwater vehicles and unmanned surface vehicles ranging from small, short-range systems to long-range autonomous systems.[47]

Ground Drones

Despite the complexity of operating in the cluttered, confusing, and entirely unpredictable ground environment, many companies are pushing hard for autonomous ground systems. From walking-paced ground-delivery systems to driverless vehicles and even to cattle-herding drones, researchers are making advances in all areas.[48]

Although driverless cars on the street are several years to a decade away, autonomous trucks are already working in closed, privately owned compounds such as mines. These trucks not only save on labor and work twenty-four hours a day, even in very remote locations, but they are also safer because few people are present in the mine.

Rob Atkinson of Rio Tinto mining reports that the company's driverless trucks have proven to be roughly fifteen percent cheaper to run than vehicles with humans behind the wheel. Because haulage is by far a mine's largest operational cost, this is a major improvement. Robotic trucks do not stop for shift changes or bathroom breaks. They are more predictable and gentler than any human in how they use brakes and other controls.[49] In 2018, Rio Tinto also delivered its first load of ore from its mines to the port using an autonomous train.[50] Diggers and bulldozers could be next to be automated.

Given the demonstrated major cost reductions, more and more businesses are operating autonomous trucks and unmanned shuttles on private property. In what may be the first movement beyond the boundaries of private property, Peloton Technology plans to sell equipment that will allow trucks to platoon. These are not autonomous trucks but rather trucks linked wirelessly to the lead truck. The driver in the lead truck controls the gas and brake inputs to several following trucks.[51] This technology has been tested in Europe and found to reduce not only labor costs but also fuel costs because of the better fuel efficiency for the following trucks which are drafting on the lead truck.

Mobile land mines and autonomous anti-vehicle weapons are also under development.[52] They require much more advanced mechanical systems and better artificial intelligence than aerial drones to operate independently. Thus, it will take significantly longer to field systems with even limited ability to move about an active battlefield autonomously.

But both states and nonstate actors have already built and are employing remotely operated land robots—and arming them. As early as 2008, the U.S. Army bought twenty-four robot patrol sentries but did not arm them.[53] The Russians, however, have no qualms about arming autonomous robots. In 2014, the Russian Strategic Missile Forces deployed mobile robots armed with heavy machine guns to guard five of its ballistic missile installations. Because these robots work in a well-defined and confined space, the Russians claim they have limited autonomy.[54] In 2014, the South Koreans put autonomous robots along the DMZ. Each robot has heat and motion sensors to detect intruders and is armed with both a heavy machine gun and a grenade launcher, but the robot cannot fire without a human's command.[55]

As always, active warfare has stimulated creativity among the combatants. In Iraq, Members of the Hashd al Shaabi (Popular Mobilization Units) in Iraq developed and used four armed robots to fight ISIS. All four used cameras so that the remote operator could see and aim the machines guns and grenade launchers. [56]

The Russians went a step further and deployed their Uran-9 remotely operated mini-tank to Syria. They claimed the "vehicle can automatically identify, detect and track enemy targets based on a pre-programmed path set by its operator."[57] However, the initial deployment did not go well. The systems remote control and sensor systems failed to operate at the specified ranges and even the track and suspension caused problems.[58] This is not surprising. All revolutionary systems encounter major problem during initial deployments

The key point is that both military and commercial drone usage is exploding. And there appear to be few limits to the uses planned for them. The global smart commercial drone market is projected to reach

$179 billion by 2025.[59] To exploit this investment fully, autonomy and GPS-free navigation will be essential.

ARTIFICIAL INTELLIGENCE

As noted in chapter 2, task specific artificial intelligence is altering the entire spectrum of human activity from leisure to work. However, two areas of artificial intelligence are of particular importance in the evolution of small, smart, and cheap weapons—navigation and target identification. The Global Positioning System (GPS) has proven satisfactory for basic autonomous drone applications such as the Marine Corps' K-MAX cargo-hauling drone helicopter in Afghanistan.[60] However, GPS will continue to be insufficient for operations where terrain blocks line of sight to the satellites, indoor environments, dense urban areas, and areas where GPS is jammed.

At the cheap end, the University of Pennsylvania has developed a quadcopter that "uses a smartphone for autonomous flight, employing only on-board hardware and vision algorithms—with no GPS involved."[61] At the top end, DARPA is working on two programs that will provide precise navigation without the need for satellites. C-SCAN (Chip-Scale Combinatorial Atomic Navigation) and QuASAR (Quantum Assisted Sensing) use variations in the Earth's magnetic field to establish the precise location of a system. If the systems work, they will provide position location data that is 1,000 times more accurate than today's GPS data.[62] The British military is also investing millions of pounds in a technology similar to DARPA's. Researchers working on the project forecast that they will have a prototype ready within five years.[63] The key point is that a vehicle equipped with non-GPS navigation is immune to GPS jamming. The huge economic potential for truly autonomous drones means that corporations are also investing heavily in GPS-independent navigation systems. Such systems can get a drone to the target area, but they will not ensure it can hit a specific target.

Thus, the second key element for truly autonomous drone-strike operations is accurate target identification. Many researchers are working on limited AI that will provide accurate identification from onboard visual or multispectral systems.[64] In 2015, Neurala, a robotics company, developed an "iOS/Android app called 'Selfie Drone' that enabled low cost Parrot Bebop and Bebop 2 drones to take hands-free videos and follow a subject autonomously."[65] By 2019, the field had advanced so rapidly that online journals were rating seven different drones as the best "follow me" drones.[66]

An app that can identify a person to follow could certainly identify a C-17 on the parking apron at Bagram and thus complete the technology needed for autonomous attack. By setting the drone to fly on a specified heading and then attack when the app identifies the designated target, insurgents can remove the requirement for remote piloting. Nor do they have to take extraordinary steps to develop the flight path for their drone. Google Maps (Earth View) can provide the azimuth and range from a launch point to the target area.

Obviously, the Department of Defense is also working to create systems that can identify targets but are light enough to be carried by a small drone. In 2017, DARPA converted a commercially available drone to an autonomous system that could examine individuals on the ground and determine if they had weapons—even if they were partially hidden.[67] Such a system has very high value for U.S. personnel operating in a stability operation. For higher end combat, the "Air Force Research Lab (AFRL) has reported good results from using a 'neuromorphic' chip made by IBM to identify military and civilian vehicles in radar-generated aerial imagery. The unconventional chip got the job done about as accurately as a regular high-powered computer, using less than a 20th of the energy."[68]

SWARMS

It is autonomy that makes the technological convergence a threat today. A truly autonomous drone will require no external input other than the signatures of the designated targets. Thus, they will not be vulnerable to jamming. Further, because they will not require human intervention, autonomous platforms will be able to operate in very large numbers. Rather than using the complex and advanced algorithms the Department of Defense is using for its self-organizing swarms, a less sophisticated enemy might simply launch a swarm that does not coordinate. Each drone would have a simple set of instructions that enables it to engage a target—hence no link to the outside world. Such a drone would also have a Faraday cage which is simply a mesh of conductive material that protects the electronic components from damage from electromagnetic energy. Some analysts think an attacker would not chance the fratricide inevitable when large numbers of drones converge on a target without any coordination mechanism. Yet military forces have never worried about fratricide when firing a time on target with a brigade of artillery simply because the rounds are relatively cheap and the vast majority will arrive at the target. If one thinks of cheap drones as rounds of ammunition, different methods of employment become obvious. Another option that AI can provide drones is the ability to fly to a preplanned location, land, and hide until a specified time or a specified target is identified.

Today the U.S. military is actively exploring the use of swarms—but focusing on smart swarms that communicate and interact with each other and other platforms.[69] Although these programs are still developmental and use a limited number of drones, recent dramatic cost reductions in each of the needed technologies will increase the number by an order of magnitude. Researchers in England have prototyped a 3D-printed drone body that costs roughly $9 a copy.[70] A team at the University of Virginia printed a more complex drone in a single day, then added a small electric motor, two batteries, and an Android phone for guidance to produce an $800 autonomous drone that had a range of fifty kilometers.[71]

A small factory with only a hundred Carbon 3D printers could make 10,000 such drone bodies a day. A Carbon 3D printing plant expanded to the 1,000 printers planned by UPS could print 100,000 of them a day. The limitation on number of weaponized drones is no longer the printing but the assembly and shipment of the finished products. Both processes can be automated with robots. In the near future, drones could be produced at a rate exceeding many types of ammunition—and often for less per round.

DARPA has also developed a cardboard cargo-delivery drone. Designed to be dropped by the hundreds from a C-17, these drones can glide over fifty miles and land close to a specified target. Inexpensive and expendable, these drones are currently configured to carry about two pounds of payload, DARPA is confident they can increase the payload to twenty-two pounds. Completely biodegradable to include the electronics, the DARPA drone is designed to deliver blood, vaccines, or other sensitive fluids and humanitarian supplies. It is not difficult to see how a similar system could be modified to carry deadly payloads.[72] In addition, their small size and ease of deployment mean they could be delivered by a wide variety of aircraft—commercial and military. The cardboard construction and lack of an engine mean little radar or heat signatures.

The U.S. Navy is also applying swarm technology to small patrol craft both to protect high-value units and for defensive patrols. In late 2016, the Navy used a swarm of rigid hull inflatable boats to patrol the Chesapeake Bay. The Office of Naval Research reported that the

> swarmboats had to seek out unknown vessels, intercept them, classify them as harmless or suspicious, and do so with the assistance of other robotic boats, which aided in tracking and trailing. In addition, the remaining swarmboats had to fill the gaps left by the intercepting vessels to carry on with the patrolling as well as sending updates to the shore supervisor.[73]

It is one thing to have access to thousands of drones, it is quite another to have the logistics and manpower available to employ them effectively in very large numbers. One method that demonstrates it can be done is a Chinese Harpy system that mounts eighteen Unmanned Combat Air Vehicles (UCAV) on a single five-ton truck.[74] Originally designed to attack radar systems, the advance version can now loiter and autonomously hunt a variety of targets using optical, infrared, and electronic sensors. The current battery of three trucks can launch fifty-four drones—a battalion one hundred and sixty-two. Although these systems can be engaged by modern ship and land based anti-air systems, the sheer numbers could overwhelm any system the U.S currently fields. Currently, six national air forces fly them. The newer Israeli version, the Harop, has a range of six hundred miles or can loiter for up to six hours.[75]

Of course, even these numbers represent a fraction of the smaller drones that could be launched by similar sized units. A five-ton truck or a twenty-foot shipping container could be configured to carry hundreds of the small U.S. Switchblade[76] or Israeli Hero[77] drones. And the Navy's LOCUST experiment used a twenty-drone launcher that is roughly the size and shape of a twenty-foot shipping container. This allows for some very interesting operational and tactical concepts that will be discussed in the next chapter.

The technology is simple enough that even small states have begun operating military drones. Israel's Aeronautics Defense Systems CEO announced his firm is producing and selling hundreds of armed Orbiter 1Ks but would not name the customers. The version they are selling flies for two to three hours and "can be deployed in a 'shoot and forget' mode, but if its planned target—either moving or stationary—is not detected, its ground operator can bring it back to perform a safe landing."[78]

Nor are small countries satisfied with just purchasing drones. Azerbaijan's Azad Systems has begun manufacturing a licensed version of Israel's Orbiter 1K named "Zarba."[79] In 2016, the Polish Army contracted for a thousand Polish manufactured combat drones with an additional thousand each following year at about $7,000 each.[80] [81] They have high explosive, high explosive anti-tank, or fuel-air explosive (also known as thermobaric) warheads. The high-explosive anti-tank round can penetrate

6–9 inches of armor.[82] This is sufficient to penetrate all but tank frontal armor. And the fuel-air explosive warhead provides a new capability for suicide drones.

SMALL WARHEADS DEVELOPMENTS

Drone design is clearly mastering the first two challenges to using drones in large numbers—autonomous navigation and target identifications. The payload limitation of small drones can be overcome by three separate approaches. The first and least technically challenging approach is "bringing the detonator." The second, the use of explosively formed penetrators as warheads, requires a bit of technical expertise, but most of it can be learned online. The third is to use swarms and count on cumulative damage to accomplish the mission.

"Bringing the detonator" uses the drone to deliver a small initiating charge to the much larger supply of explosive material provided by the target. This approach can be used against a wide variety of targets such as aircraft, vehicles, and storage facilities for fuel, ammo, or chemicals. Even a few ounces of explosives delivered directly to the right point on these targets will initiate a secondary explosion that completely destroys the target. Fixed facilities provide by far the largest potential. The 2013 explosion at the fertilizer storage plant in West Texas destroyed five hundred homes and killed fifteen people. The 1947 Texas City ship explosion, also primarily fertilizer, was a two kilo-ton equivalent blast that leveled everything for almost a mile around. Russian separatists have repeatedly dropped thermite grenades into Ukrainian ammunition storage sites and detonated hundreds of thousands of tons of explosives, causing extensive damage.[83]

To penetrate heavier targets such as a tanker truck or railroad tank car, one can use the second approach, explosively formed penetrators (EFPs). With as little as .07 pounds of explosives, a properly built thumb-sized EFP can penetrate up to half an inch of steel. Increasing the size of the

EFP to only a few pounds allows it to destroy even well-armored vehicles. The natural marriage of IEDs to inexpensive, autonomous drones is inevitable. The result will be an IED that hunts.

The convergence of new technologies proliferating these small, smart, and cheap weapons that can be based on land, sea, or air and may allow them to dominate some aspects of combat. Stationary IEDs often dominated the logistics and operational planning in Iraq and Afghanistan. The United States spent billions in an effort to defeat these stationary, crude weapons. IEDs based on drones can be mobile, smart, active hunters that will present a much greater challenge—particularly when paired with stationary IEDs.

Although numbering in the tens of thousands worldwide, the drones discussed so far represent only the first wave. Like many technologies, early versions were expensive and difficult to operate, thus only technically advanced and wealthy nations employed them. But, over time, the technology became cheaper, more reliable, and more widely employed. A major reason why drone capabilities can be expected to increase very rapidly is the fact that drone design and production is a highly competitive commercial business. Drone producers will have to consistently increase performance while keeping costs down or they will go out of business. We are at the very beginning of drone development, and almost all of the forthcoming commercial improvements will also improve military drones.

COUNTERDRONE EFFORTS

The widespread use of drones has stimulated great interest among military and civilian security services in methods to defeat drones. Like all useful civilian technologies through history, improved drones will quickly find their way on to the battlefield.

This potential for malicious use of drones did not surprise the Pentagon. Since 2002, DARPA has sponsored the annual Black Dart exercise to offer anyone with a good idea for defeating drones the opportunity to demonstrate their prototype's ability to defeat live targets. Since then anti-drone technology has taken a number of different paths:

- kinetic kill—where a system tracks, identifies, and then shoots down the target drone.
- directed energy in the form of lasers and electromagnetic pulse weapons have successfully engaged drones in flight.
- software attacks have seized control of the drone's operating system so that the defender can determine where the drone goes.
- electronic jamming has blocked the command signal from the pilot to the drone.
- GPS jamming has misdirected autonomous drones.

Lasers, software attacks, and electromagnetic pulse initially appeared to have the most potential against swarms. Unfortunately, each approach has significant limitations. Certain atmospheric conditions (dust, haze, water vapor) as well as reflective paints and ablative coatings have significantly reduced the effectiveness of lasers. Software attacks require the enemy to cooperate by leaving a path into his system to insert the software. Electromagnetic weapons can be defeated by Faraday cages or other hardening of a drone's electronics.

In a new approach, DARPA is exploring the use of drone swarms to defeat drone swarms. It sponsored a competition among teams from the U.S. service academies to see which could develop the most effective software and tactics for one swarm to defeat another. The teams then flew mixed swarms of twenty-five drones against each other with remarkable success.[84]

DARPA is not alone in the scramble to find ways to defeat drones. In June 2019, the U.S. Air Force unveiled the Tactical High Power Microwave Operational Responder (THOR). This system is designed to defeat swarms of UAVs by destroying each individual drone's electronics as the microwave beam passes through it.[85] The Air Force did not comment on its effectiveness against drones with hardened electronics.

Small-scale efforts are also proliferating. U.S. Army officers at West Point developed an inexpensive anti-drone rifle to protect dismounted units. In addition, many commercial firms are investing heavily in the technology because they see major markets in both the civil and military sectors. Lending urgency to the effort is the fact that most combatants, insurgents, and even terrorists are exploring how to use drones effectively to improve the success of their forces today.

Defense against drones is particularly tough because defenders must not only protect fixed sites but also mobile assets, and this must be done without any drastic interference with the civilian communities in the area. As the December 2018 drone disruption of Gatwick Airport demonstrated, the competition is not theoretical. Domestic agencies are scrambling to protect key facilities, large events, and even individuals. In 2017, the U.S. military had an immediate requirement to protect U.S. forces in Iraq from ISIS drone attacks. In 2015, the Russians used electronic jamming to block the control signals of the early commercial drones which some Ukrainian units had purchased. In 2016, the Russian were able to jam the control signals and even intercept the video feeds of the RQ-11B Raven drones provided by the United States. Ukrainians now assemble their own drones with components from "Australia, China and the Czech Republic for only $20,000 to $25,000 apiece ... and they are more advanced than the more pricey Ravens, which are often funded from private donations." [86] This is yet another case of civilian technology being ahead of corresponding military technology. Civilian development cycles are simply much faster than the Pentagon's.

Clearly, the drone competition is just beginning.

SPACE

In the beginning, space was the domain of major powers. Even key services provided to the public such as GPS and weather reports relied on the government-funded systems of major powers. However, over time, commercial satellite firms began to offer services such as communications but at relatively high cost with limited availability. Driven by demand, commercial firms have consistently updated the communications services they provide. Eutelsat, a satellite firm, noted "that the cost of transmission capacity will fall to a fiftieth (about $1M per gigabyte) by 2020 compared to older satellites."[87] However, the upfront cost of a major commercial satellite will still severely limit the nations or companies that can launch them.

Even as large firms squeeze more capability out of expensive satellites, cube satellites, or CubeSats, are creating viable alternatives. NASA defines CubeSats as "measuring 10×10×10 cms [about 4 inches on a side for 1 U or unit] and [are] extendable to larger sizes; 1.5, 2, 3, 6, and even 12U."[88] They were designed to take advantage of excess lift capacity on larger launch vehicles.

The speed with which CubeSats were developed and deployed demonstrates how rapidly technology is changing what is possible in space—and who can operate there. Standards for the CubeSat were developed in 1999 and the first launched in 2003. Up until 2013, CubeSats were mostly launched by universities and research organizations. Since then, the majority of launches are done by commercial firms. CubeSats now provide a cost-effective platform for science investigations, new technology demonstrations, and advanced missions using constellations, swarms, and disaggregated systems. CubeSats with basic payloads can be purchased for under $125,000 with a lead time of only a few months.[89] The low cost means that as of July 30, 2017, 829 CubeSats were in orbit —giving many nations their first presence in space.[90]

The rapid growth is part of a new industry that sells space as a service. They offer to help a wide variety of companies analyze and manage their businesses. Using a network of CubeSats, Planet, a commercial venture, has accomplished the elusive goal of taking a medium-resolution photo of every place on Earth every day. If a customer requests higher-resolution images, then Planet will use its "keg" satellites, about the size of a dorm-room fridge, to obtain an image with resolution of under a meter.[91]

Planet will add value by using the photos to predict future economic activity based on the patterns it sees in the photo. For instance, it might predict revenue "for big-box retailers such as Wal-Mart Stores, Inc, and Target Corporation based on changes in the number of cars in their U.S. parking lots, or forecasts for oil inventory based on the height of floating lids on tanks..."[92] Capella Space plans to use radar to allow its satellites to make the same measurements through any cloud cover. ICEYE, a Finnish company, already has radar-equipped CubeSats in orbit.[93]

Viasat is building its real-time earth network of satellite downlink stations that will allow customers to view images and video from the ever-increasing network of observation satellites in near real time.[94] SpyMeSat will deliver near-real-time images to your cell phone.[95]

The network of satellites is thickening rapidly. In February 2017, the Indian Space Research Organization (ISRO) launched 104 satellites on a single rocket—103 of them CubeSats.[96] Space X, a commercial company, launched sixty-four CubeSats on a single re-useable Falcon 9 rocket on December 3, 2018.[97] And on December 16, Rocketlab launched thirteen NASA CubeSats on a single 3D-printed rocket.[98]

The bottom line is that commercially available global surveillance means major powers have lost their monopoly on the use of space. Almost all nations and many nonstate actors now have access to space capabilities. The United States can no longer assume it can hide a fleet at sea or create an unexpected "left hook" like that execute in Operation Desert Storm. "Cheap space" means the globe is much more transparent, and planners must assume enemies can see their forces moving.

Even as major powers lose their monopoly on space surveillance and communications, they may be losing the monopoly on attacking space assets. In 2019, Orbital ATK is planning to launch the first in a series of satellites that will provide repair and refueling services to existing satellites.[99] Obviously if a satellite can repair or refuel another satellite, it can also destroy it.

HYPERVELOCITY

Hypervelocity missiles and projectiles, defined as those traveling at least Mach 5 (five times the speed of sound), are also potential game changers. There are two basic types of hypersonic missiles: cruise and glide missiles. Hypersonic cruise missiles are essentially very fast cruise missiles. Li Jun, a People's Liberation Army writer, notes that "a U.S. Tomahawk cruise missile takes more than an hour to strike a target 1,000 kilometers away ... while a hypersonic weapon can fly more than 1,000 kilometers in eight minutes."[100]

In contrast, hypersonic glide missiles (sometimes referred to as boost glide missiles) ride a rocket into space where the hypersonic glide vehicle (warhead) detaches and glides to the target. Current intercontinental ballistic missiles are faster (Mach 24), but the warhead cannot maneuver. A hypersonic glide vehicle combines a ballistic missile's speed and range with a cruise missile's maneuverability. Hypersonic glide missiles clearly present a very direct threat to fixed facilities such as airfields, ports, bases, missile silos, and moored ships.

The 2020 Pentagon budget has allocated $2.6 billion for hypersonic weapons, but China already has two to three times as many hypersonic research facilities as the United States. It has tested its own DF-ZF hypersonic glide repeatedly since 2014, but there is almost no public information on the results.[101]

In contrast to hypersonic glide missiles, hypervelocity projectiles are fired from either electromagnet railguns or standard powder guns. China continues to pursue an operational rail gun and has even put a test version to sea. These weapons can fire a projectile at seven times the speed of sound to a range of about one hundred miles.[102] Although apparently continuing its own railgun program, the United States has successfully fired twenty hypervelocity projectiles from a standard Mk45 5-inch naval gun.[103] By using a powder gun, the U.S. Navy has gained a significant advantage. Although operational railguns have yet to be installed on any ships, the Navy's *Ticonderoga* and *Arleigh Burke* class ships are armed with Mk45 guns and can fire the projectiles today. Just as important, many U.S. allies have Mk45 guns aboard their warships. With rounds costing about $75,000 each, they cost a fraction of current air defense and cruise missiles but can be effective in some of the missions normally assigned to those missiles. With their high rates of fire, these guns may be a partial solution to defending the fleet against drones, ballistic and cruise missiles.

It also may be possible to develop a round for the standard 155mm field artillery cannon, which would mean the United States would have more than one thousand guns that could fire hypersonic projectiles.

CONCLUSION

Clearly these advances in nano, drones, artificial intelligence, space and hypervelocity will revolutionize combat in all domains and change the tactical and operational context of conflicts. That is the subject of our next chapter.

Notes

1. Michael J. Mazarr, "The Revolution in Military Affairs: A Framework for Defense Planning," June 10, 1994, ssi.armywarcollege.edu/pdffiles/00234.pdf.
2. For a discussion of the Pentagon's view of how technology was changing warfare see Arthur K. Cebrowski and John Garstka's "Network-Centric Warfare—Its Origin and Future," *Naval Institute Proceedings,* January 1998.
3. Dr. Andrzej W. Miziolek, "Nanonenergetics: An Emerging Technology Area of National Importance," *AMPTIAC Quarterly,* Vol 6, No 1, Spring 2002, 45, http://ammtiac.alionscience.com/pdf/AMPQ6_1ART06.pdf.
4. Louis A. Del Monte, *Nanoweapons: A Growing Threat to Humanity,* (U.S.: Potomac Books, 2017), 47–48.
5. "Physicists patent detonation technique to mass-produce graphene," *K-State News,* http://www.k-state.edu/media/newsreleases/2017-01/graphenepatent12517.html; and Colin Jeffrey, "Oily alchemy: Turning soybeans into graphene," *New Atlas,* January 31, 2017, http://newatlas.com/graphene-csiro-soy-beans/47649/?utm_source=Gizmag+Subscribers&utm_campaign=fdc308c5d9-UA-2235360–4&utm_medium=email&utm_term=0_65b67362bd-fdc308c5d9–92283385.
6. Li Yi Hsu, Thomas Lepetit, and Boubacar Kante, "Extremely Thin Dielectric Metasurface for Carpet Cloaking," *Progress in Electromagnetic Research* 152 (2015): 33–40.
7. S. R. Vadera and Narendra Kumar, "Nanotechnology and nanomaterials for camouflage and stealth applications," *nanowerk,* January 30, 2015, http://www.nanowerk.com/spotlight/spotid=38899_3.php.
8. Del Monte, *Nanoweapons: A Growing Threat to Humanity,* 47–49.
9. "Canada's First International UAV Show Announces Headliners," *UAS Weekly.com,* October 28, 2016, https://uasweekly.com/2016/10/28/canadas-first-international-uav-show-announces-headliners/.
10. Tia Vialva, "Titomic develops 'largest' 3D printed titanium UAV," *3D Printing Industry,* April 30, 2019, https://3dprintingindustry.com/news/titomic-develops-largest-3d-printed-titanium-uav-154572/.
11. Winslow Wheeler, "The MQ-9's Cost and Performance," *Time,* February 28, 2012, http://nation.time.com/2012/02/28/2-the-mq-9s-cost-and-performance.

12. "New 24-Hour Endurance Hybrid Drone Developed for Monitoring and Inspection," *Unmanned Systems News*, December 12, 2016, http://www. unmannedsystemstechnology.com/2016/12/defiant-labs-announces-new-dx-3-drone-for-monitoring-inspection.

13. "Flexrotor Specifications," http://aerovel.com/flexrotor/.

14. Vanilla Aircraft VA001, https://www.militaryfactory.com/aircraft/detail. asp?aircraft_id=1917.

15. Caroline Rees, "Aerialtronics Announces New AI-Driven Camera for Drones," *Unmanned Systems Technology*, February 19, 2018, http://www. unmannedsystemstechnology.com/2018/02/aerialtronics-announces-new-ai-driven-camera-drones/.

16. "Lightweight hyperspectral imagers bring sophisticated imaging capability to drones," *ScienceDaily*, February 28, 2018, https://www. sciencedaily.com/releases/2018/02/180228112404.htm.

17. John Mannes, "Google releases new Tensor Flow Object Detection API," *TechCrunch*, June 16, 2017, https://techcrunch.com/2017/06/16/object-detection-api/.

18. Patrick Tucker, "A Criminal Gang Used a Drone Swarm To Obstruct an FBI Hostage Raid," *DefenseOne*, May 3, 2018, https://www.defenseone. com/technology/2018/05/criminal-gang-used-drone-swarm-obstruct-fbi-raid/147956/.

19. "Zephyr, the High Altitude Pseudo-Satellite," *Airbus Defence & Space*, http://www.airbus.com/defence/uav/zephyr.html?cid=psearchdef__global__us-en__br__google__ao-sem|airbusdefence-zephyr|bmm__TF.

20. Ibid.

21. Tyler Rogoway, "More Details Emerge On Kratos' Optionally Expendable Air Combat Drones," *The Warzone*, February 7, 2017, http://www.thedrive. com/the-war-zone/7449/more-details-on-kratos-optionally-expendable-air-combat-drones-emerge.

22. Aaron Gregg, "Robotic wingmen may fly next to fighter jets," *Washington Post*, June 15, 2017, A16.

23. Mike Hanlon, "Kratos to show low-cost Valkyrie and Mako 'wingman' combat drones," *New Atlas*, June 15, 2017, https://newatlas.com/kratos-valkyrie-mako-combat-drones-paris/50044/.

24. Sofia Bledsoe, "PEO workers receive Army acquisition awards," U.S. Army, May 11, 2017, https://www.army.mil/article/148323/PEO_workers_receive_Army_acquisition_awards/.

25. John Beck, "ISIL ramps up fight with weaponised drones," *Al Jazeera*, January 3, 2017, http://www.aljazeera.com/indepth/features/2016/12/isil-

ramps-fight-weaponised-drones-161231130818470.html?utm_source=
Sailthru&utm_medium=email&utm_campaign=Early+Bird+Brief+01.04
.2017&utm_term=Editorial+-+Early+Bird+Brief.

26. Tyler Rogoway, "ISIS Drone Dropping Bomblet On Abrams Tanks Is
A Sign of What's To Come," *The Warzone*, January 26, 2017, http://
www.thedrive.com/the-war-zone/7155/isis-drone-dropping-bomblet-on-
abrams-tank-is-a-sign-of-whats-to-come.

27. Eric Schmitt, "Papers Offer a Peak at ISIS's Drones, Lethal and Largely
Off-the-Shelf," *New York Times*, January 31, 2017, https://www.nytimes.
com/2017/01/31/world/middleeast/isis-drone-documents.html?_r=1.

28. Stu Robarts, "It's Take-Off for Amazon's Drone Delivery Service,"
New Atlas, December 14, 2016, http://newatlas.com/amazon-prime-air-
uk-trial-first-delivery/46960/?utm_source=Gizmag+Subscribers&utm_
campaign=a7f7e60d44-UA-2235360-4&utm_medium=email&utm_term=
0_65b67362bd-a7f7e60d44-92283385.

29. Jack Stewart, "The US Doesn't Want Drone Deliveries—So Amazon Took
Them to England," *Wired*, December 14, 2016, https://www.wired.com/
2016/12/us-doesnt-want-drone-deliveries-amazon-took-england.

30. Lora Kolodny and Darren Weaver, "These drones can haul a 20-pound
load for 500 miles and land on a moving target," CNBC, May 26, 2018,
https://www.cnbc.com/2018/05/26/volans-i-drones-can-haul-cargo-for-
500-miles-and-land-on-a-moving-ship.html.

31. Ron Struthers, "Drone Delivery Canada Leaps Ahead Of Amazon Prime
Air And Google Wing," *Seeking Alpha*, April 3, 2019, https://seekingalpha.
com/article/4252580-drone-delivery-canada-leaps-ahead-amazon-prime-
air-google-wing?page=4.

32. "FAA to team with local, state, and tribal governments and
companies to develop safe drone operations," *KurzweilAI*, May 9,
2018, http://www.kurzweilai.net/faa-to-team-with-local-state-and-tribal-
governments-and-companies-to-develop-safe-drone-operations?utm_
source=KurzweilAI+Weekly+Newsletter&utm_campaign=2f10ce3011-
UA-946742-1&utm_medium=email&utm_term=0_147a5a48c1-2f10ce30
11-282022973.

33. Martyn Wingrove, "Ferries could be remotely operated from shore,"
Passenger Technology, January 11, 2018, http://www.passengership.info/
news/view,ferries-could-be-remotely-operated-from-shore_50416.htm.

34. "Comparison of U.S. and Foreign-flag Operating Costs," U.S. Department
of Transportation Maritime Administration, September 2011, https://

www.marad.dot.gov/wp-content/uploads/pdf/Comparison_of_US_and_
Foreign_Flag_Operating_Costs.pdf, p. 5.

35. Ari Daniel Shapiro, "Remotely Piloted Underwater Glider Crosses the
Atlantic," *IEEE Spectrum*, February 26, 2010, http://spectrum.ieee.org/
robotics/industrial-robots/remotely-piloted-underwater-glider-crosses-
the-atlantic.

36. Alix Willimez, "Autonomous Submarine Drones: Cheap,
Endless Patrolling," *CIMSEC*, June 5, 2014, http://cimsec.org/
autonomous-subarine-drones-cheap-endless-patrolling/11284; Will
Connor, "Underwater Drones Are Multiplying Fast," *Wall
Street Journal*, June 24, 2013, http://www.wsj.com/articles/SBone
hundred01424127887324183204578565460623922952.

37. Kim Geiger, "Inspired by nature—Getting underwater robots to work
together, continuously," *College of Engineering Blog*, December 4,
2017, https://blogs.mtu.edu/engineering/2017/12/04/inspired-by-nature-
getting-underwater-robots-to-work-together-continuously/.

38. Dan Lamothe, "Meet Sea Hunter, the 130-Foot Unmanned Vessel the Navy
Wants to Hunt Submarines," *Washington Post*, April 8, 2016, https://www.
washingtonpost.com/news/checkpoint/wp/2016/04/08/meet-sea-hunter-
the-130-foot-unmanned-vessel-the-navy-wants-to-hunt-submarines/?
utm_term=.fd538f3ba6b4.

39. Megan Eckstein, "Navy Betting Big on Unmanned Warships Defining
Future of the Fleet," *USNI News*, April 8, 2019, https://news.usni.org/
2019/04/08/navy-betting-big-on-unmanned-warships-defining-future-
of-the-fleet?utm_source=USNI+News&utm_campaign=f55aabdfe9-
USNI_NEWS_DAILY&utm_medium=email&utm_term=0_0dd4a1450b-
f55aabdfe9-230443725&mc_cid=f55aabdfe9&mc_eid=e0ac270dd4.

40. David Smalley, "LOCUST: Autonomous Swarming UAVs fly into the
future," Office of Naval Research, April 14, 2015, http://www.onr.navy.
mil/Media-Center/Press-Releases/2015/LOCUST-low-cost-UAV-swarm-
ONR.aspx.

41. David Smalley, "The Future Is Now: Navy's Autonomous Swarmboats
can Overwhelm Adversaries," Office of Naval Research, http://www.onr.
navy.mil/Media-Center/Press-Releases/2014/autonomous-swarm-boat-
unmanned-caracas.aspx.

42. "U.S. military leaders consider $3 billion investment for unmanned
underwater vehicles (UUVs)," *Military and Aerospace Electronics*,
December 5, 2017, http://www.militaryaerospace.com/articles/pt/2016

/11/u-s-military-leaders-consider-3-billion-investment-for-unmanned-underwater-vehicles-uuvs.html.

43. Megan Eckstein, "Navy, Marines Testing Unmanned Systems to Learn Integration Lessons," *U.S. Naval Institute News,* April 12, 2018, https://news.usni.org/2018/04/12/navy-marines-testing-unmanned-systems-learn-integration-lessons?utm_source=USNI+News&utm_campaign=c26b29009d-USNI_NEWS_DAILY&utm_medium=email&utm_term=0_0 dd4a1450b-c26b29009d-230443725&mc_cid=c26b29009d&mc_eid=e0ac2 70dd4.

44. Staff Writers, "Unmanned Underwater Vehicle turns into Unmanned Aerial Vehicle," *Space Daily,* February 7, 2017, http://www.spacedaily.com/reports/Unmanned_Underwater_Vehicle_turns_into_Unmanned_Aerial_Vehicle_999.html.

45. Rob Wittman, "US Navy's unmanned vehicle efforts are the answer to deterring adversaries," *DefenseNews,* April 26, 2018, https://www.defensenews.com/unmanned/2018/04/26/us-navys-unmanned-vehicle-efforts-are-the-answer-to-deterring-adversaries/.

46. David B. Larter, "The US Navy will hit a milestone ship count in 2020; pours money into sailors, subs and unmanned tech," *DefenseNews,* March 12, 2019, https://www.defensenews.com/naval/2019/03/12/the-us-navy-will-hit-a-milestone-ship-count-in-2020-pours-money-into-sailors-subs-and-unmanned-tech/.

47. Jeffrey Lin and P. W. Singer, "The Great Underwater Wall of Robots," *Popular Science,* June 22, 2016, http://www.popsci.com/great-underwater-wall-robots-chinese-exhibit-shows-off-sea-drones.

48. Alice Klein, "Cattle-Herding Robot Swagbot Makes Debut on Australian Farms," *New Scientist,* July 12, 2016, https://www.newscientist.com/article/2097004-cattle-herding-robot-swagbot-makes-debut-on-australian-farms.

49. Tom Simonite, "Mining 24 Hours a Day with Robots," *MIT Technology Review,* December 28, 2016, https://www.technologyreview.com/s/6031 70/mining-24-hours-a-day-with-robots.

50. "Rio Tinto achieves first delivery of iron ore with world's largest robot," Rio Tinto, July 13, 2018, https://www.riotinto.com/media/media-releases-237_25824.aspx.

51. Elizabeth Woyke, "FedEx Bets on Automation as It Prepares to Fend off Uber and Amazon," *MIT Technology Review,* February 3, 2017, https://www.technologyreview.com/s/602896/fedex-bets-on-automation-as-it-prepares-to-fend-off-uber-and-amazon.

52. "Fire Ant EFP Tank Killer," *YouTube,* January 5, 2013, https://www.youtube.com/watch?v=JNboWkzKGkg.

53. Noah Shachtman, "24 More Armed Robots Sentries for Base Patrol," *Wired,* February 28, 2008, https://www.wired.com/2008/02/army-gets-more.

54. David Hambling, "Armed Russian robocops to defend missile bases," *New Scientist,* April 23, 2014, https://www.newscientist.com/article/mg2 2229664-400-armed-russian-robocops-to-defend-missile-bases/.

55. Mark Prigg, "Who goes there? Samsung unveils robot sentry that can kill from two miles away," *Daily Mail,* September 15, 2015, http://www.dailymail.co.uk/sciencetech/article-2756847/Who-goes-Samsung-reveals-robot-sentry-set-eye-North-Korea.html.

56. Adam Rawnsley and Austin Bodetti, "The Warbot Builders of the Middle East Spill Their Secrets," *Wired,* February 2, 2017, https://www.wired.com/2017/02/warbot-builders-middle-east-spill-secrets.

57. Sean Rayment, "Russia to deploy drone tank," *Times,* January 8, 2017, http://www.thetimes.co.uk/article/russia-to-deploy-tank-drone-lst20 jwzq.

58. Daniel Brown, "Russia's Uran-9 robot tank reportedly performed horribly in Syria," *Business Insider,* July 9, 2018, https://www.businessinsider.com/russias-uran-9-robot-tank-performed-horribly-in-syria-2018-7.

59. "Global Smart Commercial Drone Market Size, Share & Industry Expected to Reach 179600 Million US$ by 2025," *Reuters,* Nover 14, 2018, https://www.reuters.com/brandfeatures/venture-capital/article?id=62679.

60. Alex Davies, "The Marines' Self-Flying Chopper Survives a Three-Year Tour," *Wired,* July 30, 2104, https://www.wired.com/2014/07/kmax-autonomous-helicopter/.

61. Evan Ackerman and Celia Gorman, "A Qualcomm Processor in This Stock Android Phone Is Powerful Enough to Autonomously Fly This Robot," *IEEE Spectrum,* April 9, 2015, http://spectrum.ieee.org/video/robotics/aerial-robots/this-drone-uses-a-smartphone-for-a-brain.

62. Brian Wang, "Quantum Assisted GPS Would Be One Thousand Times More Accurate Than Any Existing GPS and Other High Potential DARPA Projects," *nextBIGFuture,* May 23, 2014, http://www.nextbigfuture.com/2014/05/quantum-assisted-gps-would-be-one.html.

63. Jonathan O'Callaghan, "Could a 'quantum compass' replace GPS? British military develops system to navigate WITHOUT using satellites," *Daily Mail,* May 15, 2014, http://www.dailymail.co.uk/sciencetech/article-262 9088/MoD-quantum-compass-GPS-without-satellites.html.

64. "Agricultural UAV Drones: Photos—Multi-Spectral Camera," Homeland Surveillance & Electronics LLC, http://www.agricultureuavs.com/photos_multispectral_camera.htm.
65. "This app lets autonomous video drones with facial recognition target persons," *KurzweilAI,* November 15, 2015, http://www.kurzweilai.net/this-app-lets-autonomous-video-drones-with-facial-recognition-target-persons.
66. "The 7 Best Follow You Drones – [2019] Follow Me Drone Review." *DroneEnthusiast,* May 30, 2019, https://www.dronethusiast.com/drones-that-follow-you/.
67. Matt Rosenberg and John Markoff, "The Pentagon's 'Terminator Conundrum': Robots That Could Kill on Their Own," October 25, 2016, https://www.nytimes.com/2016/10/26/us/pentagon-artificial-intelligence-terminator.html?_r=2.
68. Andrew Rosenblum, "Air Force Tests IBM's Brain-Inspired Chip as an Aerial Tank Spotter," *MIT Technology Review,* January 11, 2017, https://www.technologyreview.com/s/603335/air-force-tests-ibms-brain-inspired-chip-as-an-aerial-tank-spotter/?utm_source=MIT+TR+Newsletters&utm_campaign=69627754d1-The_Download&utm_medium=email&utm_term=0_997ed6f472–69627754d1–154257029.
69. Kris Osborn, "Air Force Developing Swarms of Mini-Drones," *Military.com,* May 27, 2015, http://defensetech.org/2015/05/27/air-force-developing-swarms-of-mini-drones.
70. Victoria Woollostan, "Cheap Drones Are Coming! Researchers Successfully Build and Fly a Low-Cost 3D Printed DISPOSABLE Aircraft," *Daily Mail,* March 28, 2014, http://www.dailymail.co.uk/sciencetech/article-2591533/Cheap-3D-printed-drones-coming-Researchers-successfully-build-fly-low-cost-DISPOSABLE-aircraft.html.
71. Jordan Golson, "A Military-Grade Drone That Can Be Printed Anywhere," *Wired,* September 16, 2014, http://www.wired.com/2014/09/military-grade-drone-can-printed-anywhere.
72. Nick Lavars, "Cardboard delivery drone has a one-way ticket," *New Atlas,* January 18, 2017, http://newatlas.com/cardboard-delivery-drone/47419.
73. David Szondy, "Autonomous, unmanned swarmboats secure harbor approaches for US Navy," *New Atlas,* December 15, 2016, http://newatlas.com/us-navy-autonomous-swarmboats-demonstration/46965/?utm_source=Gizmag+Subscribers&utm_campaign=a7f7e60d44-UA-2235360–4&utm_medium=email&utm_term=0_65b67362bd-a7f7e60d44–92283385.

74. "UAV/UCAV—Harpy," Chinese Military Aviation, http://chinese-military-aviation.blogspot.com/p/uav.html.
75. IAI Harop (Harpy) Disposable Unmanned Aerial Combat Vehicle, *Military Factory*, April 18, 2016, http://www.militaryfactory.com/aircraft/detail.asp?aircraft_id=1288.
76. "Switchblade Overview," Aeroenvironment, https://www.avinc.com/images/uploads/product_docs/Switchblade_Datasheet_032712.pdf.
77. "Hero 30," Uvision, http://uvisionuav.com/portfolio-view/hero-30.
78. Arie Egozi, "Aeronautics producing 'hundreds' of armed Orbiter 1Ks," *FlightGlobal*, March 3, 2017, https://www.flightglobal.com/news/articles/aeronautics-producing-hundreds-of-armed-orbiter-1k-434771.
79. Arie Egozi, "Azerbaijan starts producing Zarba armed UAV," *Flight Global*, January 10, 2017, https://www.flightglobal.com/news/articles/azerbaijan-starts-producing-zarba-armed-uav-433014.
80. "Misiewicz: 1000 Attack Drones for the Polish Army in 2017," *Defense24*, December 5, 2016, http://www.defence24.com/503694,misiewicz-one hundred0-attack-drones-for-the-polish-army-in-2017.
81. "Polish Ministry of Defence: 16 Kruk Attack Helicopters and 200 UAV Systems—To Be Acquired before 2022," *Defense24*, December 2, 2016, http://www.defence24.com/502668,polish-ministry-of-defence-16-kruk-attack-helicopters-and-200-uav-systems-to-be-acquired-before-2022.
82. "Macierewicz: Thousands of UAV Systems for the Territorial Defence Component and for the Operational Units of the Polish Army," *Defence24*, November 14, 2016, http://www.defence24.com/488869,macierewicz-thousands-of-uav-systems-for-the-territorial-defence-component-and-for-the-operational-units-of-the-polish-army.
83. Kyle Mizokami, "Another Ukrainian Ammo Dump Goes Up in Massive Explosion," *Popular Mechanics*, September 27, 2017, https://www.popularmechanics.com/military/weapons/news/a28412/ukrainian-ammo-dump-explosion/.
84. "Service Academies Swarm Challenge Pushes the Boundaries of Autonomous Swarm Capabilities," DARPA, May 11, 2017, https://www.darpa.mil/news-events/2017-05-11.
85. Andrew Liptak, "The US Air Force has a new weapon called THOR that can take out swarms of drones," *The Verge*, June 21, 2019, https://www.theverge.com/2019/6/21/18701267/us-air-force-thor-new-weapon-drone-swarms.

86. Phil Stewart, "Exclusive: U.S.-supplied drones disappoint Ukraine at the front lines," *Reuters,* December 22, 2016, http://www.reuters.com/article/us-usa-ukraine-drones-exclusive-idUSKBN14A26D.
87. "Continental disconnect: Mobile phones are transforming Africa," *Economist,* December 10–16, 2016, 48.
88. "What Are SmallSats and CubeSats?" NASA, February 26, 2015, https://www.nasa.gov/content/what-are-smallsats-and-cubesats.
89. Paolo Quaranta, "Nanosatellites: Low-Cost Future Constellations," *Military Technology* 40, no. 2 (2016): 66.
90. Nanosatellite & Cubesat Database, http://www.nanosats.eu.
91. Robinson Meyer, "Google Remakes the Satellite Business, by Leaving It," *Atlantic,* February 7, 2017, https://www.theatlantic.com/technology/archive/2017/02/google-gets-out-of-the-satellite-business/515841.
92. Bradley Hope, "Investors Can Get an Eye in the Sky," *Wall Street Journal,* August 15, 2016, C1.
93. "Orbital ecosystem," *Economist,* June 15–21, 2019, 71.
94. Kent Leka, "Viasat will enable near-instant satellite images and video delivered anywhere," Viasat, May 15, 2018, https://corpblog.viasat.com/viasat-will-enable-near-instant-satellite-images-and-video-delivered-anywhere/.
95. SpyMeSat, https://spymesat.com/.
96. Jay Menon, "India Launches Record 104 Satellites On One Mission," *Aviation Week & Space Technology,* February 22, 2017, http://aviationweek.com/commercializing-space/india-launches-record-104-satellites-one-mission.
97. Hanneke Weitering, "Watch SpaceX Launch 64 Satellites Into Orbit on a Really Used Rocket Today!" *Space.com,* December 3, 2018, https://www.space.com/42604-spacex-falcon9-ssoa-launch-webcast.html.
98. Mike Wall, "Rocket Lab Launches 13 Cubesats on 1st Mission for NASA," *Space.com,* December 16, 2018, https://www.space.com/42714-rocket-lab-launches-cubesats-nasa.html.
99. Sandra Erwin, "In-orbit services poised to become big business," *Space News,* June 10, 2018, https://spacenews.com/in-orbit-services-poised-to-become-big-business/.
100. Margot van Loon, Dr. Larry Wortzel, and Dr. Mark B. Schneider, "Defense Technology Program Brief: Hypersonic Weapons," American Foreign Policy Council, May 2019, 5.
101. "Hypersonic boom," *Economist,* April 6–12, 2019, 67–69.

102. David Axe, "China's Navy Railgun Is Out for Sea Trials. Here's Why It's a Threat to the U.S. Navy," *National Interest,* January 6, 2019, https://nationalinterest.org/blog/buzz/chinas-navy-railgun-out-sea-trials-heres-why-it%E2%80%99s-threat-us-navy-40812.

103. Sam Legrone, "Navy Quietly Fires 20 Hyper Velocity Projectiles Through Destroyer's Deckgun," *USNI News,* January 8, 2019, https://news.usni.org/2019/01/08/navy-quietly-fires-20-hyper-velocity-projectiles-destroyers-deckgun.

CHAPTER 6

TACTICAL AND OPERATIONAL IMPLICATIONS

This chapter will examine the impact that the convergence of technology will have on warfare in each domain and the operational implications, concluding with a discussion of how the character of war will change over the next one to two decades.

TACTICAL IMPACT

The fourth industrial revolution will have major tactical impacts on each of the different domains of combat—and more importantly on cross-domain operations.

Ground Domain

Offense clearly dominated the conventional phases of Operations *Iraqi Freedom*. However, the 2006 Israeli-Hezbollah Summer War showed that, under the right conditions, well-trained, determined irregular forces armed with advanced anti-tank weapons could make the defense much more formidable. Since then, defensive conventional ground warfare has become both deadlier and cheaper. Direct-fire gunnery systems have improved, as have wire-guided and fire-and-forget missile systems. All are proliferating but slowly because they are very expensive. U.S. artillery can provide precision fire with either the M712 Copperhead laser guided round or the M982 Excaliber GPS guided round, but they cost about $70,000 each.[1] Looking for a cheaper precision weapon, the U.S. Army issued a contract in 2015 for a new $10,000 fuze that makes any 155mm artillery round a precision weapon.[2] And artillery is only one element of the growing global capability of guided rockets, artillery, mortars, and missiles (GRAMM) systems.

To bring truly affordable mass precision to the battlefield, the ground forces may have to turn to inexpensive drones. For less than the price of a precision fuze, commercially available autonomous drones already provide greater range than artillery without artillery's large logistics and training tails. Such drones, deployed in large numbers, will provide a particularly nasty challenge for ground forces. And because they fly, rather than move along the ground, the AI is simpler and the range longer. Further, if packaged in standard commercial containers or trucks, they will be very difficult to identify prior to launch so counterbattery fire will be ineffective. The key is to think of and develop some drones as expendable rounds of ammunition.

When deployed widely, drones will have a major impact on how U.S. ground forces operate. Even light forces are dependent on vehicles and helicopters that are vulnerable to small drones. As early as 2013, a drone hobbyist tracked and closed with moving vehicles under conditions very similar to those needed to engage a military convoy. He was filming his friends racing off-road vehicles. The only thing his drone lacked to be a hunter was an EFP mounted alongside his GoPro camera. Veterans of Iraq and Afghanistan will find the video chilling.[3]

When one combines simple drones, additive manufacturing, autonomous navigation and target identification, what ground forces may have to confront is thousands or even tens of thousands of smart drones. Although some may think this is impractical, a Switchblade UAV is small enough that more than five hundred could be mounted on a single five-ton truck or 150 on a single HMMWV. Both U.S. and international manufacturers have already demonstrated the ability to produce fire and forget drones.

These expendable strike drones are only one element of the drone force needed for ground combat. Reconnaissance, surveillance, electronic warfare, and logistics aerial drones will also become an integral part of ground forces. Defenders will also use mines, GRAMM fires, and other precision weapons to create a deep zone denied to movement by either side. Consider how difficult it will be to move in an area where hundreds of autonomous, loitering drones are hunting.

Today, ground forces are in the first stage of the assistant to partner to replacement process. Infantry squads are fielding small drones as assistants and working out the practical matters of employing them effectively. As drones become partners, different tactical concepts will evolve. Ground forces will have to work out how they coordinate the maneuver and fire of these disparate elements even as the drones achieve higher levels of autonomy and much longer ranges. Today, the infantry squad could have a strike drone with a range of thirty miles. Division commanders may soon have drones and cruise missiles with a range of one thousand miles. Joint doctrine will have to adjust if ground forces control weapons that exceed the range of fighter bombers.

The final step—replacement—will require careful consideration of what ground-combat functions can be allocated to autonomous drones. The AI limitations of such autonomous systems indicate they will be better at conventional conflict than unconventional conflict where determining human intention is much more problematic. This is an area that requires extensive wargaming, computer simulation, field experiments, and air-ground coordination.

Sea Domain

At sea, it will soon be possible to pit very large numbers of relatively cheap drones, cruise, and ballistic missiles against the few and exquisite platforms of the U.S. Navy. Studies by the Navy's Assessment Division indicate that in naval combat the first salvo wins.[4] Although winning the first salvo works against another conventional fleet, it is less applicable for a fleet fighting a land-based force. If the ground force chooses to use launchers that look like standard shipping containers, it can hide among the thousands of such containers found in most urban and even many rural areas. Even if it uses standard military vehicles, the ground force can hide in garages, barns, tunnels, or hundreds of other manmade or natural features that provide concealment from observation—and sometimes protection from weapons. The ground force will not have to emit any signal until it fires. In contrast, ships and aircraft will create signatures by moving. This both provides surprise for the ground forces and makes it much more difficult to find and suppress the ground force's weapons.

Using a similar concept, the Joint Force could deploy a widely dispersed mix of warships, missile armed merchant ships, and ground forces. By having more weapons dispersed among similar commercial ships and in complex littoral terrain, this force will have a much higher survivability against a first salvo than a conventional navy. The good news is the U.S. Navy's Distributed Lethality ("If it floats, it fights") seeks to upgrade the current surface fleet's combat power.[5] The Navy is also exploring the concept of missile-armed merchant ships.[6]

Russia, China, and Israel have already produced containerized cruise missiles, which can provide a wide variety of platform with ship-killing weapons. Further, using commercial ships can dramatically reduce the cost of putting a lethal force to sea. Container ships could be converted to warships by the addition of containerized weapons and a simple command-and-control system. In late 2018, new merchant ships were available for $50 million.[7] Even if it cost $75 million to convert and add forty containerized missiles, the $125 million total is a fraction of the

$400 million purchase price of a Littoral Combat Ship (LCS) hull.[8] Rather than the one-hundred-sailor LCS crew, a missile-equipped container ship would need fewer than forty sailors. The ship would be expendable with the crew abandoning ship if it takes a serious hit—much like the LCS. Unlike the LCS, container ships are very strongly built due to the requirement to resist hogging and sagging of their long hulls in heavy seas. Many even have double hulls. Most important, this much more survivable and cheaper class of ship could add a vast number of missiles to the fleet.

In addition to increasingly capable cruise missiles, vertical takeoff and landing drones like the *Valkyrie* mean almost any seagoing vessel can be a small aircraft carrier. Highly capable drones will provide the U.S. Navy with great advantages. Drones do not have to carry weapons large enough to sink a ship to achieve a mission kill. A drone detonating against an aircraft on the deck of a carrier or firing a fragmentation charge against an Aegis's phased array radar will significantly degrade that platform's capabilities. In addition, many U.S. warships carry weapons in box launchers topside. These both provide easily identifiable target points and great potential for secondary explosions. Aircraft carriers may well be the most vulnerable. The fires on the *USS Oriskany, USS Forrestal,* and the *USS Enterprise* all demonstrate that a small explosive on a deck full of armed, fueled aircraft can result in a carrier being put out of action for weeks to months.

Undersea weapons pose an even greater challenge to navies. China, Vietnam, Japan, South Korea, Australia, and Indonesia are all upgrading their submarine forces. However, a submarine force is expensive, complex, and difficult to operate. The wide array of commercial unmanned underwater vehicles may provide a much cheaper alternative. If developed as weapons systems, they could dramatically change naval combat. Obviously, swarms of autonomous drones can threaten any naval force trying to project power ashore. For the cost of one *Virginia*-class submarine, a nation could purchase 170,000 commercial glider drones.[9] [10] Armed oceanic gliders will cost more, but even at ten times the price they can provide a cheap, naval swarm. Of more importance, the skills and organization needed to build and employ a glider are orders of magnitude less than those needed for a submarine force.

Currently unable to intercept ships underway, gliders can navigate to a harbor entrance or other maritime chokepoint. With the right warhead and fuze, they could wait for a specific class of ship before attacking. Defensive minefields could even be launched from the beach simply by driving truckloads of these mines to the shore and having people carry each glider to the water and push it out.

Mines have the distinction of being the only weapon that has denied the U.S. Navy freedom of the seas since World War II. Mines defeated a U.S. amphibious assault at Wonson, Korea, in October 1950. Not much changed in forty years. During Operation Desert Storm, the U.S. Navy was unable to maneuver in northern Arabian Gulf because the Iraqis had sown more than 1,300 mines[11]—and these were simple moored and contact mines.

Mines have become more difficult to find and much better at target discrimination. They have sensors which can use acoustic, magnetic, and other signals to attack a specific type of ship.[12] Nor does a ship have to actually run over a sea mine in order to sustain damage. New mines can attack from a distance. The Chinese are selling the EM-52,

> a multiple-influence (acoustic, magnetic, pressure) rocket-propelled straight-rising mine, armed with a 600-pound high-explosive warhead that can be deployed by surface vessels in waters as deep as 600 feet.[13]

Drones and mines can also be used against commerce. Although these systems cannot stop trade, damaging a few ships will may cause maritime insurance rates to be prohibitively expensive thus forcing commercial ships to stay out of the threatened seas. To date, no nation is capable of rapidly clearing smart mines with a high degree of confidence. In short, mines provide another major advantage to the defense.

The arrival of large numbers of autonomous air and sea drones that are relatively cheap, will drastically change war at sea. U.S. and Allied navies are already working through the assist, partner, and replacement process. The key is to conduct rigorous and ruthless wargames to examine how a near-peer competitor will use large numbers of cruise missiles and autonomous drones as well as a limited number of hypervelocity missiles. The wargames must also provide realistic evaluations of submarine capabilities against U.S. carriers. Despite the fact that diesel submarines have "sunk" aircraft carriers ten times in exercises over the last decade, the Navy still builds its force around its very limited number of fleet carriers.[14]

Finally, hypervelocity missiles will make major platforms extremely vulnerable to destruction by a single hit. Games and exercises must explore new mixes of ships and weapons to sustain the U.S. Navy's combat power during this difficult period of transition. In particular, they must look at how the Navy can distribute capabilities over more platforms at sea, in the air, undersea, and even ashore so that its primary combat power cannot be eliminate by a few dozen hits.

Air Domain

The fourth industrial revolution presents both enormous opportunities and challenges in the air domain. The rapid advances in 3D printing, new materials, and AI in particular will assist in developing hyper-velocity missiles and perhaps new manned aircraft. But like all major weapons procurement projects, these will take years—and, if the F-35 is a model, perhaps decades to bring into full service. The revolution will present two enormous challenges on a much shorter timeline—how to protect critical high-demand, low-density assets and how to protect aircraft at their bed-down sites.

Clearly, the Chinese see U.S. enablers as a critical vulnerability and have dedicated major resources to crippling American airpower by defeating the enablers with long-range, air-to-air missiles. Prudent planners must assume they will also experiment with anti-aircraft missiles in shipping containers. Mounted on a wide variety of commercial ships, these could ambush tankers en route to the fight. Without tanker support, the short-range F-35s are rendered impotent in the Pacific.

Although building its own fourth- and fifth-generation fighters, China sees another way of defeating America's advanced aircraft, which is to destroy them on the ground. It is working very hard to extend its cruise- and ballistic-missile ranges to force the United States to base its enablers and fighters so far from China's shore that they are no longer a threat. The Center for New American Security recently published a study that indicated in the first hours of a conflict a Chinese first strike on U.S. facilities in Japan could heavily damage:

> —Almost every major fixed headquarters and logistical facility struck with key headquarters struck within the first minute of the conflict

> —Almost every U.S. ship in port in Japan

> —Every runway and runway-length taxiway at all major U.S. air bases in Japan

> —More than two hundred U.S. aircraft trapped on the ground.[15]

The study did not examine the Chinese potential for an attack on Guam. However, China just announced the activation of a brigade of twenty-two DF-26 missile launchers that can range bases on Guam.[16] The study also did not consider Chinese use of any of its hundreds of long-range drones in the initial attack. And if China develops hypervelocity-boost glide missiles, the airfields of Guam can be deeply crated.

The F-35A, which will be the mainstay of U.S. fighter strength in the next decade, has a range of only eight hundred statute miles. An opponent does not have to challenge it in the air. Instead he can send hundreds of drones after each base to destroy these advanced aircraft on the ground. Even if the aircraft are protected by shelters, radars, fuel systems, and ammunition dumps will be highly vulnerable. Currently, range is a problem for many cheap drones. However, more expensive ones, such as the Aerovel Flexrotor has a range of 1,500 miles, the DX-3 nine hundred miles, the Harop over six hundred miles, and numerous other drones are exceeding five hundred miles.

Destroying air bases will not affect these mobile, vertical-launch drones, which can hide easily in urban or most rural terrain. Even more alarming, they can turn any oceangoing vessel into an aircraft carrier—particularly if they are employed as suicide drones and the ship does not have to be around for recovery. Small ships will carry only a limited number of containers, but it is important to remember that eighteen Harpy drones fit in a single twenty-foot container. Thus, the sheer number of drones could overwhelm defensive systems. Complicating the problem, China has more than 200,000 oceangoing fishing vessels.[17] Obviously, they cannot all be armed and controlled in a coordinated attack, but the sheer number will prevent Allied forces from preempting attacks launched from these platforms.

Although manned aircraft will become vulnerable due to basing issues, a mix of cruise missiles and unmanned vertical take-off and landing (VTOL) aircraft like the QX-222 could free allied airpower from airfields and thus dramatically improve their survivability. For two million dollars, the QX-222 will be able to deliver ordnance out to 1,500 miles and potentially conduct multiple missions.

Cruise missiles deliver a larger payload, and their cost may decrease significantly. Lockheed expects to be able to cut the cost of two new satellites by forty percent using additive manufacturing.[18] If the Department of Defense (DoD) can obtain similar cost savings on cruise missiles, Tomahawk Land Attack Missiles could cost about $1 million each. These missiles carry a thousand-pound warhead out to a thousand miles.[19]

Having withdrawn from the 1987 Intermediate Range Nuclear Forces Treaty, the United States can now develop land based, long-range cruise missiles to augment its existing sea-based capability.

Although somewhat expensive, missiles such as these can provide long-range heavy-strike capabilities—particularly if the warhead uses nano-explosives. The combination of cheap drones and much more capable cruise missiles may offer small- and medium-sized states anti-access/area-denial (A2/AD) and precision, long-range strike capabilities. The United States could develop them as a cheaper but much more robust capability than the B-21. The United States can no longer assume that its domestic air bases will be sanctuaries. Kaliber-class cruise missiles fired from a merchant ship in the Gulf of Mexico range most U.S. bomber bases. In short, the capability to cheaply destroy the B-21s on the ground exists today even though the B-21 could well be a decade away from operational capability.

Airpower is facing enormous change. Relatively cheap, autonomous drones and somewhat more expensive but more capable cruise and ballistic missiles and, potentially, hypervelocity missiles are rendering manned aircraft obsolete. There is currently no way to defend airbases and aircraft carriers against this new generation of weapons. Nor can current or envisioned systems find and attack these mobile systems to preempt them. Drones are beginning to assume various roles in the air domain, but airmen must embrace them and work rapidly to move them from their current status as partners to that of replacements.

Space Domain

In space, the advent of micro and cube satellites, paired with commercial-launch platforms, will allow a middle power to develop an effective space program for surveillance and eventually attack of other space assets. Surveillance services are already being provided by commercial firms and, if cubesat capabilities continue to improve and launch costs decline, even small states will be able to afford a proprietary surveillance system.

Attack in space is a more difficult proposition but, as noted earlier, Orbital ATK plans to launch a satellite to provide in-orbit repair services to other satellites in 2019.[20] The possibility of severe degradation of space is a major driver of the U.S. effort to develop rapid replacement options for space capabilities.

Because China has demonstrated the ability to use both kinetic and soft kill on satellites, one must assume the United States is developing similar capabilities. This evinces a clear understanding that any major conflict will involve fighting in space to defend one's own assets. Resilience is also required. A combination of small satellites, long-endurance solar-powered drones, and perhaps even balloons can mitigate the loss of current space assets and is being actively explored by the United States. It is good news that the U.S. Air Force is shifting the emphasis of Space Command from that of a service provider to that of a warfighting command.[21]

Thus, conflict will occur *in* space as each side protects its own assets while trying to degrade its opponents. It remains an open question as to whether space assets will be used to attack targets on the earth.

Cyber Domain

Any detailed discussion concerning the software or technical aspects of cyber conflict would have to be classified. However, there is a wealth of information about cyberattacks in open-source literature. From the "I love you" worm that introduced the world to cyberattacks in 2000 to the Stuxnet virus used against Iranian centrifuges to the Sony hack to Russian attacks on the Ukrainian power system to the more powerful NotPetya malware, they have spanned the globe. Attacks have been conducted by individual hackers, criminal groups, and states. Results have varied from causing physical damage to a system to quietly stealing everything from personal data to intellectual property to vast amounts of money.

In March 2018, the U.S. government protested that Russian state hackers had been in U.S. energy, manufacturing, nuclear, water, and aviation systems for two years.[22] Clearly, advanced attacks represent a real threat to infrastructure. However, to date, cyber has been most effective for theft, gathering intelligence, and disrupting systems temporarily.

Not surprisingly, criminal gangs pioneered cyber theft. As early as 2015, Kaspersky Labs reported that an international cybercriminal gang had succeeded in stealing over $1 billion from more than one hundred banks around the world.[23] North Korea seems to have pioneered cybertheft to fund its government, stealing hundreds of millions in the last few years.[24] Cybercrime will continue to be a major driver of advances in cyberattack methods for the simple reason that enormous profits will attract some of the best minds in the field. Cybersecurity experts expect that cybercrime will cost the world $6 trillion by 2021—a one-hundred-percent increase since 2015.[25]

China has been at the forefront of cyber espionage. Its cyberespionage teams focused "on the satellite, aerospace, and communications sectors"[26] and enjoyed remarkable success. The Snowden files confirmed that China had penetrated Lockheed Martin's top-secret data on the F-35.[27] The fact that China gained access to decades of technological advancements indicates how powerful a tool cyberespionage is. There is no question that many nations continue to pursue cyberespionage today.

There is also no question that cyberattacks can also cause significant physical damage. As early as 2007, U.S. researchers had successfully destroyed an alternating current generation in its Aurora cyber exercise.[28] But Russia has led the way in using cyberattacks to disrupt enemy infrastructure. It has dedicated significant assets to finding and exploiting vulnerability is industrial control systems.[29]

In response, the United States government is working to develop the offensive and defensive skills needed to deal with cyberattacks. On May 17, 2018, U.S. Cyber Command announced it had reached full operational capability, which meant all 6,800 personnel were aboard and trained. The command is responsible for offensive, defensive, intelligence collection, and analysis globally for the Department of Defense.

In May 2018, the Department of Homeland Security released its strategy for cybersecurity. In September 2018, the White House released the U.S. National Cyber Strategy. Both clearly recognized that cyber defense is much bigger than just the U.S. government. DHS stated that a "core guiding principle underlying the DHS strategy approach is collaboration across the cybersecurity community, including with our partners in the federal government, state and local governments, industry, and the international community."[30]

Even as governments, businesses, and individuals struggle to cope with rising cyberattacks, researchers are making rapid advances in machine learning to provide improved capabilities in attack, defense, and exploitation of information systems.[31] Clearly, advances in AI will fundamentally change cyber warfare as autonomous systems begin to emerge. This is an area in which the U.S. government has been working closely with civilian cyber security firms—and must continue—in order to protect the key infrastructure that is essential to the functioning of almost every economy.

Perhaps the only reassuring aspect of the increasing state-sponsored cyber activity is that it may be reducing the chance of a major surprise. Historically, devastating surprise attacks have usually taken place after a long period of peace when new operational concepts clash for the first time. For over two decades, the Germans worked to create a fluid offensive concept that came to be known as Blitzkreig. For their part, the French concentrated on a firepower intensive defensive concept based on methodical battle. Both sides were convinced their approach was best. The question was not resolved until, after twenty years of peace, the two concepts were tested on the battlefield and the flexible offense won.

In contrast, cyber warfare is constant, global, ongoing, and evolving. The many sides in these contests are constantly sharpening both offensive and defensive skills and testing them against each other. In addition, cyberattacks focused on societies are, by definition, attacking complex adaptive systems. These systems show remarkable resilience and power of recovery. Perhaps that is why that even the best cyber actors (Russia, Israel, and the United States) have achieved relatively modest results despite months or even years of intensive efforts. The ongoing conflict in cyberspace will accelerate as the fourth industrial revolution continues. However, it is virtually impossible to predict if a specific attack will succeed or how long it will remain effective.

One aspect not normally thought about when discussing cyber warfare is the potential for physical attacks on an enemy's cyber capability. When discussing conflict in cyberspace, it is important cross-domain attacks are possible. All networks have nodes in the real world. For instance, satellite downlinks and points where fiber optic networks come ashore are vulnerable. Many cyber-network maps are available in the public domain, so a smart attacker would be able to select nodes to maximize damage. In 2004, Sean Gorman, a college student, successfully mapped the entire U.S. fiber-optic network for his doctoral thesis.[32]

Using a map like this, an enemy could select key nodes to attack. Unlike cyberattacks which have a high degree of uncertainty, physical attacks on known locations can cause more predictable major damage to an opponent's cyber networks. It is also easier to coordinate real-world attacks than to mix cyber and real-world attacks. This is an area ripe for cross-domain exploitation.

Electromagnetic Spectrum
Although not yet officially defined as a domain of warfare by the Pentagon, use of the spectrum is essential to warfare in every other domain. If a force can dominate the spectrum, then it can severely limit or even defeat an enemy's efforts in air, land, sea, space, and even cyber domains. It is pretty obvious that an inability to use the EM spectrum renders most air and sea combat systems inoperable because they rely on sensors to find the enemy and communications links to guide weapons to their targets. With proper and constant training, naval and air forces can operate in emission-controlled environments, but this severely reduces

their capabilities. Land forces can fight without communications but, unless well trained and practiced in maneuver warfare, the result is a series of disconnected local engagements. If an enemy truly dominates the EM spectrum, they can make it extremely difficult to communicate with space assets. And cyber systems often rely on EM communications links, which could be subject to jamming, degradation, or deception.

Although the United States has not yet decided the electromagnetic spectrum is a domain of war, China has made it a key element of its newly organized Strategic Support Force (SSF). The SSF not only integrates space, cyber, information, and electronic warfare (EW) in support of Chinese operations, it also directs advanced research in EW.[33] For its part, its experience in Georgia drove Russia to dedicate millions to updating its EW capabilities. As a result, the Russians have been able to make aggressive use of EW to damage or destroy Ukrainian command networks, as well as jam radios, radars, and GPS signals.[34] They also used EW to develop targeting information for engagement by artillery. General Raymond Thomas noted that Russia has created the most aggressive EW environment in the world in Syria.[35] Clearly, both China and Russia have assigned high priority to operating in this environment.

Perhaps the most important aspects of conflict in the EM spectrum is the need to reduce the vulnerability of other systems to EM interference. One solution will be to create autonomous weapons that once launched do not require any external signals to operate. In fact, they can be sealed and protected from any external energy reaching their critical components. The growing capability of EM weapons remains a closely guarded secret, but the logical conclusion is that it will increase the value of truly autonomous, sealed combat systems.

OPERATIONAL IMPLICATIONS

Technological convergence is driving the "democratization" of military power by providing small states—and even groups—capabilities that used to be the preserve of major powers. This will greatly complicate U.S. responses to various crises. Five factors will have direct impact on the operational level of war: range obsolescence, the loss of immunity to attack, the tactical dominance of defense, the return of mass, and the requirement to mobilize.

Range Obsolescence

Range obsolescence is not a new phenomenon. The battleship is a classic example. A battleship could deliver more firepower faster than a carrier and was much more survivable. But it simply could not get within range of a carrier to deliver its devastating firepower. By 1942, the battleship's lack of range made it irrelevant in most naval fights. Today, the most obvious U.S. systems at risk of range obsolescence are its fighter bombers and thus its carriers.

The fundamental problem is that U.S. tactical aircraft are outranged by hypervelocity, ballistic, and cruise missiles, as well as a growing variety of drones. As you look at figure 9, it is critical to remember these ranges reflect individual aircraft flying point to point. Operational requirements shorten these ranges significantly. The U.S. Naval Institute reports the strike range of the F-18 carrier air wing is currently about 450 nautical miles. With the addition of the MQ-25 Stingray unmanned tanker, the U.S. Navy expects the strike range to be extended only to seven hundred nautical miles and the MQ-25 will not be in service until 2026.[36] The range disparity is starkly illustrated in figure 9.

Some drones can also carry significant payloads. The QX-222 Valkyrie and UTAP–22 Mako each carry five hundred pounds. The Israeli Harop delivers fifty-one pounds. Although the manufacturers do not list payload weights for the Aerovel Flexrotor Mk2 or Defiant Labs DX-3, they can certainly carry an explosively formed penetrator capable of penetrating a half-inch of steel. Such a device, weighing only half a pound, can destroy aircraft on the ground/flight deck or cause secondary explosions at fuel and ammunition dumps. Thus, at a cost of only $200,000 each, the autonomous VTOL Flexrotor or DX-3 could provide affordable, long-range, precision strike.[37]

Figure 9. Ranges of Missiles, Drones, and Aircraft in Nautical Miles.

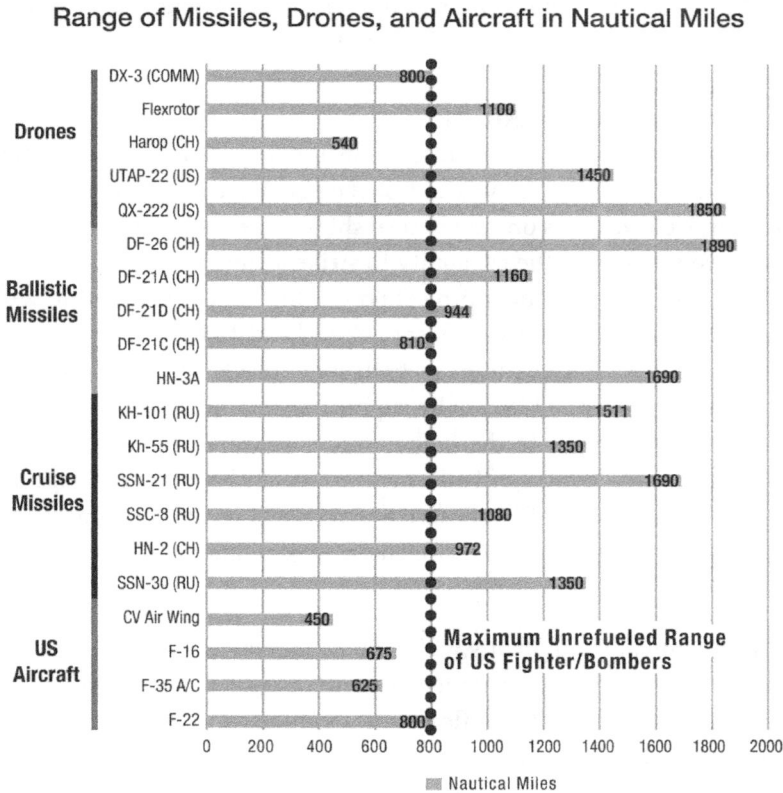

Range of Missiles, Drones, and Aircraft in Nautical Miles

Category	System	Range
Drones	DX-3 (COMM)	800
	Flexrotor	1100
	Harop (CH)	540
	UTAP-22 (US)	1450
	QX-222 (US)	1850
Ballistic Missiles	DF-26 (CH)	1890
	DF-21A (CH)	1160
	DF-21D (CH)	944
	DF-21C (CH)	810
Cruise Missiles	HN-3A	1690
	KH-101 (RU)	1511
	Kh-55 (RU)	1350
	SSN-21 (RU)	1690
	SSC-8 (RU)	1080
	HN-2 (CH)	972
	SSN-30 (RU)	1350
US Aircraft	CV Air Wing	450
	F-16	675
	F-35 A/C	625
	F-22	800

Maximum Unrefueled Range of US Fighter/Bombers

Nautical Miles (0, 200, 400, 600, 800, 1000, 1200, 1400, 1600, 1800, 2000)

Missiles and drones have two other major advantages over manned aircraft. First, many land-based cruise missiles are truck mobile, as are a growing number of drones. Second, they are relatively cheap. Kratos is offering the QX-222 for $2 million a copy or 1/50th the cost of an F-35. The cost advantage actually increases with time. As an unmanned, vertical takeoff and recovery system, the QX-222 not only has minimal monthly training costs and does not require an airfield, but it also does not require a training pipeline for pilots and maintainers and does not have staff-related costs, such as pilot bonuses, retirement income, and healthcare. But the primary advantages for missiles remain range and flexible basing. Today's missiles and drones can reach most U.S. in-theater airfields.

Loss of Immunity to Attack

More and more states, and even some insurgent or terrorist groups, will soon be able to project power out of theater. Very long-range drones, containerized weapons on commercial ships, sea mines, and submersible drones could provide the capability to strike airports and seaports. The United States will no longer project power anywhere in the world with impunity. This will create significant political and diplomatic problems in sustaining a U.S. military campaign both domestically and internationally. Domestically, will the U.S. public support distant actions if they result in a significant threat to the homeland? Politicians will soon have to ask how an intervention will affect all Americans beyond the budgetary and human cost of conflict. Future enemies will be able to impose real costs that directly affect U.S. citizens, and they may not be shy about employing them.

Internationally, opponents will have an increased ability to threaten intermediate bases. For instance, a great deal of our support for the campaigns in Iraq and Syria flowed through Kuwait. Suppose ISIS had demonstrated to Kuwait that it could hit an airliner sitting at Kuwait International Airport? If threatened, would Kuwait allowed U.S. forces to use its facilities? The United States may have to protect commercial airfields, key government facilities, key economic assets, and other such areas throughout the Middle East and Europe, and it currently lacks the capability to do so.

Of more immediate concern will be the far larger number of weapons that can hit critical operational support bases, particularly large logistics facilities such as Bagram, Afghanistan. Because these bases are adjacent to Afghan communities, very cheap, short-range, and unsophisticated drones could be used to strike them. Defending against this threat is possible but expensive—particularly when the cost of defending against these weapons is compared to the cost of employing them. Even if the United States can develop systems that defend fixed bases, can it create defenses for the convoys that move personnel, equipment, and supplies within the theater? Can it protect all patrol bases, gathering of local leaders, and host-nation facilities?

Increasing cyber capability have also distinctly reduced U.S. immunity to counterattack when it gets involved in a conflict overseas. Both state and nonstate actors have repeatedly demonstrated the ability to damage key elements of civilian networks and even critical components like power systems.

This loss of immunity is not entirely new. Terrorist attacks have caused America to spend billions to protect both domestic and overseas facilities. Unfortunately, current barriers are all focused at stopping a ground-based attack. To protect against aerial attacks will dramatically increase the cost of protecting everything from embassies to transit airfields to patrol bases.

Tactically Dominant Defense

These emerging autonomous systems will provide an inherent advantage to defenders because they do not have to generate an active signature until they choose to fire. Finding a defender's system hidden in urban clutter, underground facilities, or even the complex littoral environment is much harder than finding the aggressor's system as it moves to attack, especially if it moves in the air or on the sea.

This may create a situation similar to World War I where any person in range above the ground could be easily killed. The result was static, trench warfare. Able to reach out a thousand miles in the surface, subsurface, and air domains these systems, drones, cruise and ballistic missiles may again make defense the tactically dominant form of warfare. Power projection may be limited to strike operations using a family of drones, as well as cruise and hypervelocity missiles.

Proponents of directed-energy weapons—lasers and microwave systems —suggest their systems will defeat such drone and missile swarms and thus return offense to the tactical battlefield. Unfortunately, these systems are still expensive and power hungry, ineffective under some environmental conditions, and may be subject to defeat by relatively inexpensive countermeasures. They will also favor defenders who have the huge advantage of fixed-power facilities and the ability to blend into complex terrain.

At this point it is impossible to tell which mix of systems will dominate. Again, it will be essential that the U.S. Defense Department run rigorous experiments to understand the character of such conflicts. It is imperative that these systems be tested against a thinking, reacting "enemy" team that employs countermeasures such as autonomy, smoke, and electromagnetic shielding. If such systems become capable of defeating thousands of drones, they may also be able to defeat the much smaller number of conventional aircraft, guided bombs, and missiles the United States can deploy. This would reinforce the dominance of the defense. A key question that must be explored is whether land power, by making use of the advantages of complex terrain, unlimited magazines, massive power networks, and ever-increasing range and speed of land based weapons will come to dominate the air, sea, and space domains.

The Return of Mass
Mass played a major role in the outcomes the U.S. Civil War, World War I, World War II, and the Korean War. However, in the 1980s, the Pentagon realized NATO could not match the Warsaw Pact in mass. Therefore, it invested heavily in precision weapons to defeat mass.[38] However,

technological convergence means that mass with precision has arrived. Additive manufacturing will make large numbers of cheap drones and advanced GRAMM systems available. Sheer numbers of cheap, mass-produced, unmanned, precision weapons may simply overwhelm the exceptionally capable but few manned U.S. systems.

The Return of Mobilization

Today, the U.S. defense industry lacks the surge capacity to equip a mobilized population rapidly. It is not possible to ramp up production quickly for weapons like the F-35s. With a planned peak production of only seventeen F-35s per month, it is difficult to see how the United States could hope to replace combat losses in a war lasting more than a few weeks. [39] Unfortunately, since 1750, wars between healthy states have lasted years rather than weeks.

Mobilization in World War II was possible because civilian industry could rapidly convert to military production. By 1990, the complexity of modern military weapons systems made rapid mobilization difficult, if not impossible. [40] Advanced manufacturing—particularly 3D printing, robotics, and task-specific artificial intelligence—may radically change this situation. 3D printing is inherently flexible because the product produced depends only on the materials the printer can use, the design of the printer, and the software that is loaded. With a change of software, these printers can go from producing commercial products to producing weapons. Thus, as 3D printing assumes a greater role in industry, the possibility of industrial mobilization will reemerge. However, successful mobilization cannot be accomplished quickly without a significant planning effort. The Pentagon must be prepared to provide the computer files for the 3D printers as well as produce the required government-furnished equipment. The Pentagon must also be prepared to enlist and train new personnel, build them into coherent units, and then move those units and the weapons to an overseas battlefield. Unfortunately, the Pentagon is only just beginning to think about the issue. [41]

CUMULATIVE IMPACT ON MILITARY OPERATIONS

The convergence of technology over the next ten to twenty years means everyone—even nonstate actors—will have precision-strike capabilities. Five years ago, a cheap drone demonstrated its ability to fly autonomously to a range of thirty miles. Nations with access to as few as one hundred 3D printers could have access to tens of thousands of these drones. The operational implications of this type of proliferation has not escaped our senior leaders. General Robert Neller, Commandant of the Marine Corps, asked "How do you mask your signature, make your adversary raise his? If your signature can be detected, you can be killed."[42] Because it is easier to find a moving object than a stationary one hiding in a cluttered environment, a prepared defense will be tactically dominant.

Unfortunately, because of the huge physical and electronic signature of major bases, they will prove the exception to the dominance of the defense. Rapidly improving inexpensive drones can reach five hundred miles today. Relatively inexpensive cruise missiles reach a thousand miles or more. Both can be deployed on platforms that will offer new opportunities for surprise, mass attacks on the U.S. bases at home and overseas.

The combination of these factors means that states and nonstates will be able to impose significant casualties and even economic damage to opponents who try to land ground forces in their home territories. Intervention is going to be much more costly in human and financial terms than today.

But the technologies of the fourth industrial revolution will not change the fundamental nature of war. It will still be driven by Clausewitz's primary trinity of passion, chance, and reason. It will remain the domain of fog, friction, and uncertainty. Technology will not bring clarity or brevity. For millennia, political and military leaders have embarked on wars where they thought they understood the situation and would win a short and decisive war—and subsequently paid the price for ignoring the true nature of war. [43]

CHANGING CHARACTER OF WAR

In contrast to the unchanging nature of war, the character of war—how it is fought—has changed continually. Yet, despite our American love of technology, how people fight wars will remain based more on the social, economic, and political aspects of their societies than the technology involved. Historically, each society's employment of new technology has been heavily shaped by its political, economic, and social conditions. Take, for example, the Swiss pikemen who dominated the battlefields of Europe for over two hundred years. There was no technological mystery to making or even using pikes, but only the Swiss had the political, economic, and social structure that allowed them to employ the pike most effectively. The Swiss had the necessary social cohesiveness and trust to fight in tight formations under elected leaders. The more hierarchical political entities of Europe could not.

We should expect each society to use the emerging technologies in unique ways that are best suited to its society. Further, conflict will not be based solely on those aspects of one society but the interactions of all the societies in the conflict. Wars are likely to bloodier, longer, and more financially ruinous. The next chapter will examine how the United States should transition to a force that exploits the technologies of the fourth industrial revolution.

NOTES

1. Sean Gallagher, "Long-range projectiles for Navy's newest ship too expensive to shoot," *ARS Technica,* November 7, 2016, https://arstechnica.com/information-technology/2016/11/long-range-projectiles-for-navys-newest-ship-too-expensive-to-shoot/.
2. Joe Gould, "US Army 'Dumb' 155mm Rounds Get Smart," *Defense News,* March 13, 2015, http://www.defensenews.com/story/defense/land/weapons/2015/03/13/orbital-atk-wins-us-army-deal-for-pgk/70222932.
3. "XP2 Quadcopter Off Road Racing Demo Reel—Aerial Video and Photography," *YouTube,* July 3, 2013, https://www.youtube.com/watch?feature=player_embedded&v=QRrSriR5b6s.
4. Megan Eckstein, "Panel: Navy Must Invest in Counter-ISR, Unmanned Boats, Railgun to Prepare for Future Fight," *USNI News,* March 9, 2017, https://news.usni.org/2017/03/09/panel-navy-must-invest-counter-c4isr-unmanned-boats-railgun-prepare-future-fight.
5. Thomas Rowden, "Surface Warfare Strategy: Return to Sea Control," https://news.usni.org/2017/01/09/document-u-s-navy-surface-force-strategy.
6. H. Robinson Harris et al., "Converting Merchant Ships to Missile Ships for the Win," *Proceedings,* January 2019, https://www.usni.org/magazines/proceedings/2019/january/converting-merchant-ships-missile-ships-win.
7. Ibid.
8. Ronald O'Rourke, "Navy Littoral Combat Ship (LCS)/Frigate Program: Background and Issues for Congress," Congressional Research Service, June 14, 2016, https://fas.org/sgp/crs/weapons/RL33741.pdf.
9. Robert Farley, "Ú.S. Navy Orders 10 *Virginia*-class Submarines at a Record Cost of $17.6 Billion," *The Diplomat,* May 3, 2014, http://thediplomat.com/2014/05/us-navy-orders-10-virginia-class-submarines-at-a-record-cost-of-17-6-billion.
10. Daniel Kelley, "Michigan Tech's ROUGHIE Gliders Will Follow Their Own Path," *Environmental Monitor,* June 17, 2014, https://www.fondriest.com/news/michigan-techs-roughie-gliders-will-follow-path.htm.
11. Scott C. Truver, "Taking Mines Seriously: Mine Warfare in China's Near Seas," *Naval War College Review* 65, no. 2 (Spring 2012), 30.

12. Andrew S. Erickson, Lyle J. Goldstein, and William S. Murray, *Chinese Mine Warfare: A PLA Navy's 'Assassin's Mace' Capability*, (Newport, RI: Naval War College, June 2009), 14.

13. Truver, Scott C., "Mine the Gap: Iranians and the Strait of Hormuz," *Proceedings*, February 28, 2013, https://news.usni.org/2012/06/17/mine-gap-iranians-and-strait-hormuz.

14. Winslow Wheeler, "More Than the Navy's Numbers Could Be Sinking," *Time*, December 4, 2012, http://nation.time.com/2012/12/04/more-than-the-navys-numbers-could-be-sinking/.

15. Thomas Shugart and Javier Gonzalez, "First Strike: China's Missile Threat to U.S. Bases in Asia," Center for New American Security, June 2017, https://s3.amazonaws.com/files.cnas.org/documents/CNASReport-FirstStrike-Final.pdf.

16. Zachary Keck, "China's DF-26 'Carrier-Killer' Missile Could Stop the Navy in Its Track (without Firing a Shot)," *The National Interest*, April 20, 2018, http://nationalinterest.org/blog/the-buzz/chinas-df-26-carrier-killer-missile-could-stop-the-navy-its-25493.

17. Zhang Hongzhou, "China's Fishing Industry: Current Status, Government Policies, and Future Prospects," CNA Maritime Power Conference, July 9, 2015, https://www.cna.org/cna_files/pdf/China-Fishing-Industry.pdf.

18. Andrea Shalal, "Lockheed aims to build satellites 40 percent quicker, lower costs," *Business Insider*, March 8, 2016, http://www.businessinsider.com/r-lockheed-aims-to-build-satellites-40-percent-quicker-lower-costs-2016-3.

19. "Tactical Tomahawk Cruise Missile," https://comptroller.defense.gov/Portals/45/documents/defbudget/FY2017/FY2017_Weapons.pdf#page=63.

20. Sandra Erwin, "In-orbit services poised to become big business," *SpaceNews*, June 10, 2018, https://spacenews.com/in-orbit-services-poised-to-become-big-business/.

21. Matthew Bienart, "Air Force Space Command Shifting To Warfighting Operational Mindset," *Defense Daily Network*, March 2, 2018, http://www.defensedaily.com/air-force-space-command-shifting-warfighting-operational-mindset/.

22. Dustin Volz and Timothy Gardner, "In a first, U.S. blames Russia for cyberattacks on energy grid," *Reuters*, March 15, 2018, https://www.reuters.com/article/us-usa-russia-sanctions-energygrid/in-a-first-u-s-blames-russia-for-cyber-attacks-on-energy-grid-idUSKCN1GR2G3.

23. "Cyber bank robbers steal $1bn, says Kaspersky report," *BBCNews*, February 16, 2015, http://www.bbc.com/news/business-31482985.
24. "How North Korean hackers became the world's greatest bank robbers," *Public Radio International*, May 16, 2018, https://flipboard.com/@flipboard/-how-north-korean-hackers-became-the-wor/f-37dc572867%2Fpri.org.
25. Steve Morgan, "Cybercrime Damages $6 Trillion By 2021," *Cyber Security Ventures*, October 17, 2017, https://cybersecurityventures.com/hackerpocalypse-cybercrime-report-2016/.
26. Adam Segal, "Chinese Cyber Espionage: We Know the Who, How, Why, and Why it Matters—We're Missing the What to Do," Council on Foreign Relations, June 11, 2014, https://www.cfr.org/blog/chinese-cyber-espionage-we-know-who-how-why-and-why-it-matters-were-missing-what-do.
27. Franz Stefan-Gady, "New Snowden Documents Reveal Chinese Behind F-35 Hack," *The Diplomat*, January 27, 2015, https://thediplomat.com/2015/01/new-snowden-documents-reveal-chinese-behind-f-35-hack/.
28. Joe Weiss, "Industrial control systems: The holy grail of cyberwar," *Christian Science Monitor*, March 24, 2017, https://www.csmonitor.com/World/Passcode/Passcode-Voices/2017/0324/Industrial-control-systems-The-holy-grail-of-cyberwar.
29. Dustin Volz and Timothy Gardner, "In a first, U.S. blames Russia for cyberattacks on energy grid."
30. "Department of Homeland Security Unveils Strategy to Guide Cybersecurity Efforts," Department of Homeland Security, May 15, 2018, https://www.dhs.gov/news/2018/05/15/department-homeland-security-unveils-strategy-guide-cybersecurity-efforts.
31. Lily Hay Newman, "AI can help cybersecurity—if it can fight though the hype," *Wired*, April 29, 2018, https://www.wired.com/story/ai-machine-learning-cybersecurity/.
32. Matthew Cole, "A Dissertation So Good It Might Be Classified," *Wired*, January 1, 2004, https://www.wired.com/2004/01/a-dissertation-so-good-it-might-be-classified/.
33. John Costello, "The Strategic Support Force: Update and Overview," Jamestown Foundation China Brief, December 21, 2016, https://jamestown.org/program/strategic-support-force-update-overview/.
34. Sergey Sukhankin, "Russian Electronic Warfare in Ukraine: Between Real and Imaginable," *Eurasia Daily Monitor*, Volume: 14 Issue: 71, May

24, 2017, https://jamestown.org/program/russian-electronic-warfare-ukraine-real-imaginable/.

35. Colin Clark, "Russia Widens EW War, 'Disabling' EC-130s OR AC-130s In Syria," *Breaking Defense,* April 24, 2018, https://breakingdefense.com/2018/04/russia-widens-ew-war-disabling-ec-130s-in-syria/.

36. Jane Edwards, "Vice Adm. Mike Shoemaker: Carrier-Based Tanker Drone Could Extend Fighter Jets' Operational Range," *ExecutiveGov,* September 1, 2017, https://www.executivegov.com/2017/09/vice-adm-mike-shoemaker-carrier-based-mq-25a-stingray-tanker-drone-could-extend-fighter-jets-operational-range/.

37. T. X. Hammes, "America is well within range of a big surprise, so why can't it see it?, War on the Rocks, March 12, 2018, https://warontherocks.com/2018/03/america-is-well-within-range-of-a-big-surprise-so-why-cant-it-see/

38. Robert Work, "The Third U.S. Offset Strategy and its Implications for Partners and Allies," U.S. Department of Defense, January 28, 2015, http://www.defense.gov/News/Speeches/Speech-View/Article/606641/the-third-us-offset-strategy-and-its-implications-for-partners-and-allies.

39. Matthew Richardson and Evan Hoopfer, "Lockheed Martin lands $5.5B contract for dozens of F-35s — more to come," *Dallas Business Journal,* July 11, 2018, https://www.bizjournals.com/dallas/news/2017/07/11/lockheed-martin-lands-5-5b-contract-for-dozens-of.html.

40. Richard Danzig, "Driving in the Dark: The Propositions About Prediction and National Security," Center for New American Security, October 2011, http://www.cnas.org/files/documents/publications/CNAS_Prediction_Danzig.pdf.

41. Daniel Goure, "The First Signs Of A National Mobilization For War Are Appearing," *RealClearDefense,* May 12, 2017, https://www.realcleardefense.com/articles/2017/05/12/the_first_signs_of_a_national_mobilization_for_war_are_appearing_111371.html.

42. Otto Kreisher, "Neller: 'We Need a Fifth-Generation Marine Corps,'" *Seapower Magazine Online,* January 12, 2017, http://seapowermagazine.org/stories/20170112-neller.html.

43. Cathal J. Nolan, *The Allure of Battle: A History of How Wars Have Been Won and Lost,* (United Kingdom: Oxford Press, 2017).

CHAPTER 7

TRANSITION AND RESTRUCTURING OF U.S. FORCES

Planners must accept new technologies will be integrated into U.S. force structure. The key uncertainties are how long it will take and how the United States will restructure its forces to gain maximum advantage. Should the United States invest heavily in land and air forces for a potential confrontation in Europe with Russia? Or focus on the maritime and air domains for the potential conflict with China? Are Iran and North Korea considered lesser included cases? Where does the war against terrorists fall in the priority? Given the centrality of cyber, space, and electronic warfare to the American military's combat capabilities, do they get priority?

The challenge is to modify our concepts, doctrine, and organizations to address these issues by taking advantage of the fourth industrial revolution. This chapter will take a brief look at historical examples of transition, then examine how new technologies are being integrated today, and finally make recommendations on how to continue the process.

The body of academic research on innovation both is rich and deep. However, the unique challenges of military innovation due to the mix of national cultures, service cultures, service competition for resources, the political-military-industrial complex, the enormous uncertainties inherent in warfare, and the deep conservatism of most military leaders require a somewhat different approach to innovation than that required for business.

A Rand Corporation paper focused on the political science schools of military innovation and concluded there are five primary models: the Civil-Military Model, the Interservice Model, the Intraservice Model, the Cultural Model, and the Bottom-up Model.[1] As indicated by their titles, each of these models attribute innovation to a primary driver with smaller secondary factors.

Historians take a different approach. Rather than trying to create a model that explains many examples of innovation, they examine each case independently and see if any characteristics appear consistently in the various cases. This approach is particularly appropriate for those decision makers trying to guide today's peacetime military innovation. The current level of technological change and its application to defense strategy is not unprecedented. It occurred as recently as 1914–1941. Military professionals should consider how their predecessors dealt with that era's rapid technological breakthroughs in metallurgy, explosives, steam turbines, internal combustion engines, radio, and radar. How did they combine them to create new concepts such as armored warfare, strategic bombing, carrier task forces, and amphibious assaults? Why did some organizations figure out how to exploit these changes and others failed, some miserably?

In their edited volume, *Military Innovation in the Interwar Period*, Professors Allan Millett and Williamson Murray convened noted historians to study how six nations succeeded or failed at innovation during this period. This continued the tradition of Geoffrey Parker, the historian who first used the term "Revolution in Military Affairs," and Steve

Rosen. Both studied historical cases of innovation to determine why some attempts succeeded and other failed.

In examining the six nations that attempted to innovate successfully between the wars, Millett and Murray noted that even the visionaries only had a vague idea of how their concepts could develop in conjunction with the technological changes. The outcome was often contingent on decisions senior leaders made early that locked their nations into a path. But, within these paths, it was essential that senior leader bought into the concepts and provided both resources for experiments and a path to promotion for the proponents of change. Both were essential to those services that succeeded. It is also important to understand that many of the innovations failed. The militaries that developed the processes to thoroughly explore, test, and refine the vague concepts of the thought leaders were more successful. And they had to be willing to discard favored theories that failed the tests. Their theories were the ones survived in combat. Those that accepted the visions but did not thoroughly test them or biased the tests to senior leaders wishes, failed when tested in combat.

The fundamental truth that evolves from the case studies is that, as with all complex adaptive systems, there is no simple formula to guide change. Political, social, cultural, and economic factors will have major impacts on the success or failure of military innovations.

Remember the pre–World War II U.S. leaders faced high levels of uncertainty, massive budget cuts, and isolationist sentiments as they tried to build their forces for future fights. Yet they were able to conceptualize, wargame, and experiment to generate completely new and highly effective forces. However, the process was not smooth. The technological advances were, for the time, sudden. And it took time for even the progressive thinkers to adjust to the new reality—and more time for them to bring their institutions along. Like all human events, it was contingent on having the right people in the right places at the right times.

Consider the problem of warfare at sea. World War I's single major fleet action, the Battle of Jutland, was dominated by battleships. Accordingly, during the interwar period, battleships received the lion's share of U.S., British, French, and Japanese naval investments. The displacement of a battleship almost tripled, main batteries grew from 15-inch to 18.1-inch, range doubled, secondary batteries improved, radar arrived, speed increased by fifty percent, cruising range more than doubled, and armor was thickened.[2] Yet none of these advances changed the fundamental capabilities of the battleship. They only provided incremental improvement on existing strengths. This is the key problem with mature technology—even massive investment leads to only incremental improvement.

In contrast, aviation was in its infancy in 1914. Aircraft were slow, had limited range, were mostly unarmed, and were used primarily for reconnaissance. Despite the limitations, military aviation made great strides in tactics, technology, and operational concepts during World War I. The Royal Navy actually commissioned its first five aircraft carriers. Yet, after the war, naval aviation remained an auxiliary force in the Royal Navy. Britain would not commission a new aircraft carrier until 1937.[3] Senior navy and army officers wanted aircraft relegated to supporting ships at sea and armies on land.

For their part, air-power enthusiasts had other ideas but unfortunately focused most of their limited air-power investment on land-based, heavy bombers. Yet despite neglect of air-power enthusiasts, sea-based dive and torpedo bombers dominated naval warfare in the Pacific by 1942. Fortunately for the United States, most of the critical advances in aircraft design and production that made naval aviation dominant were initially developed for civilian uses by private companies. Because aircraft production was a highly competitive business, entrepreneurs drove rapid technological advances. And as is often the case with emerging technology, relatively modest investment in these new technologies resulted in massive increases in aircraft capability. Thus, when military innovators understood the potential of naval aviation, the technology was ready. Obviously, there are some interesting parallels with today.

The transition from battleships to carrier aviation still took almost twenty years. Between 1919 and 1939, the U.S. Navy contracted for twenty-one battleships[4] but only eight carriers.[5] When the war came, these few carriers led the fleet through the first eighteen months of conflict until the new *Essex* class carriers arrived in mid-1943. With their arrival, the U.S. Navy came to dominate the Pacific Ocean. Its investment in carriers and the policies and facilities to support them paid huge dividends. In contrast, its massive investment in new battleships mostly resulted in very expensive anti-aircraft escorts for the fleet carriers. In fact, if not in the hearts of surface line officers, battleships were reduced to near irrelevance before the war. In contrast, the rapid improvements in carrier aircraft meant that they were able to swarm and destroy the Japanese battle fleet.

This highlights one of the major problems facing decision makers during a period of rapid technological change. When should investment shift from the dominant legacy system to the new systems challenging it? And how can you be sure you are picking the right new system? For instance, the investment in battleships from 1919 to about the mid-1930s was the correct decision. Until then, naval aircraft and tactics had not advanced enough for the carrier to dominate the seas. Had war in the Pacific broken out then, battleships would likely have dominated the fleet actions. However, U.S. naval officers continued contracting for battleships through 1941. This was even after obsolete carrier-based bi-planes had sunk an Italian battleship and heavily damaged two others in the port of Taranto in November 1940 and then crippled the German battleship *Bismarck* in May 1941. Despite the success of their aircraft at Pearl Harbor, the sinking of the *Repulse* and the *Prince of Wales* near Singapore, and the Battle of Coral Sea—which was fought entirely by naval aviation, Japanese admirals still planned for battleships to strike the decisive blow at Midway in June 1942. As a result, Japan lost four carriers and their irreplaceable frontline pilots.

Land forces took a similar view of aircraft and worked to limit them to supporting ground forces through aerial reconnaissance, close air support, and interdiction. In sharp disagreement, those officers pushing for an independent role for air power seized upon the concept of "strategic bombing" described by Giulio Douhet as a war-winning idea.[6] This concept had particular appeal to the British who were desperately looking for a way to achieve strategic objectives without the horrendous losses of World War I. Bomber enthusiasts believed the bomber would always get through and could win the war in a short, sharp campaign.

France had a different problem. It shared a border with Germany, so any war would involve major ground combat. France therefore invested heavily in the Maginot Line to defend that border while minimizing casualties. In contrast, Germany felt it had to take the offensive because it would most likely fight a two-front war again. The World War I Schlieffen Plan was based on the idea Germany could quickly defeat France and then concentrate its forces against Russia. It failed. Although the political situation had changed significantly since the start of World War I, its strategic problem remained the same. Once again, German forces focused on the offensive, specifically how to exploit the breakthroughs they were able to achieve on the Western front late in World War I.

The different approaches chosen by each nation highlights another particularly wicked problem that inevitably arises during a period of change. Various theories will evolve. No nation can afford to pursue all the theories, and so they will have to choose where to invest. Proponents will argue about which will work best. Militaries will even test them through wargaming and field exercises. Unfortunately, but not surprisingly, the wargames are often biased to validate the beliefs of the senior officers of the service conducting the game or exercise. This, of course, reinforces their belief in their chosen approach. Which approach is correct cannot be verified until the fighting begins. Thus, Germany's maneuver triumphed over France's static defense, carriers defeated battleships, and bombers did not always get through.

TECHNOLOGICAL TRANSITION

Obviously, a key question is how will forces integrate fourth industrial revolution weapons—and even more important, how quickly? History provides numerous examples. Two such examples are firearms replacing pikes in infantry formations and the carrier and its aircraft replacing the battleship in the Pacific—these demonstrated the same pattern. In each case, the technology started out as an experiment. As the inventors and military innovators worked together, they figured out how the new technology could assist the old. Even as it served as an assistant to the old technology, the new technology improved to the point it became a full partner and finally replaced the old technology. The pattern was thus assistant to partner, and then partner to replacement.

For instance, during the first part of the sixteenth century, some forward thinkers saw how even primitive muskets could support the dominant pike formations. The Spanish placed muskets at the edge of their pike formations where the muskets could assist by firing into the massed enemy pikemen. Despite a very slow rate of fire, the Spanish felt the muskets were valuable. As muskets improved, they were integrated into the pike formations to fight as full partners. Replacement of the pike came with the development of the socket bayonet that allowed a musket to fire even with a fixed bayonet.

Aircraft followed a very similar path in replacing the battleship. At first, they assisted battleships with scouting and gunnery. The aircraft became the eyes of the fleet. As the carrier's air wing evolved into a mix of capable fighters, dive bombers, and torpedo bombers, the carriers moved from being assistants to being full partners with the battleships. When World War II proved conclusively that carrier aviation could destroy battleships at range, the carriers replaced the battleship.

Both weapons systems displayed the same evolutionary pattern. Each moved from assistant to partner to replacement. Each became dominant because it outranged the systems that it replaced. However, neither was a straight replacement. The time required for these two transitions ranged from over a century for the musket to just over two decades for the aircraft carrier. However, the fourth industrial revolution is happening faster than any previous revolution, the new generation of small, smart, and many weapons will quickly replace the old generation of few and exquisite ones. As with these two examples, success or failure will be based on the ability to develop concepts and organizations that play to a society's strengths while optimizing the use of new capabilities.

U.S. Response to the Changing Character of War Today

The United States' major defense programs for the next two decades are already underway, but they do not appear to have been designed with the fourth industrial revolution in mind.

Procurement Challenges to Replacing U.S. Equipment

The F-35 program officially started in 1993, but the Marine Corps did not declare initial operational capability (IOC) until 2015, the Air Force in 2016, and the Navy in 2018. Even after two services had declared IOC, the Pentagon's own Office of Operational Testing and Evaluation noted "276 deficiencies in combat performance" and that the planned Block 3FR6 improvements will only address about half of them.[7] In June 2019, *Defense News* obtained DoD documents that provided details on thirteen category-one deficiencies that still impact safety or mission effectiveness.[8]

Thus, twenty-six years after it was initiated, the F-35 program is still not fully operational. The F-35 program is not alone in the slow lane. The first steel was cut for the CVN 78 *USS Ford* in 1995. The Navy did not accept delivery of the much-delayed ship until June of 2017 and projects it to be operational in 2020. Given this pattern, it is unlikely that the major new weapons systems the United States is investing heavily in today will be ready in two decades.

It is therefore essential to think through the security implications of the fourth industrial revolution before the nation commits to multibillion dollar procurement programs that may be irrelevant two decades later. The fact is that once a program of record begins, it seldom substantially modifies its key attributes. Worse, once defense contractors begin spending billions of dollars in targeted Congressional districts, it becomes extremely difficult to terminate a program even if it becomes obvious it is no longer a viable combat system. The Littoral Combat Ship (LCS) is a classic example. Almost every outside evaluation shows these ships cannot fight and have major reliability problems.[9] Yet the LCS remains in production. Simply reducing the number of LCSs from the previously planned fifty-two to the currently planned thirty-two required a major effort.

The recent Pentagon procurement record should be of great concern because the expensive new programs are particularly vulnerable to evolving weapons systems. The B-21 bomber contract was not awarded until October 27, 2016, but the Air Force reported spending a billion dollars a year in preparation for the program and has increased it to $2 billion since the contract was signed.[10] Yet, as noted, the major bases and special hangers needed for the existing B-2 bombers are already within range of cruise missiles launched from off the coast of the United States. Because the B-21 is being procured specifically to provide the ability to penetrate the airspace of the near-peer competitor, the fact that it is already vulnerable to a much cheaper countermeasure should be cause for the Department of Defense to reconsider this major investment.

Where are U.S. forces on the Assistant-Partner-Replacement Path?

Given the notoriously slow and expensive Pentagon procurement process, it is useful to consider where the various new technologies are on the path from assistant to partner to replacement today in each of the domains.

In the air domain, the mission of long-duration surveillance in a low-threat environment has largely been assumed by drones. To be fair, drones have not flown in the high-threat environments, so drones remain a partner rather than a replacement in this area. However, newer drones with much greater range and stealth characteristics are already being tested and may soon take over this mission even in high-threat environments.

For the aerial-strike mission, cruise missiles are already full partners and, in some situations, have replaced manned aircraft. Drones are also already assisting in the strike mission. As demonstrated by U.S. Switchblade drones in Afghanistan and ISIS's use of commercial and hand-built drones in Syria, inexpensive strike drones are beginning to appear in various conflict arenas. Today, Kratos drones are being developed as partners, and potentially replacements, for manned strike aircraft in high-threat environments. Soon hypervelocity missiles might join the strike capability.

Cruise missiles and drones are already full partners and have replaced manned aircraft for many missions. It is not a stretch to say that the day will come soon when they can replace manned aircraft almost completely in the strike mission. The fact the operational range of these missiles and drones can be greatly extended with much less investment, compared to achieving a minor increase in range for the F-35, is of critical importance. Even more important, these weapons do not need the vulnerable runways, maintenance, and support facilities associated with manned aircraft. Unfortunately, the United States continues to invest heavily in platforms that require large fixed bases that are easy to find and very difficult to defend against swarm attacks.

For air superiority, Kratos-type drones are being considered as partners with manned aircraft. In fact, they may actually be more effective at the Air Force's preferred method for achieving air superiority—destroying enemy aircraft on the ground. With twice the range of the F-35 and costing orders between one and two percent as much, long-range, highly capable, autonomous drones that can be launched from hundreds of unimproved locations may well prove more effective in causing destruction to enemy aircraft. Numbers matter.

At sea, cruise missiles and inexpensive drones are not only augmenting strike but providing a much wider set of basing options. The teaming of surface ships and expeditionary land bases with the evolving family of drones and missiles points to these systems replacing the carrier. Proponents of maintaining an eleven-carrier fleet note the last of the planned *Ford* class is projected to still be serving in 2099. Two obvious questions arise: First, will a ship as large as a carrier still be viable eighty years from now? Second, what is the opportunity cost?

Given the sharply increasing missile and submarine threat to carriers today, it is difficult to see them surviving even another two decades in anything but a low-threat environment. Their aircraft either require extensive refueling assistance from the limited number of Air Force tankers or must launch from well within range of China's ballistic missiles, cruises missiles, and family of drones—to include strike variants. If it comes within range of shore-based systems, the ships will be in a magazine-capacity competition against the shore. This is particularly important against Chinese DF-21D anti-ship ballistic missiles. For the cost of one carrier and its air wing, the Chinese could buy up to two thousand DF-21s or a large number of hypervelocity missiles.[11] And, of course, the Navy has not solved the diesel-submarine problem that has led to the sinking of the carrier in so many exercises.[12]

Bombers can strike from long range, but they generate extremely low sortie rates. Assuming a fifty percent readiness rate for the nineteen B-2s, which may be optimistic, they could generate about six sorties from Guam per day.[13] Given that Chinese systems can already strike Guam, B-2s may have to operate from much farther away—and thus provide even fewer sorties. Although the Chinese will hesitate to engage our stateside bomber bases with ballistic missiles for fear that the attack might be misinterpreted as an escalation to nuclear weapons, new cruise missiles and drones packaged in standard shipping containers launched from merchant ships in the Gulf of Mexico offer another feasible and less risky approach. The cost of defending against such attacks will be very high.

In contrast to bomber-basing limitations, Kratos-type vertical-launch drones can range China's coast from thousands of locations in Japan and the Philippines as well as a wide variety of sea platforms. We do not know the eventual cost of such systems, but Kratos announced a target price of $2 million for its XQ-222 drone if purchased in lots of more than a hundred.[14] Even if it follows the pattern of recent DoD procurements and doubles in price, Kratos still provides an interesting option to manned aircraft—with no requirement for major bases or maintenance facilities.

Within the next two decades, surface and aerial drones will be full partners and may well be replacements for some surface Navy missions such as patrol, underway replenishment, cargo delivery, and survey. If the underwater drones mature into self-deploying mines or transport systems for advanced torpedoes, they will seriously challenge surface ships' ability to leave port or approach a hostile shore.

Submarine warfare is already demonstrating several innovative uses for drones. In addition to their use as surveillance, reconnaissance, and even underwater-attack systems, Innocorp drones have shown the potential for a subsurface-launched drone to transition to an airborne surveillance or strike weapon. Currently unmanned underwater vehicles (UUVs) are partners in undersea warfare and may soon replace submarines for risking inshore missions. They could also greatly expand U.S. capability in offensive mine warfare.

In the ground domain, cheap small aircraft drones have become effective partners in the reconnaissance. For strike, relatively cheap drones have moved from the experimental phase to that of assistant. The U.S. Army and Marine Corps used the Switchblade successfully in Afghanistan both to look ahead for patrols and, because it is an expendable platform, to provide a way to deliver a small explosive on insurgents discovered by the drone. The Russians and Ukrainians have demonstrated that drones effectively assist with heavier fires by spotting for everything from mortars to long-range heavy rockets.

The near-exponential increase in range over the last few years indicates autonomous, inexpensive drones will soon vastly outrange current tube artillery and even most rocket artillery. And as has been the case historically with other emerging technologies, drones will do so quickly and for much less investment than needed to extend the range of the very mature artillery and rocket technologies.

As these new systems mature, the key issue for both offensive and defensive ground combat will be maintaining the logistic support essential to any fight. K-MAX helicopter drones have already demonstrated that drones can be partners in aerial delivery. Commercial air-freight companies are pushing hard to perfect fully autonomous large cargo aircraft. Commercial shipping firms are working on autonomous ships ranging from ferries to super tankers. Drones have even reached the experimental stage in ground delivery. Still the key question remains, can U.S. forces resupply in a combat zone with hundreds of drones actively hunting its logistics forces?

In space, CubeSats are becoming partners because they can provide more frequent and less expensive coverage than conventional satellites. Today's versions lack the resolution and variety of sensors of major platforms, but rapid progress on nano sensors, power systems, and networking means they may soon equal satellites in many functions.

As noted earlier, the Pentagon has to think about space superiority differently. It has to assume that U.S. forces will suffer significant attrition. Thus, in space, the most important aspect of superiority may be the ability to launch quickly systems that can provide space services—geolocation, timing, communications, early warning, optical and electronic surveillance. A sustained campaign of hard kills may even render the current orbits unusable due to debris. The ability to rapidly replace space capabilities with non-space-based systems will be a crucial part in U.S. deterrence of space conflict.[15]

OPPORTUNITY COSTS OF CONTINUING CURRENT PROCUREMENT PLANS

The cost of a legacy systems is not just monetary; there is also the opportunity cost of not devoting those funds to developing and buying the new systems. In short, if we do not buy this system, what else could we have? Would it be more effective in future fights? The *U.S.S. Ford* and embarked air wing will cost roughly $20 billion dollars just to procure—this does not include the necessary escorts that make up a carrier strike group. At the $2 million the Navy paid for each Tomahawk in 2016, it could buy 10,000 for just the procurement cost of the carrier and its airwing.[16] Operating cost for the carrier and air wing are over $1 billion dollars per year. These are just the operations and maintenance costs for the carrier and air wing and do not include personnel costs, training pipeline costs, basing costs, major overhauls and updates, or the cost of operating the escorts and support ships. Thus, for every year it operates a carrier and its air wing (without escorts) the Pentagon could buy up to hundreds, if not thousands, more missiles or drones per year. These newer weapons will not need tankers or AWACs to guide their strike packages. Even the relatively ancient TLAM can provide heavy strike at more than twice the range of the current carrier air wing.

Using a different measuring stick, the United States could buy six new Virginia-class submarines and 3,500 Tomahawks instead of the carrier and its air wing. In both cases, the Navy would phase out the carriers over time. Using the existing carriers until their end of life, it will still have six carriers in service in 2050. Unfortunately, the air wing's range will not extend much during the era of the F-35, even as the range of missiles and drones is increasing quickly and dramatically. And the missiles provide a much wider set of basing options that would vastly complicate a near peer competitor's attempts to preempt.

If the Pentagon rethinks its procurement plan, rather than being faced with a single class of threat (fighter bombers) concentrated on a very few carriers, any opposition would face a mix of supersonic cruise missiles, subsonic cruise missiles, a variety of drones, and the legacy aircraft still in our inventory. Another major consideration is the fact personnel costs would be much lower. Six Virginia-class submarines require only about nine hundred sailors compared to the single carrier and air wing, which needs more than four thousand staff. Given the serious concern over the rapid rise of personnel costs ($132,243 per person per year in 2017) and increasing difficulties of recruiting and retaining sailors, this is a major savings.[17] Replacing manned aircraft with autonomous systems will also relieve the major pilot shortages all services are suffering today. It will also reduce downstream costs. The Veterans Administration 2018 budget of $185 billion[18] exceeded the Pentagon's $141 billion budget for personnel.[19] The most certain way to reduce VA costs is to reduce the number of veterans by reducing the number of people in U.S. forces.

Because cruise missiles can be containerized, they will greatly complicate any enemy's targeting problem. Even with ten carriers, the Navy will have a maximum of six in any conflict at any one time. This reduces the enemy's target problem to six major platforms that provide incredibly lucrative targets—more than four thousand sailors and sixty aircraft in one place. If the Navy chooses instead to buy missile-equipped merchant ships at $125 million each, it could have forty ships with 1,600 missiles at sea manned by only 1,600 sailors for $5 billion or one quarter the price of a carrier and its air wing.[20] Clearly these ships can be partners with the carriers both in delivering ordnance in low-threat environments and the missile-volley contest critical to large-scale conventional war.

Similarly, if the services chose to buy autonomous drones developed from the Kratos QX222, they could buy about fifty of the $2 million

drones for the reduced price agreed to for the eleventh lot of F-35s[21]
Moreover, they will be able to buy more each year they do not have to
pay for the F-35 operating, support, and personnel costs. Their VTOL
capability will also greatly complicate an enemy's targeting problem
while dramatically reducing the value of each enemy hit.

Another opportunity cost that must be considered is the fact that new
technology has both the greater potential to grow and to come down
in costs. Mature technology has historically required more and more
investment for even incremental improvement in its performance as
illustrated by the major cost increases in the Ford-class over the Nimitz-
class carriers. In contrast, new technology often comes down in price
even as capabilities increase.

Autonomy is Here

Even as AI capabilities are improving rapidly, cost is coming down.
The proposed autonomous drones would be driven by the same kind
of limited AI used in smart sea mines. They will be tasked to attack
specified targets and use multiple sensors to positively identify them.
When they have done so, they will attack—just as today's smart sea
mines do. Unfortunately, the Department of Defense continues to have
laborious discussions centered on two approaches to autonomy—"human-
in-the-loop" or "human-on-the-loop." "Human-in-the-loop" requires a
person to give specific permission before a drone can kill a target. The
glaring problem with "human-on-the-loop" is that it is too slow for
today's combat. Long ago, the Navy admitted human decision-making
was too slow when it built automatic modes for both the Aegis and the
Phalanx defensive systems. Although these are theoretically "human-
on-the-loop," the reality is humans simply are not fast enough to keep
up in high-intensity conflict. In effect, it is an argument of which of two
failed systems the United States should apply to modern weapons.

This is particularly odd because of what the United States has already built, which are "human-starts-the-loop" systems such as Aegis, Captor, or modern air-to-air missiles. Human operators set the parameters under which these systems can engage. By applying appropriate and thoughtful parameters, the operator can maximize the effectiveness of the system while minimizing the danger the system will engage a target that it should not. Once the parameters are set, the human starts the loop and turns the fighting over to the system. This is effectively the most ethical use of autonomy. By accepting humans are not able to keep up, the engineers and operators can focus on the technical, procedural, operational, and training requirements necessary to ensure that the system executes according to the law of warfare.

Oddly, the fact that the United States already has autonomous weapons in its arsenal and has used them does not seem to be speeding up the policy discussion about continued development, procurement, and use of autonomous systems. It should be noted, to the disadvantage of the United States, that other nations are not waiting to explore the possibilities of using limited AI to operate autonomous drones.

RETHINKING FORCE STRUCTURE

To sustain its military power, the U.S. military must lean forward to develop the concepts, organizations, training, and technology to exploit emerging capabilities. The transition to new systems has already started and must be sustained. This will not require sudden changes but rather a continuation of the ongoing shift. With procurement, the DoD should logically start by phasing out old systems and programs and replacing them with new ones. By simply ceasing to buy obsolete systems and in their place buying new ones, it can phase in the shift. Further if the new systems are bought in small batches, the DoD should be able to purchase upgrades with each batch. Much like computers and cell phones, improvements will be continuous and cause minimum disruption. Such a system can also keep production lines hot while continually updating the advanced manufacturing systems to sustain U.S. and allied forces during a long conflict.

Procurement should be based on operational concepts. Due to air-base vulnerability and the range deficiencies of the F-35, the United States should not buy all 2,400 planned F-35s. The F-35's range limitations, maintenance issues, and base vulnerability problems are simply too big to overlook. Maintenance costs have been an issue since the beginning of the program. In February 2018, Undersecretary of Defense for Acquisition and Sustainment Ellen Lord stated "right now, we can't afford the sustainment costs we have on the F-35." In January 2018, Will Roper, the current Assistant Secretary of the Air Force for Acquisition, Technology and Logistics for the U.S. Air Force, expressed the same reservations.[22]

Fortunately, although China has developed a mix of weapons to come after U.S. air bases, they do not seem to be prepared for the United States responding in kind. The Pentagon can take advantage of this Chinese failure. U.S. Air Force doctrine calls for destroying enemy air power on the ground. As long as opponents continue to use large number of conventional aircraft, they will be easy to find. Thus, rather than replacing current fighters with F-35s, the Department of Defense needs to start phasing in the drones and cruise missiles that will soon replace them. But it should consider most of the drones as expendable rounds of ammunition and build accordingly.

Even as their bases become more vulnerable, China is developing systems to neutralize the stealth capabilities of U.S. aircraft. Although such aircraft will still be harder to locate and engage than non-stealthy aircraft, the extraordinary premium the United States pays for stealth aircraft may no longer be worth the investment. Thus, the next step is to accept that the F-35 is the last manned fighter for any service. By the time its successor can be built, autonomous drones will execute manned-fighter missions for a fraction of the cost.

The Pentagon needs to accept that the B-21 is based on a twentieth-century concept and is not a good investment for twenty-first-century defense. Proponents of the B-21 argue that the United States must be able to "contend with more mobile sets of targets,"[23] "hit hardened and deeply buried targets,"[24] and finally, "hold targets at risk."[25] Let us consider each in turn. In Operation Desert Storm, strike aviation was given the mission of defeating/suppressing Saddam's Scud mobile missile launchers. Despite having absolute air supremacy and hundreds of strike aircraft dedicated to the mission, the *Gulf War Air Power Survey* concluded that "there is no indisputable proof that Scud mobile launchers —as opposed to high-fidelity decoys, trucks or other objects with Scud-like signature—were destroyed by fixed-wing aircraft."[26] Allied forces failed to get a single confirmed kill, even though the Scuds were liquid fueled and took at least thirty minutes to erect, fuel, and launch. Today, even long-range missiles have solid fuel systems, so the time from breaking cover until the missile is away is as little as ten minutes.

The earlier discussion concerning the Iraqi Scuds should put to rest the idea that manned aircraft can pursue mobile targets effectively. But deep-strike advocates still insist bombers can find and kill Chinese mobile systems in the complex mix of rural, urban, and industrial environments protected by China's integrated air-defense system. Even if our intelligence systems can find the hides, the United States would have to maintain sufficient aircraft in contested air space to ensure it could find and hit a target in less than ten minutes. We simply do not own enough stealthy aircraft to maintain the hundreds of aircraft in the air around the clock just to suppress missiles. Further, stealthy aircraft are just as visible in daylight as non-stealthy ones, so even stealthy aircraft will not be able to hunt mobile systems in daylight.

Next, the requirement to "hit hardened and deeply buried targets"[27] seems to refer to command-and-control centers or nuclear-weapons facilities. Unfortunately, no one has explained how to prevent the enemy from simply digging deeper or moving into commercial mines, which go miles into the ground. It makes little sense to invest heavily in a capability so easily sidestepped by an enemy. In fact, efforts to neutralize such a target will most likely continue to focus on destroying the target's connectivity to the outside world, which does not require manned aircraft.

As for "holding targets at risk,"[28] proponents have never explained why manned bombers or strike aircraft are necessary to "hold targets at risk." Do cruise missiles not hold targets at risk? More importantly, air-power proponents have also never shown how "holding targets at risk" has been a particular deterrent. When Ghaddafi chose to destroy PanAm 103, did he think the United States could not bomb Libya in response? What about Saddam when he refused to allow UN inspectors to enter? Did Milosevic not believe NATO could strike his assets? Lacking historical proof, it seems that the claimed need for conventional assets to "hold targets at risk" is more faith-based than fact-based.

Finally, it is a relatively short step for the Chinese to put containerized Kaliber-type cruise missiles on commercial ships to attack bomber bases in the United States without launching ballistic missiles. Anyone with access to the internet can use Google Maps to precisely locate the B-2 hangers at Whiteman Air Force Base, Missouri.

Instead of sinking enormous funds into the B-21 and a sixth-generation manned fighter, the United States should invest in drones and a family of missiles that could provide long-range strike at a fraction of the cost. With steadily increasing range, speed, and payload capability, autonomous drones offer an affordable, effective alternative. China and Russia's ever-growing ability to strike U.S. airbases can be largely neutralized by short take-off and landing (STOVL) or vertical take-off and landing (VTOL) drones. Enemies will also be forced to build defenses that can deal with mixed raids of legacy manned aircraft, drones of various types and capabilities, and missiles. In short, they have to defend against both today's and tomorrow's threats.

At sea, dispersion and range will be vital for survival. Concentrating striking power in carrier aviation is simply unwise. Instead of buying more carriers, the Navy should start buying systems like the Kratos and advanced missiles which can turn every ship into a combatant. If it designs these systems into the footprint of standard twenty- or forty-foot shipping containers, every seagoing vessel can become a warship. The Navy will no longer need to think in terms of a 355-ship Navy but rather in terms of a thousand or more from the merchant ships and seagoing fishing boats it could buy, arm, and crew in a crisis. Just as important, systems like these could be used from ashore to help defend U.S. facilities, allied territory, or advanced bases if U.S. forces seize them.

On the ground, the Pentagon is going to have to start adapting to the idea that defense will be dominant. Future systems must be selected based on the ability to move rapidly, hide, or dig in easily. Once in place, they must not emit until they engage enemy units. As with air and sea systems, the change will take place over time. But rather than continuing to invest in minor improvements to legacy ground systems —tanks, infantry fighting vehicles, artillery, and heavy trucks—we shift investment into systems optimized for the new environment.

Perhaps the most challenging military aspect of the transition to a world with thousands of smart drones will be sustaining our logistics. In the very near future, defending fixed facilities will be expensive and difficult. U.S. forces must work much harder to minimize logistics requirements. At the same time, logistics units must be reinforced so they can mount their own defense against an increasing variety of threats even while on the move. In addition to protecting its own logistics units and lines of communication, the United States will face the challenge of protecting high-value host-nation targets as well as the intermediate airfields and ports that sustain our efforts. Everything from political leaders to public gatherings to economic infrastructure will be vulnerable to attack and thus will require protection.

In all cases, logistics are the key vulnerability of U.S. forces. Fixed bases, forward logistics sites, and logistics systems moving into and in the battlespace will be the most exposed parts of the power projection force. Since the fall of the Soviet Union, the United States has had the luxury of not funding defensive capabilities nor expending time and effort training to use them. We need to focus on that now because the threat will continue to escalate.

The understanding that Air Force Space Command has to be a warfighting command is a major step forward. Space provides vital support to all operational forces, but it cannot assume space will be a sanctuary in the event of a major war. China's has already demonstrated ground-based kinetic interceptors and is developing "ground-based directed energy weapons, ground-based satellite jammers, computer network operations, and co-orbital ASAT systems."[29] Thus, the U.S. effort to develop systems to replace space-based capabilities rapidly are essential to both deter enemy action in space and to recover if enemies choose to attack U.S. space assets.

The United States currently ties the cyber and electromagnetic domains together. Although the DoD is improving it capabilities in both domains, the investment is a fraction of that dedicated to the traditional air, land, and sea domains. Yet, cyber and EW remain key U.S. vulnerabilities. Establishing Cyber Command and starting the discussion about designating the electromagnetic spectrum as a domain are both positive first steps. However, given the heavy investments by China and Russia, it is essential the Pentagon assign them a higher priority. This will mean reallocating resources from other programs. By reducing the F-35 buy, terminating the B-21 program, and stopping carrier construction after the *USS Enterprise,* the third *Ford-class* carrier, the Pentagon could free up major funds to invest very heavily in the critical cyber and electronic warfare fields.

SUMMARY

Each technology discussed in this book is already challenging U.S. legacy systems and will defeat them within the next two decades. At the same time, defense budgets will be squeezed by other demands. The Joint Force has to think and operate differently. It must start by accepting that new systems are ready to replace some of the legacy systems like carriers and bombers that are central to service cultures. When the Pentagon chooses to terminate these programs, the services can continue to operate existing systems as they phase in their replacements. Next, the services have to examine where relatively small investments in systems that are now partners with their legacy systems can expedite their becoming replacements. Last, the Department of Defense has to scan the horizon continuously to see which of today's experimental systems can become assistance for our legacy systems.

These technologies are still in the infancy stage, but within a decade they will have major impacts and within two decades are likely to dominate the battlefield. Further, advanced manufacturing with 3D printing will allow massive numbers of these systems to be produced.

Perhaps the biggest question the United States has to ask is whether the products of the fourth industrial revolution will allow ground-based swarms of drones and missiles to force legacy air and sea systems to withdraw so far that they are no longer effective. In short, do families of missiles teamed with ground-based air, sea, underwater, and ground drones come to dominate all fighting domains?

NOTES

1. Adam Grisson, "The future of military innovation studies," *Journal of Strategic Studies*, 29:5, 905–934.
2. See Siegfried Breyer, *Battleships and Battlecruisers, 1905–1970*, (New York: Doubleday, 1973) for a detailed history of battleship development.
3. "HMS Ark Royal," http://www.naval-history.net/xGM-Chrono-04CV-Ark%20Royal.htm.
4. "U.S. Navy Battleship list," http://www.navy.mil/navydata/ships/battleships/bb-list.asp.
5. "U.S. Navy Carrier list," http://www.navy.mil/navydata/ships/carriers/cv-list.asp.
6. See Guilio Douhet, *Command of the Air* published in 1921 for his initial arguments.
7. Patrick Tucker, "Pentagon Tester: F-35 Program Rushing Tests, Delays Still Likely," *Defense One,* January 11, 2017, http://www.defenseone.com/technology/2017/01/pentagon-inspector-f-35-program-rushing-testing-delays-still-likely/134531.
8. Valerie Insinna, "The Pentagon is battling the clock to fix serious, unreported F-35 problems," *DefenseNews,* June 12, 2019, https://www.defensenews.com/air/2019/06/12/the-pentagon-is-battling-the-clock-to-fix-serious-unreported-f-35-problems/.
9. "Cancel the Littoral Combat Ship Program," Congressional Budget Office, https://www.cbo.gov/budget-options/2013/44771.
10. Jeremiah Gertler, "Air Force B-21 Raider Long-Range Strike Bomber," Congressional Research Service, June 7, 2017, https://fas.org/sgp/crs/weapons/R44463.pdf.
11. Dan Grazier, "How Not to Build an Aircraft Carrier: The pricey history of USS 'Ford'," *War is Boring,* June 5, 2017, https://warisboring.com/how-not-to-build-an-aircraft-carrier/.
12. Wheeler, "More Than the Navy's Numbers Could Be Sinking."
13. Tara Copp, "Less than half of the US bomber fleet is ready to 'fight tonight'," *Air Force Times,* August 12, 2017, https://www.airforcetimes.com/news/your-air-force/2017/08/12/less-than-half-of-the-us-bomber-fleet-is-ready-to-fight-tonight/.

14. James Drew Washington, "Kratos Combat Drones Go On The Offensive," *Aviation Week & Space Technology*, February 7, 2017, http://aviationweek.com/combat-aircraft/kratos-combat-drones-go-offensive.

15. Air University Research, "Fast Space: Leveraging Ultra Low-Cost Space Access for the 21st Century," Air University, 2017, http://www.airuniversity.af.mil/Portals/10/Research/documents/Space/Fast%20Space_Public_2017.pdf.

16. "United States Department of Defense Fiscal Year 2017 Budget Request Program Acquisition Cost By Weapon System," Office Of The Under Secretary Of Defense (Comptroller) /Chief Financial Officer. January 2016, 63, https://comptroller.defense.gov/Portals/45/documents/defbudget/FY2017/FY2017_Weapons.pdf#page=63.

17. Katherine Blakeley, "Analysis of the FY 2017 Defense Budget and Trends in Defense Spending," Center for Strategic and Budgetary Assessment, 2017, 52, https://csbaonline.org/uploads/documents/CSBA6196-2017-Budget-Analysis_PRINT.pdf.

18. "President Trump Seeks $12B Increase in FY2019 VA Budget to Support Nation's Veterans," Veterans Administration Press Release, February 12, 2018, https://www.va.gov/opa/pressrel/pressrelease.cfm?id=4007.

19. "DoD Releases Fiscal Year 2018 Budget Proposal," Department of Defense Press Release, May 23, 2017, https://www.defense.gov/News/News-Releases/News-Release-View/Article/1190216/dod-releases-fiscal-year-2018-budget-proposal/.

20. R. Robinson Harris, "Converting Merchant Ships to Missile Ships for the Win."

21. Valerie Insinna, "F-35 price falls below $90M for first time in new deal," *DefenseNews*, September 28, 2018, https://www.defensenews.com/air/2018/09/28/f-35-price-falls-before-90m-for-first-time-ever-in-new-deal/.

22. Aaron Methta, "Pentagon 'can't afford the sustainment costs on F-35, Lord says," *DefenseNews*, February 1, 2018, https://www.defensenews.com/air/2018/02/01/pentagon-cant-afford-the-sustainment-costs-on-f-35-lord-says/.

23. J. Randy Forbes and Chris Stewart, "Prioritize the Long-Range Strike Mission," *National Interest*, November 20, 2013, http://nationalinterest.org/commentary/prioritize-the-long-range-strike-mission-9432.

24. Ibid.

25. "Hardened and deeply buried targets," *Effects of Nuclear Earth-Penetrators and Other Weapons*, National Academies Press, 2005, 13, https://www.nap.edu/read/11282/chapter/4.

26. T. A. Keaney and Eliot Cohen, *Gulf War Air Power Survey*, Department of the Air Force, Washington DC, 1993, 89–90, http://www.dtic.mil/dtic/tr/fulltext/u2/a273996.pdf.
27. Forbes and Stewart, "Prioritize the Long-Range Strike Mission."
28. "Hardened and deeply buried targets," 13.
29. Staff, "China's Position on a Code of Conduct in Space," U.S.-China Security and Economic Review Commission, September 8, 2017, https://www.uscc.gov/sites/default/files/Research/USCC_China%27s%20Position%20on%20a%20Code%20of%20Conduct%20in%20Space.pdf.

CHAPTER 8

CONCLUSION

We stand on the brink of a technological revolution that will fundamentally alter the way we live, work, and relate to one another. In its scale, scope, and complexity, the transformation will be unlike anything humankind has experienced before.

—Klaus Schwab[1]

The previous chapters examined how the convergence of technology is changing the character of war and driving major changes in international trade and security structures. This chapter will explore how the United States may preserve those critical alliances without bankrupting itself.

DECLINING POPULAR SUPPORT FOR GLOBAL ENGAGEMENT

Starting in the 1950s, there had been a general consensus among Americans that U.S. security was closely tied to our international alliances. However, in the last few years that attitude has been changing. A 2016 Pew Research Center poll on the issue reported that

> Nearly six-in-ten Americans (57%) want the U.S. "to deal with its own problems and let other countries deal with their own

problems as best they can." Just 37% say the U.S. should help other countries deal with their problems.[2]

In 2019, the Eurasian Group Foundation reported two primary conclusions it derived from a nationwide survey of Americans of voting age:

> First, the public desire for a more restrained U.S. foreign policy is significant and diverse. It crosses party lines and generational boundaries...The second conclusion is that a chasm persists between what American believe is their country's appropriate role in the world and what foreign policy leaders believe.[3]

The costly, repeated failures in Vietnam, Afghanistan, Iraq, Syria, and Somalia have made the U.S. population increasingly reluctant to intervene overseas. In addition, the continuing failure of allies to spend what many Americans perceive to be their fair share in their own defense remains a high-profile issue in the Trump administration.

It appears four factors will reinforce the decline in U.S. public support for overseas intervention—the employment changes being driven by the revolution, the reduced reliance on overseas trade, the increasing cost of intervention, and budgetary pressures which will force the United States to choose between funding domestic programs or defense/international programs.

EMPLOYMENT CHANGES

The 2016 presidential election campaign and the 2018 midterms revealed the depth of concern and anger over changes in the labor market. Even though unemployment was declining and manufacturing jobs were increasing, it did not feel that way to many Americans. In addition, the failure of the minimum wage to keep up with inflation means that many cannot make a decent living even working full time. The explosive growth of robotics combined with the gig economy look to exacerbate these problems.

Previous revolutions all saw major increases in wealth but primarily to the owners of capital. The fourth industrial revolution will see the same happen. However, unlike previous revolutions, the fourth industrial revolution is deepening the knowledge and skills necessary for employment. The negative impact will be suffered most by the older, the less educated, and the poor.

REDUCED RELIANCE ON INTERNATIONAL TRADE

A central theme of this book has been the reshoring of manufacturing and service jobs to the economies they serve. Unlike other regions, North America's large markets, energy reserves, strong manufacturing base, advanced services industry, and food security mean it can become essentially self-reliant. Its increasing independence and overall wealth will reduce Americans' interest in intervening to maintain global security.

Even as industries such as energy, agriculture, aircraft manufacturers, and information technology expect to see their overseas markets grow, the fact that the United States will be importing less will reduce American interest in foreign affairs. The oil shocks of the 1970s got the attention of many Americans and resulted in much greater U.S. diplomatic and military focus on the region. However, today's multiple crisis in the Middle East—Syria, U.S.-Iran confrontation, Qatar versus Saudi Arabia, and instability in Iraq—have generated much less attention and even less willingness to get involved. Although some of the reluctance can be attributed to fatigue after eighteen years of war in the region, a good deal of apathy seems to be driven by how American citizens perceive these conflicts as having had minimal impact on them.

THE COST OF FUTURE INTERVENTION: MORE BLOOD AND TREASURE

Future interventions are likely to be more costly in both blood and treasure. Not only will the enemy forces have capabilities that used to be reserved for major powers, but the United States will also have to defend the entire length of its deployment channels. Host nations that provide facilities will require guarantees of U.S. protection from the type of long-range, precision strikes the U.S. has employed for decades. The technologies which are enabling small powers and insurgent groups to mount effective defenses are still in their infancies. Within a decade they will have major impacts, and within two decades are likely to dominate the battlefield. The increasing power and density of defensive weapons will increase other nations' ability to hold U.S. forces at bay.

Even as the cost of projecting power goes up, the cost of defending against terrorism and cyberattacks will increase and thus will consume more government and commercial resources.

BUDGETARY PRESSURES

As the DoD recovers from six years of sequestration and eighteen years of war, the current force is becoming increasingly expensive. According to the Congressional Budget Office, the three major categories of defense spending are all increasing rapidly:

—Costs of developing and buying weapons have been, on average, 20 percent to 30 percent higher than DoD's initial estimates.

—Costs for compensation of military personnel—including their active and retired healthcare benefits—have been rapidly increasing since 2000.

—Costs of operations and maintenance per active-duty service member have been steadily increasing since at least 1980.[4]

The major price increases in new equipment present challenges for the DoD as its conventional forces face major modernization requirements at the same that the nuclear triad of bombers, ballistic missile submarines, and intercontinental ballistic missiles all require replacement due to age.

The years of war combined with the Budget Control Act of 2011 resulted in dangerously low-readiness rates for all the services. In March 2018, the Air Force reported a mission-capable rate of 71.2% for all its aircraft. However, critical platforms had much lower readiness rates with half the F-22, F-35, B-1, and B-2A aircraft non-mission capable.[5] Naval aviation saw similar readiness rates with only sixty-two percent of its F-18s mission capable and only thirty-one percent fully mission capable in 2017.[6] Only twenty-six percent of the Marine Corps F-18s were mission capable.[7] Even the nuclear submarine force faced major maintenance backlogs with fifteen submarines idled.[8] Budget cuts forced the Navy to prioritize funding of forward deployed ships and those deploying next. Army ground and air units also suffered from readiness issues.

Even with the significant increases in the 2018 and 2019 budgets, it will take years to return to normal readiness levels. Army leadership believes that with the increased budgets it can reach readiness goals by 2022. It will then turn to modernization.[9] The Chief of Naval Operations reported to Congress that even with the budget increase it will be only in 2021 or 2022 before the Navy gets back to normal readiness status.[10] Exacerbating the budget situation, the systems the DoD is fielding today are not only vastly more expensive to purchase but also cost much more to operate. Current procurement plans indicate this will not change significantly.

Further, annual costs per active duty service person "increased from $58,240 per service member to $132,243 per service member" between 2001 and 2017.[11] In addition, Veterans Administration costs, although not part of the official DoD budget, are projected to continue their steep rise. When the Afghan War began in 2001, the VA budget was $49 billion. The Trump administration's 2019 Budget proposal for the VA is $196 billion.[12]

The DoD projects the defense budget will continue to grow at about two percent per year through the fiscal year 2023.[13] However, with the shift of control in the House of Representatives, this may be an optimistic projection. In April 2018, then Secretary of Defense James Mattis told Congress that the current National Defense Strategy is not sustainable if the budget caps return.[14]

Debt and Deficit Add to Budget Issues

Of particular concern is the rapid growth of U.S. debt, which is driving up debt interest payments, that will impact the U.S. budget strongly in the next few years. The Congressional Budget Office projects that the national debt will grow from $16 trillion in 2018 to $29 trillion by 2028. By 2020, mandatory interest payments on the national debt will roughly equal DoD's projected budget. The U.S. annual deficit is expected to increase to $1 trillion dollars per year by 2022.[15]

Even as debt and interest payments continue to rise, demands on social welfare programs will increase sharply. The Congressional Budget Office's (CBO) long-term spending projections indicate that by 2041 spending on Social Security, healthcare, and interest will exceed all revenue.[16]

With the cost-benefit ratio of intervention increasingly in the red, less perceived integration with the global economy, and rising entitlement and debt payments severely restricting available options, Americans may be tempted to return to the isolationism that was the standard prior to 1941. Exacerbating the problem is the cost of maintaining U.S. forces overseas, which will inevitably increase until the Pentagon transitions to forces that do not require large bases that must be defended. Although isolationism is not currently U.S. policy, Trump's rhetoric about "America First" and "obsolete" alliances can lead it in that direction. Once an alliance is dissolved it can be very hard to resurrect, thus it is essential the United States find a way to sustain alliances at significantly less cost.

SUSTAINING THE INTERNATIONAL SECURITY ORDER

On February 1, 2016, former CIA Director and Commander Central Command David H. Petraeus recognized this danger in testimony to the House Armed Services Committee

> As important as *those* various threats are, however, the world order has also been undermined by something perhaps even more pernicious—a loss of self-confidence, resolve, and strategic clarity on America's part about our vital interest in preserving and protecting the system we sacrificed so much to bring into being and have sacrificed so much to preserve.[17]

Petraeus' warning could well become reality as the fourth industrial revolution unfolds. To encourage American to remain engaged, U.S. leaders will be able to point to the export markets which will likely continue to grow such as aircraft, high technology, and agriculture. (Although agriculture will have to recover from the significant damage done by the Trump trade dispute with China.)[18] They will also be able to highlight the need for certain imports to maintain U.S. production but the argument to intervene overseas to establish stability in another nation or region will be very difficult to make.

WHY REMAIN ENGAGED?

If the changes I suggest in this book take place, then a legitimate question might be "Why should America remain engaged overseas?" American security planners must clearly express the value of the international security arrangements that have prevented major interstate war since 1945. Rooted in the idea that it is cheaper to sustain peace than to fight a war, the United States has consistently invested in the alliances that have prevented major wars. However, the United States cannot do so in the same way it has for the last seventy years. If we are to succeed, the United States must exploit the opportunities presented by the fourth industrial revolution to maintain the international security system at a sustainable cost. Fortunately, as a status quo power, the United States is well situated to benefit from the defense dominant aspects of the revolution.

KEY THREATS

An analysis of the threats and potential U.S. responses show that, with planning and political will, the United States can head off these threats even with flat or reduced budgets. The 2018 National Defense Strategy shifted the focus of U.S. defense to great power competition with China and Russia. The document also listed Iran, North Korea, and terrorism as threats that the United States must contain.[19] The strategy reiterated that the United States requires the help of our allies or at least use of their territories if the United States is to deal with these threats.

To support the National Defense Strategy, it is clear the United States has to maintain its position in Europe against Russia; in Asia in response to China and North Korea; and in the Middle East to contain Iran and terrorism. However, budget realities mean it must do so differently.

Fortunately, Russia's actions in Crimea and the Ukraine breathed some life back into NATO. At its 2014 summit in Wales, NATO members pledged to raise defense spending to two percent of their respective GDPs —although not until 2024. Unfortunately, although the United States continues to spend 3.6 percent, only five of the other twenty-seven NATO members have met the two-percent goal to date.[20] Even with Russia providing the incentive of an elevated threat, NATO leaders have to contend not only with their voters' reluctance to spend on defense but with strong disagreements about the source and severity of the threat. Northern and Eastern European nations see Russia as the clear and present threat and thus have been willing to spend more on their militaries. In contrast, Southern Europeans see mass refugee migration as a much more serious challenge and prefer to spend on border control and police. Further complicating NATO's calculation is the uncertainty created by the stark contrast between President Trump's declarations that

"NATO is obsolete" and statements by the vice president's and secretary of defense that U.S. commitment to NATO is unwavering.

European nations clearly have the population and wealth to create forces that can fend off both Russian pressure from the east and migration from the south and southeast. However, there is very little indication they have the collective political will to do so. Each NATO state faces its own major challenges and prioritizes threats and responses according to its unique conditions. Europe has never acted as a unified force. Even when faced with the very real possibility of a Soviet invasion, Europeans often disagreed sharply on defense issues—to the point France removed its forces from NATO command in 1967. It is unlikely they will agree in the future. With over seventy percent of European trade, capital investment, information, and travel conducted within the European Union, aging populations, and the accompanying increasing social budget costs, Europeans will have to decide how they want to provide for their national defenses—individually, collectively as NATO with limited U.S. commitments, or in smaller coalitions. Only two NATO nations— Britain and France—have independent nuclear capabilities. Europeans understand that the U.S. nuclear umbrella only serves as a deterrent if it is unconditional. Trump appears to be making it conditional. Europeans could turn to the British but former Prime Minister Teresa May hinted she "might make its nuclear shield a subject of negotiation during the upcoming Brexit talks."[21] At the time of this writing, Boris Johnson had just assumed his position as prime minister. Given his position on Brexit, it is unlikely he will dedicate Britain's nuclear security forces to European needs. For its part, France has been very clear that it will not share "sovereignty over its nuclear arms and has always been skeptical about shared deterrence."[22] Thus these deterrents would, at best, also be conditional.

Asia is already working through the impact of the U.S. withdrawal from the Trans-Pacific Partnership (TPP). The signing of the Comprehensive and Progressive Agreement for the Trans-Pacific Partnership (CP-TPP) is the key effort by the other eleven members in the now-dead TPP to capture its benefits. The good news is that it provides the possibility the United States could join the pact. But the CP-TPP members will not necessarily make it easy. Australia, traditionally one of America's closest allies in Asia, noted that the members would not be willing to undo the deal to accommodate new U.S. requirements.[23]

As complex as the issues are on the trade side, they are much more complex on the security side. Asia is home to two of the nations of concern to the United States—China and North Korea. U.S. allies and friends desire U.S. protection of the region remain in place because security arrangements in the absence of the United States will be very difficult. The United States provides both a nuclear umbrella and highly capable conventional forces to maintain stability in the region. Should China's aggressive actions in the East and South China Seas foreshadow a drive to hegemony, the other nations in the region will have serious cause for alarm. North Korea's growing nuclear arsenal and delivery systems are even more unsettling and currently the most likely source of major conflict in the region. If Japan and South Korea believe the U.S. commitment will fail, they may have to develop independent nuclear forces to confront either China or North Korea. The alternative would be to accept China as regional hegemon and place themselves at the mercy of a mercurial North Korean regime.

Iran, the last nation identified in the National Defense Strategy, and many violent extremist organizations are resident in the Middle East. Iran is clearly perceived as a threat to the Sunni nations in the region and Israel. There are quiet indications these nations are assisting each other in the long-drawn out conflict that is spreading across the region. Based on its negative experiences with previous "nation-building" efforts, most Americans remain very reluctant to get engaged in stabilization efforts. Yet instability is the primary threat to the region as various groups are attempting to redraw colonial boundaries to conform to the social and ethnic realities on the ground. The nature of these conflicts ensures they will produce high numbers of refugees, which will lead to southern Europeans focusing even more on the immigration threat and reducing their interest in investing in additional conventional forces to contain Russia. Worse, the historical record shows that instability based on nation formation creates very long conflicts—many of which have lasted centuries.

Even as Middle Eastern nations struggle with internal stability, confrontation between states is growing. The June 2017 imposition of an embargo of Qatar by a coalition of Arab states led by Saudi Arabia shows that longstanding tensions continue to plague the region. Increasing instability in the area combined with the financial fragility of several of the regimes indicate the Middle East will remain a source of anti-Western terrorist organizations. It is clear the United States cannot solve the problems in the region, so the best it can do is manage the toxicity that will leak out. The only viable, affordable option may be to remain engaged in what is essentially its "mowing the grass" strategy for the region.[24] The expense and long timelines may make other approaches unworkable.

Unfortunately, the Trump administration's increasing efforts to control Iran's behavior has increased the potential for U.S-Iranian open conflict. These actions are placing increased demand on U.S. conventional forces even as they struggle to regain readiness levels.

The National Defense Strategy does not assign a high priority to either Latin America or Africa. Latin America migration is rapidly becoming a key Trump campaign issue and the administration increased Department of Homeland Security action against illegal immigrants as well as committing to building a wall. However, it has not yet tasked the Department of Defense with a major role in dealing with these issues other than reprograming appropriated funds and sending a limited number of troops to the border.

The undergoverned areas of sub-Saharan Africa will continue to provide fertile soil for terror groups despite the trillions the United States has spent addressing global terrorism. However, terror based in sub-Saharan

Africa does not represent a major threat to the United States. Instability and poverty in sub-Saharan and North Africa will generate large numbers of refugees, but the vast majority will try to migrate to Europe. These regions have been, and remain, at the bottom of U.S. priorities.

To deal with the apparently increasing global insecurity, the United States has a range of grand strategic options, from restraint to aggressive interventionism.[25] No matter what security policy the United States selects, either globally or for each region, the diffusion of power inherent in the fourth industrial revolution will make it more difficult. The viability of projecting power from the United States becomes questionable when almost any enemy can strike selectively at U.S. facilities from in-theater to the United States. America will find its options limited and will be required to rethink how it projects power. Our enemies and allies will know this.

RECOMMENDATIONS

The government can no longer assume Americans are going to support our alliance commitments. To sustain them, it must reduce the cost to the United States and increase the visible contributions of its allies. Fortunately, if intelligently applied, the remarkable advances being created by the fourth industrial revolution and the inherent geographic and economic strengths of our alliances provide a path to stronger alliances at a lower cost. In both Asia and Europe, our alliances are essentially defensive in nature and occupy terrain that favors the defense. Therefore, the technological advances of the fourth industrial revolution actually favor U.S. alliances.

To take advantage of these advances, the United States needs to develop a comprehensive plan for phasing in the replacements for the extremely expensive and increasingly vulnerable weapons systems it is currently purchasing. If the United States leads the way in this transition, allied nations are much more likely to follow. If the United States insists on continuing to purchase exquisite but very expensive weapons, it is likely allied nations will also focus their limited funds on these systems in an effort to sustain interoperability and connections with the United States.

One of the first steps should be to stop investing so heavily in expensive assets that require large, mature bases to operate effectively. The cost of defending such bases will soon exceed the benefits of having them. Long-range, increasingly stealthy drones that do not require large bases are already in the design-and-test phase. Combined with existing and improved ballistic and cruise missiles, they will make bases extremely expensive to defend or even untenable. The arrival of hypersonic weapons will mean that any major airbase will simply be a trap for the aircraft stationed there.

Some of those at the Pentagon charged with conceptualizing the future force have pointed out this is the direction the U.S. military should move. William Roper, when he was Director of the Pentagon's Strategic Capabilities Office, predicted that "future wars will be fought with swarms of expendable, disaggregated, intelligent systems rather than the big, expensive weapons platforms the U.S. has relied on for fifty years."[26]

The Pentagon has started on this path already. It simply must make this a conscious procurement strategy rather than the current system of random evolution. There is no question the current force needs to modernize, but it needs to do so by embracing entirely new concepts of operations and supporting equipment. Using the assistant-to-partner-to-replacement model, it will be able to get maximum use out of legacy systems even as it replaces them.

For instance, the highly centralized Geographic and Functional Combatant Commands as well as the service components' operational headquarters are housed in massive, exposed headquarters. Several are in geographically exposed locations that can be subjected to physical destruction. All are subject to electronic warfare and cyber warfare. Protecting these facilities against the rapidly evolving fourth industrial revolution weapons will be extremely expensive. Both the physical and software elements of the communications links are also extremely vulnerable. The United States needs to conduct free-play wargames where the enemy is allowed to disrupt or destroy these headquarters. In addition to developing defensive measures, both active and passive, to protect these facilities, the commands must learn to operate when heavily disrupted. This clearly means doing without the daily teleconference briefings and perhaps even without a centralized air-tasking order. To date, the armed forces have not seriously challenged the operations of these facilities in our exercises. It must be a priority to do so—and then adapt to the new reality that our headquarters are not sanctuaries.

The most important national security step the United States can take is to reinforce and reassure our allies in both Asia and Europe. Given the United States current situation, the nation should focus its declining security resources on sustaining its alliances, and hence the status quo, in the truly strategic areas of East Asia, Eastern Europe, and the Gulf while managing the worldwide terror threat.

Asia

Even as the United States and its allies continue to invest heavily in legacy systems, China is refining numerous weapons systems specifically to attack their prime vulnerabilities—the need for major fixed bases and the limited range of most U.S. aircraft. To be blunt, the United States and its allies are spending vast sums on systems for which China is already fielding increasingly effective counters. It has already demonstrated the ability to use missiles to strike fixed bases[27] and claims it can target carriers at sea with anti-ship ballistic missiles.[28]

A shift from the few, vulnerable, and very expensive current platforms to the future force of smaller, cheaper, autonomous weapons can allow the United States to maintain a forward presence but at a much lower cost.

A second major benefit of shifting to an arsenal of small, smart, and many weapons is that the United States can push its Asian allies to follow suit. Japan and South Korea both have sophisticated, capable defense industries. Korea is already spending heavily on defense, so for them it is a matter of shifting investment from legacy platforms to emerging ones. Unfortunately, despite six years of budget increases, Japan's defense budget[29] did not reach even one percent of its GDP in 2018.[30] The United States must push Japan to achieve at least the NATO goal of two percent. It will be less difficult for Japan to increase its defense budget if the additional funds are spent on systems built in Japan by Japanese firms.

Smaller Asian nations could also afford a limited number of these systems. Although Vietnam, the Philippines, or Indonesia will not field enough cruise missiles and drones to overwhelm the defenses of a Chinese naval task force, they could close their adjacent waters to merchant ships. The ability to threaten China's foreign trade can serve as a powerful deterrent. Further, the geography of Vietnam, the Philippines, and Indonesia lends itself well to dispersion and protection of limited assets. The use of small, smart and many weapons offers these nations an affordable way to protect their sovereignty.

Against China, the dominance of the defense actually works for allied forces if they choose to hold the First Island Chain, the chain of islands that stretch from northern Japan through Taiwan and the Philippines to Indonesia, while denying China's use of the waters inside the First Island Chain or access to the ocean beyond.[31] Under this concept, the allies will not seek to win by striking into China but by choking Chinese international trade and thus exhausting China's ability to fight. This recognizes the reality that wars between major, capable powers have usually lasted years rather than months. It is also informed by the inherent limitations of a strike campaign against a continental-sized enemy.

If the United States leads, a key strength in this approach can be allied mobile land-based air and ground systems fighting from the First Island Chain. They restrict China's access to the Pacific Ocean. U.S. and Japanese naval forces can act as linebackers behind the Chain to block Chinese efforts to breakout through one of the straits or overwhelm the defenses at a specific point.

However, to survive today, allied air forces and logistics facilities must be dispersed. U.S. and Japanese forces have begun limited exercises to demonstrate they can operation their air forces from a wider range of bases. It is essential that all allied forces practice dispersed operations regularly to ensure their legacy systems retain some deterrent value. Demonstrating this capability will have a deterrent effect on China by greatly reducing the probability of a successful preemptive attack on allied legacy forces even as the allies begin moving to mobile systems of missiles and drones.

As long as air power is tethered to bases inside range of China's missile and drones, they remain vulnerable to preemption. It is essential that the United States and Japan cooperate in rapidly designing and procuring long-range, advanced cruise and hypersonic missiles as well as vertical takeoff and landing drones. The United States already has promising military designs such as the QX222 and adaptable civilian designs like the DX-3 and Flexrotor. The key is shifting investment from current systems to accelerate the development and fielding of these new systems.

Forces fighting on the defensive from the First Island Chain already have a wide range of advantages against attacking Chinese air and sea forces. The most obvious is that Chinese forces will be fighting inside the Allied Air Defense zone. The second is the fact that many of China's forces lack the range to reach the islands and thus the allies will only have to fight a portion of the People's Liberation Army forces. These advantages will grow as conflict shifts from few and exquisite platforms to the small, smart, and many. Using this strategy, the allies gain the advantage of thousands of smart drones launched from commercial trucks and ships. It will also take advantage of fact that land forces will have much larger magazines and access to massive power infrastructure for directed energy weapons when they are developed.

North Korea is the other Asian threat identified in U.S. strategic documents. It is the most likely country to cause a major disruption by initiating a major war with South Korea. Although North Korea would lose such a war, the war would inflict massive devastation on both sides. Even in the highly unlikely case that Trump succeeds in terminating North Korea's nuclear program, Pyongyang will still have thousands of artillery pieces that can wreak havoc on South Korea. Thus, deterrence will remain an essential element to maintaining peace on the peninsula. If the United States military can make the transition to the small, smart, and many systems of the fourth industrial revolution, it will eliminate the possibility of North Korea destroying allied air power on the ground with its rocket and missile forces. A force based on a mix of legacy systems and small, smart, and many autonomous systems will be well positioned to deter and, if necessary, assist South Korea in defeating the north. And, if the Japanese and Koreans make the same shift, they will be able to contribute more to the defense of the Korean Peninsula.

Europe
Much of the same approach can work for NATO. It is fairly clear that barring a full Russian invasion, most NATO members are not going to meet the two-percent pledge.[32] Fortunately, NATO's mission is inherently defensive, and the fourth industrial revolution offers relatively inexpensive defensive systems. The addition of GRAMM munitions, smart mines, autonomous drones, and the creative use of improvised explosive devices (IEDs) can relatively cheaply increase deterrence against Russian aggression. For instance, a twenty-foot shipping container filled with ammonium nitrate (fertilizer) creates a cheap 50,000-pound improvised explosive device. By shifting to less expensive, defensive systems, even small nations can become porcupines. Although a bear can certainly eat a porcupine, it will not.

For NATO the key question will remain one of unity. An essential element of keeping America tightly engaged in NATO is for those nations to demonstrate an increased willingness and ability to defend the Alliance against Russia. NATO nations can do so by exploiting the cheaper but highly capable weapons evolving out of technological advances.[33] Combined with thoughtful tactics, focused organizations, and some U.S. support, they can clearly deter and, if necessary, defeat Russian conventional forces. Once again to make this happen, the United States needs to lead the way in the transition.

Iran

Iran will retain both the capability to employ irregular forces throughout the region and to fire volleys of ballistic missiles at targets across the region. The proliferation of small autonomous drones will significantly increase the reach and power of its irregular forces even as it increases the ability of its defensive forces to keep other forces out of the Persian Gulf. These advances will also provide sophisticated-but-simple-to-operate weapons that Iran, or any state sponsor of terror, can provide to a terrorist group. If it chooses, Iran can continue to cause instability in the Middle East thorough its support of Shia insurgent and terrorist groups.

Fortunately, if they take advantage of the small, smart, and many weapons revolution, the Gulf States can defend their sovereign territory from Iranian conventional forces. Given the budget problems caused by continuing relatively low oil prices, the Gulf States no longer have unlimited assets to spend on expensive Western weapons systems. They can choose the same path available to the Europeans. These states could buy the containerized autonomous drones and missiles systems that can provide deterrence and assured retaliation against any Iranian conventional aggression. Besides being cheaper than legacy weapons, they will reduce manpower and training requirements which always present a challenge to these nations.

Violent Islamic Extremists

Stability in the Middle East presents a serious challenge. The energy revolution's impact on petro-dependent states has already been dramatic. Oil prices have been cut in half. Even with the collapse of Venezuelan oil, crude oil inventories falling below the five-year average, allied missile strikes into Syria, Iranian attacks on oil tankers, the threat of war in the Middle East, and the summer driving season, the price a barrel of West

Texas Intermediate remained near $60 in July 2019.[34] This is well below the levels petro-states need to sustain their current social contracts with their people. They simply cannot continue the cradle-to-grave social systems that were put in place when oil prices were high.

As this economic crisis unfolds among petro-states, the United States will have less reason to support most nations in the Middle East. Daniel L. Byman of the Brookings Institute observed in March 2016 that U.S. interests in the Middle East historically hinged on keeping oil prices down, working toward Israeli-Palestinian peace, pushing democracy, fighting communism, and counterterrorism. He notes the U.S. shale oil boom has reduced the first. The prospects for Israeli-Palestinian peace are very low. Pushing democracy has gone out of favor and Communism has disappeared. Thus, only counterterrorism and the security of Israel are still supported by a majority of Americans.[35] The good news is that Israel has repeatedly demonstrated that it is capable of providing its own security with U.S. technical and financial assistance.

However, the petro-states' inability to keep their social contracts with their citizens will mean increasing instability in some of these states. As demonstrated in Syria and Iraq, instability not only causes violence within a country but spills over into adjacent states through violent exiles and large numbers of refugees.

This is of concern as traditional societies throughout the region struggle to reconcile their relatively new state boundaries with the much older ethnic, religious, and social connections. It is beyond the power of the United States and its allies to resolve these issues. Historically, disputes based on ethnic, religious, social, and traditional relations have taken decades to centuries to settle. Thus, Pentagon planners will have to assume that this region will remain a source of instability and terror —potentially for decades. Similar conditions in several nations in sub-Saharan Africa will yield the same results.

Terrorism represents a very small threat to American statistically, but the political reality is that American citizens demand that their government take action. Thus, U.S. planners must assume that the demand for Special Operations Forces to conduct "mowing-the-grass" operations will remain high and the demand for advisors will continue. The good news is that Special Operations Command is already at the leading edge of exploiting new technologies to increase the effectiveness of its forces. It can serve as a model for the services.

CONCLUSION

> When compared with previous industrial revolutions, the Fourth is evolving at an exponential rather than a linear pace. Moreover, it is disrupting almost every industry in every country. And the breadth and depth of these changes herald the transformation of entire systems of production, management, and governance.[36]

The convergence of these technologies is fundamentally altering the structure of international trade by returning manufacturing and services to the markets where they are consumed. At the same time, energy production is becoming more local and regional as it moves to renewables. As a result, deglobalization is occurring.

At the same time, it is very likely that all nations—including the United States—will have to contend with significant decreases in military spending over the next two decades. To be in position to exploit the new technologies and encourage our allies to do so, the United States must lead their development. Because the overwhelming majority of the investment in fourth-industrial-revolution technologies is already coming from the commercial section, the focus for the Department of Defense must be to identify key niche technologies unlikely to draw commercial money —such as nano-explosives, smart mine fuzes, and weapons that ensure the small, smart, and many weapons have maximum combat power. For instance, the Poles took existing drone technology and paired it with small thermobaric warheads the Russians developed over a decade ago. This mashup between old technology and new will greatly increase the effective combat power of each and is exactly the type of program that will provide highly capable but relatively cheap weapons.

One of the biggest obstacles to the transition to a new generation of weapons systems and new methods of warfare will remain the political constituencies that benefit from the current systems. They represent thousands of high paying jobs in hundreds of Congressional districts nationwide. The beneficiaries will not give up these benefits without a fight.

Compounding the problem, military leaders have been conservative about the adoption of new concepts and technologies. Over their careers they have developed confidence both in the existing capabilities and in their ability to use them effectively. Given the very high risk to the nation, its military personnel, and their own careers involved in employing military force, military leaders tend to be slow to adopt new approaches. The key question is whether the Department of Defense can get ahead of the changes or be overrun by an enemy who has embraced them.

The United States cannot meet these security challenges by continuing to operate as it has since the Cold War. Instead, the United States must lead its allies is seizing the significant advantages the new generation of small, smart, and inexpensive systems can provide. Combined with the allies' natural geographic advantages, these systems paired with the right strategic and operational approaches can provide affordable, effective, and sustainable deterrence, and if necessary, defense.

The fourth industrial revolution is a good news story. And the United States is the nation best positioned to derive maximum economic benefits. American natural advantages of geographic location, exceptional natural resources, friendly neighbors, a large talented population, and a propensity for innovation mean U.S. businesses are uniquely positioned to develop the ideas, funding, tools, and workforce to lead the revolution.

The bad news is that America's progress toward a fourth industrial revolution economy could become easily derailed by three major issues

—immigration policy, trade policy, and political gridlock. The first, immigration policy, remains a hot political issue. Unfortunately, one element that is not broadly discussed in the U.S. immigration debate is the intellectual nature of the fourth industrial revolution. To progress into the fourth industrial revolution requires large number of smart, skilled, and educated people. Innovation at the top of the scale requires advanced education in STEM skills. The 330 million people of the United States cannot hope to stay ahead of the seven billion people in the rest of the world. However, it can significantly improve its chances by encouraging the best STEM students from around the world to come to America for an education and then stay to work. In 2017, foreign nationals accounted

> for 81 percent of the full-time graduate students in electrical engineering and petroleum engineering, 79 percent in computer science, 75 percent in industrial engineering, 69 percent in statistics, 63 percent in mechanical engineering and economics, statistics, 59 percent in civil engineering and 57 percent in chemical engineering.[37]

The United States is generally recognized as having the finest university system in the world, and it attracts very large numbers of the best foreign students. This is a major advantage, but what really counted is the number of foreign STEM graduates who chose to remain in the United States to work increased by four hundred percent from 2008 to 2016. In essence, the United States was attracting and keeping some of the finest minds in the world.

In 2017, two things happened that dramatically reversed the flow of foreign students into U.S. universities. First, the Trump administration made it much harder for students to obtain visas or to be certain they could renew them year to year. At the same time, the administration restricted the number of graduates who can remain in the country to work. The result has been a major downturn in the number of foreign students enrolled in U.S. universities. Other countries have seen the success the United States was having and have started their own aggressive recruiting programs to attract foreign students. Current U.S. policy is assisting those foreign programs in attracting top students. It makes no sense for a foreign student to invest heavily in a U.S. education when the visa might not be renewed and thus the investment will not pay off in a degree. Even if one succeeds in getting a degree, the U.S. job market, which needs STEM graduates, will be closed. It makes much more sense to go to school in Canada, Australia, or the United Kingdom. Canada and Australia in particular are encouraging overseas students.

Not only do these policies deprive the United States of intelligent, productive students and potential citizens, they are also hurting U.S. universities. Overseas students pay higher tuitions that U.S. citizens so in effect subsidize their education. Universities across the country are having to cut STEM programs due to the reduction in funds flowing in from overseas.[38]

In short, current U.S. immigration policies are directly responsible for reducing the flow of the people America needs to thrive in the fourth industrial revolution. By failing to distinguish effectively between types of potential immigrants, the United States is excluding a great deal of exceptional talent. In sharp contrast, forward-thinking governments are striving to entice the best and brightest from around the world to move to their nations. Current immigration policies are damaging American prospects for success in a rapidly changing global economy.

Trade policy is a second area that could well hamper U.S. transition to the fourth industrial revolution. The North American market is large. The combined U.S., Canadian, and Mexican populations totals 486 million. This market is also wealthy: Mexico's GDP per capita is $19,500. Canada's is $48,100 and the United States' is $59,500. (Canada and Mexico's per capita GDP uses purchasing power parity figures.)[39] Thus North American is ideally situated to thrive in a world of regional markets. Unfortunately, the current trade disruption and failure to ratify the United States Mexico Canada Agreement is causing great uncertainty as CEOs try to make investment decisions to exploit these advantages.

Finally, the alarming political dysfunction that has characterized American politics for the last couple of decades is perhaps the biggest threat to U.S. prosperity in the emerging revolution. A widely identified and lamented development, the dysfunction clearly threatens American security. The Executive and Legislative Branches inability to pass defense spending bills for years deepened the readiness and modernization crises now facing the U.S. military. The recent increases in defense spending help, but the fact they are funded by an increasing deficit simply highlighted the political impasse. Whereas the defense implications are painfully obvious, the inability to take steps to assist U.S. businesses and educational institutions to thrive in the fourth industrial revolution will cause much greater, longer-term economic damage. American political leaders face a choice: They can continue the divisive "us-against-them" politics that have dominated the last decade, or they can lead the American people to recognize we are in this together. There is no question that this will be an extremely challenging leadership issue. It will also be the central leadership issue of the next two decades.

Notes

1. Klaus Schwab, "The Fourth Industrial Revolution: what it means, how to respond," World Economic Forum, January 14, 2016, https://www.weforum.org/agenda/2016/01/the-fourth-industrial-revolution-what-it-means-and-how-to-respond.

2. Bruce Drake and Carroll Doherty, "Key findings on how Americans view the U.S. role in the world," Pew Research Center, May 5, 2016, http://www.pewresearch.org/fact-tank/2016/05/05/key-findings-on-how-americans-view-the-u-s-role-in-the-world.

3. Mark Hannah, "Worlds Apart: U.S. Foreign Policy and American Public Opinion," Eurasia Group Foundation, February 2019, 19.

4. David E. Mosher, "Prospects for DoD's Budget Over the Next Decade," Congressional Budget Office, February 5, 2018, https://www.cbo.gov/system/files/115th-congress-2017-2018/presentation/53542-presentation.pdf.

5. Stephan Losey, "Fewer planes are ready to fly: Air Force mission-capable rates decline amid pilot crisis," *Air Force Times*, March 5, 2018, https://www.airforcetimes.com/news/your-air-force/2018/03/05/fewer-planes-are-ready-to-fly-air-force-mission-capable-rates-decline-amid-pilot-crisis/.

6. Hope Hodge Seck, "Navy Cutting Maintenance, Cannibalizing Planes Amid Readiness Crisis," *Military.com*, November 9, 2107, https://www.military.com/dodbuzz/2017/11/09/navy-cutting-maintenance-cannibalizing-planes-amid-readiness-crisis.

7. Sydney J. Freedberg, Jr., "62 % Of F-18 Hornets Unfit To Fly, Up To 74% In Marines," *Breaking Defense*, February 7, 2017, https://breakingdefense.com/2017/02/62-of-f-18-hornets-unfit-to-fly-dod-hill-focus-on-readiness/.

8. Sydney J. Freedberg, Jr., "15 Subs Kept Out of Service: 177 Months Of Drydock Backups," *Breaking Defense*, October 31, 2017, https://breakingdefense.com/2017/10/15-subs-kept-out-of-service-177-months-of-drydock-backups/.

9. Matthew Cox, "Army Aims to Reach Readiness Goal by 2022, Then Shift to Modernization," *Military.com*, March 7, 2018, https://www.military.com/dodbuzz/2018/03/07/army-aims-reach-readiness-goal-2022-then-shift-modernization.html.

10. Megan Eckstein, "CNO: Navy to Restore Readiness Levels by 2022 After Years of Insufficient Funding," *USNI News,* April 19, 2018, https://news.usni.org/2018/04/19/cno-navy-restore-readiness-levels-2 022-years-insufficient-funding?utm_source=RC+Defense+Morning+ Recon&utm_campaign=bbfb7fd317-EMAIL_CAMPAIGN_2018_04_19& utm_medium=email&utm_term=0_694f73a8dc-bbfb7fd317-83981957.

11. Katherine Blakeley, "Analysis of the FY 2017 Defense Budget and Trends in Defense Spending," Center for Strategic and Budgetary Assessment, 2017, 52.

12. Leo Shane III, "VA spending up again in Trump's fiscal 2019 budget plan," *Military Times,* February 12, 2018, https://www.militarytimes. com/veterans/2018/02/12/va-spending-up-again-in-trumps-fiscal-2019-budget-plan/.

13. "U.S. Department of Defense Fiscal Year 2019 Budget Request Briefing," Office of the Undersecretary of Defense (Comptroller)/CFP February 2018, 6.

14. Joe Gould, "Mattis: New defense strategy won't work under budget caps," *DefenseNews,* April 26, 2018, https://www.defensenews.com/congress/20 18/04/26/mattis-new-defense-strategy-wont-work-under-budget-caps/.

15. Jeff Stein, "Deficit to top $1 trillion per year by 2020, CBO says," *Washington Post,* April 9, 2018, https://www.washingtonpost.com/ business/economy/deficit-to-top-1-trillion-per-year-by-2020-cbo-says/20 18/04/09/93c331d4-3c0e-11e8-a7d1-e4efec6389f0_story.html?utm_term= .020002545131.

16. "CBO's 2018 Long-Term Budget Outlook," June 26, 2018, Committee for a Responsible Federal Budget, https://www.crfb.org/papers/cbos-2018-long-term-budget-outlook.

17. David H. Petraeus, "The State of the World," House Armed Services Committee, February 1, 2017, http://docs.house.gov/meetings/AS/AS00/ 20170201/105509/HHRG-115-AS00-Wstate-PetraeusD-20170201.pdf.

18. Brittany Shoot, "America's Farmers Face Challenging Times. Loan Delinquencies Hit a Nine-Year High," *Fortune,* February 28, 2019, http:// fortune.com/2019/02/28/agriculture-farm-fsa-loan-delinquency-usda/.

19. "Summary of the 2018 National Defense Strategy of the United States of America," https://dod.defense.gov/Portals/1/Documents/pubs/2018-National-Defense-Strategy-Summary.pdf.

20. "Military spending by NATO members," *Economist,* February 16–22, 2017, https://www.economist.com/blogs/graphicdetail/2017/02/daily-chart-1.

21. "Germans are debating getting their own nuclear weapon," *Economist,* March 4–10, 2017, https://www-economist-com.libproxy.smu.edu.sg/ europe/2017/03/04/germans-are-debating-getting-their-own-nuclear-weapon?zid=310&ah=4326ea44f22236ea534e2010ccce1932.
22. Ibid.
23. "Australia says 'no appetite' for major TPP changes after Donald Trump signals US may want to rejoin," *South China Morning Post,* April 15, 2018, http://www.scmp.com/news/asia/diplomacy/article/2141781/australia-says-no-appetite-major-tpp-changes-after-donald-trump.
24. Efraim Inbar and Eitan Shamir, "Mowing the Grass in Gaza," Begin-Sadat Center for Strategic Studies, July 20, 2014, https://besacenter.org/ perspectives-papers/mowing-grass-gaza.
25. Frank G. Hoffman, "Forward Partnership: A Sustainable U.S. Strategy," *Orbis* 57, no. 1 (Winter 2013): 20–40.
26. Aaron Mehta, "DoD weapons designer: Swarming teams of drones will dominate future wars," *DefenseNews,* March 30, 2017, http://www. defensenews.com/articles/dod-weapons-designer-swarming-teams-of-drones-will-dominate-future-wars.
27. Oriana Skyler Mastro and Ian Easton, "Risk and Resiliency: China's Emerging Air Base Strike Threat," Project 2049 Institute, November 8, 2017, https://poseidon01.ssrn.com/delivery.php?ID=5 83078083024093003122115099096102124033019081079037056018099 one hundred07509902201408509108706202060960280one hundredone hundred4702200509602511011106403307303708508810807802312712311 6 104088040081094123115097116001081085070021081115026092074104001 019077095078080118099094067114&EXT=pdf.
28. Harry Kazianis, "Did China Test its 'Carrier-Killer?'" *The Diplomat,* January 24, 2013, https://thediplomat.com/2013/01/did-china-test-its-carrier-killer/.
29. "Defense Programs and Budget of Japan Ministry of Defense, Overview of FY2018 Budget," Ministry of Defense Japan, 7, http://www.mod.go. jp/e/d_budget/pdf/300329.pdf.
30. "Gross Domestic Product for Japan," FRED, https://fred.stlouisfed.org/ series/JPNNGDP.
31. T.X. Hammes, "Offshore Control: A Proposed Strategy for an Unlikely Conflict," *Institute for National Strategic Studies,* June 2012, http://www. dtic.mil/dtic/tr/fulltext/u2/a577602.pdf; Andrew F. Krepinevich, "How to Deter China: The Case for Archipelagic Defense." *Foreign Affairs,*

March/April 2015, https://www.foreignaffairs.com/articles/china/2015
-02-16/how-deter-china.

32. "Wales Summit Declaration," September 5, 2014, North Atlantic Treaty
Organization, https://www.nato.int/cps/ic/natohq/official_texts_11296
4.htm.

33. T. X. Hammes, "Melian's Revenge: How Small, Frontline European States
Can Employ Emerging Technology to Defend Against Russia," *Atlantic
Council,* June 27, 2019, https://www.atlanticcouncil.org/programs/brent-
scowcroft-center/transatlantic-security/publications.

34. "Oil (WTI) Price Commodity," http://markets.businessinsider.com/
commodities/oil-price?type=wti.

35. Daniel L. Byman, "Shifting U.S. interests in the Middle East," Brookings,
March 2, 2016, https://www.brookings.edu/blog/markaz/2016/03/02/
shifting-u-s-interests-in-the-middle-east.

36. Klaus Schwab, "The Fourth Industrial Revolution: what it means, how
to respond."

37. "The Importance of International Students to American Science and
Engineering," National Foundation for American Policy, October
2017, 3, http://nfap.com/wp-content/uploads/2017/10/The-Importance-
of-International-Students.NFAP-Policy-Brief.October-20171.pdf.

38. Stephanie Saul, "As Flow of Foreign Students Wanes, U.S. Universities
Feel the Sting," *New York Times,* January 2, 2018, https://www.nytimes.
com/2018/01/02/us/international-enrollment-drop.html.

39. CIA World Factbook, https://www.cia.gov/library/publications/
resources/the-world-factbook/.

SELECT BIBLIOGRAPHY

BOOKS

Allen, Douglas W. *The Institutional Revolution: Measurement and Economic Emergence in the Modern World.* Chicago: The University of Chicago Press, 2012.

Anderson, Chris. *Makers: The New Industrial Revolution.* New York: Crown Business, 2012.

Avent, Ryan. *The Wealth of Nations.* New York: St. Martin's Press, 2016.

Bartlett, Jamie. *The Dark Net: Inside the Digital Underworld.* London: William Heinemann, 2014.

Berstein, William J. *A Splendid Exchange: How Trade Shaped the World.* New York: Atlantic Monthly Press, 2008.

Bobbitt, Philip. *The Shield of Achilles: War, Peace, and the Course of History.* New York: Anchor Books, 2003.

Coker, Christopher. *Future War.* Cambridge, UK: Polity Press, 2015.

Copeland, Dale C. *Economic Interdependence and War.* New Jersey: Princeton University Press, 2015.

Diamandis, Peter H. and Kotler, Steven. *Abundance: The Future Is Better Than You Think.* New York: Free Press, 2012.

Domingos, Pedro. *The Master Algorithm: How the Quest for the Ultimate Learning Machine Will Remake Our World.* New York: Basic Books, 2015.

Ferguson, Niall. *The Ascent of Money.* New York: Penguin Press, 2008.

Franklin, Daniel, ed. *Megatech: Technology in 2050.* United States: Profile Books, 2017.

Judis, John B. *The Populist Explosion.* New York: Columbia Global Reports, 2016.

Juma, Calestrous. *Innovation and Its Enemies: Why People Resist New Technologies.* United States: Oxford Press, 2016.

Kaplan, Fred. *Dark Territory: The Secret History of Cyberwar.* New York: Simon & Schuster, 2016.

Kelly, Keven. *The Inevitable: Understanding the 12 Technological Forces That Will Shape our Future.* New York: Viking, 2016.

King, Stephen D. *Grave New World: The End of Globalization, The Return of History.* New Haven, CN: Yale University Press, 2017.

Kramer, Franklin D., ed. *Cyberpower and National Security.* Washington DC: Potomac Books.

Lee, Wayne E. ed. *Empire and Indigenes: Intercultural Alliance, Imperial Expansion, and Warfare in the Early Modern World.* New York: New York University Press, 2011.

Malcomson, Scott. *Splinternet: How Geopolitics and Commerce are Fragmenting the World Wide Web.* New York: OR Books, 2016.

Markoff, John. *Machines of Loving Grace.* United States: Harper Collins, 2015.

Millett, Allan R. and Williamson Murray. *Military Innovation in the Interwar Period.* United Kingdom: Cambridge University Press, 1996.

Mitchell, Melanie. *Complexity: A Guided Tour.* United Kingdom: Oxford University Press, 2011.

Murray, Williamson. *Military Adaptation in War: With Fear of Change.* United Kingdom: Cambridge University Press, 2011.

Parker, Geoffrey. *The Military Revolution: Military Innovation and the Rise of the West 1500–1800.* United Kingdom: Cambridge University Press, 1996.

Porter, Michael E. *The Competitive Advantage of Nations.* New York: Free Press, 1998.

Raynor, Christensen. *The Innovators Solution.* Harvard: Harvard Business Review, 2003.

Rosen, Stephen Peter. *Winning the Next War: Innovation and the Modern Military.* Ithaca, NY: Cornell University Press, 1994.

Ross, Alec. *The Industries of the Future.* New York: Simon & Schuster, 2016.

Shadlow, Nadia. *War and the Art of Governance.* Washington, DC: Georgetown University Press, 2017.

Susskind, Richard and Susskind, Daniel. *The Future of the Professions: How Technology Will Transform the Work of Human Experts.* United Kingdom: Oxford University Press, 2015.

JOURNALS AND PUBLICATIONS

Campbell, Kurt, et.al. "Extending American Power: Strategies to Expand U.S. Engagement in a Competitive World Order." Washington, DC: Center for New American Security, May, 2016.

Donovan, Sarah A. and Marc Labonte. "The U.S. Income Distribution: Trends and Issues." Congressional Research Service, December 8, 2016.

Ellman, Jesse, Lisa Samp, and Gabriel Coll. "Assessing the Third Offset Strategy." Center for Strategic & International Studies, March 2017.

Inbar, Efriam, and Eitan Shamir. "Mowing the Grass in Gaza." Ramat Gan, Israel: Begin-Sadat Center for Strategic Studies, July 20, 2014.

Mahbubani, Kishore, and Lawrence H. Summers. "The Fusion of Civilizations: The Case for Global Optimism." *Foreign Affairs,* May/June 2016.

Mearsheimer, John J., and Stephen M. Walt. "The Case for Offshore Balancing." *Foreign Affairs,* July/August 2016.

Potember, Richard. "Perspectives on Research in Artificial Intelligence and Artificial General Intelligence Relevant to DoD." McLean, VA: Mitre Corporation, January 2017.

Rana, Pradumna B., and Ji Xianbai. "TPP12 vs TPP11: Gainers and Losers." Singapore: Rajaratnam School of International Studies, February 15, 2017.

Ratha, Dilip. "Trends in Remittances, 2016: A New Normal of Slow Growth." Washington, DC: World Bank, Oct 6, 2016.

Signoret, Jose, et. al. "Trans-Pacific Partnership Agreement: Likely Impact on the U.S. Economy and on Specific Industry Sectors." Washington, DC: U.S. International Trade Commission, May 29, 2016.

Staff. "China's Position on a Code of Conduct in Space." U.S.-China Security and Economic Review Commission, September 8, 2017.

INDEX

ABOUT THE AUTHOR

T. X. Hammes is a Distinguished Research Fellow at the National Defense University. He holds a DPhil in Modern History from Oxford University, a Masters in Historical Research from Oxford, and a BS from the U.S. Naval Academy. In addition to two other books, Dr. Hammes has published more than 160 articles. He has lectured at conferences, war, and staff colleges in the U.S., Europe, and Asia. During his thirty years in the Marine Corps, Dr. Hammes commanded an intelligence battalion, an infantry battalion, and the Chemical Biological Incident Response Force. He also participated in stability operations in Iraq and Somalia and trained insurgents in various locations.

CAMBRIA RAPID COMMUNICATIONS IN CONFLICT AND SECURITY (RCCS) SERIES

General Editor: Geoffrey R. H. Burn

The aim of the RCCS series is to provide policy makers, practitioners, analysts, and academics with in-depth analysis of fast-moving topics that require urgent yet informed debate. Since its launch in October 2015, the RCCS series has the following book publications:

- *A New Strategy for Complex Warfare: Combined Effects in East Asia* by Thomas A. Drohan
- *US National Security: New Threats, Old Realities* by Paul R. Viotti
- *Security Forces in African States: Cases and Assessment* edited by Paul Shemella and Nicholas Tomb
- *Trust and Distrust in Sino-American Relations: Challenge and Opportunity* by Steve Chan
- *The Gathering Pacific Storm: Emerging US-China Strategic Competition in Defense Technological and Industrial Development* edited by Tai Ming Cheung and Thomas G. Mahnken
- *Military Strategy for the 21st Century: People, Connectivity, and Competition* by Charles Cleveland, Benjamin Jensen, Susan Bryant, and Arnel David
- *Ensuring National Government Stability After US Counterinsurgency Operations: The Critical Measure of Success* by Dallas E. Shaw Jr.
- *Reassessing U.S. Nuclear Strategy* by David W. Kearn, Jr.
- *Deglobalization and International Security* by T. X. Hammes
- *American Foreign Policy and National Security* by Paul R. Viotti